GENDER, ETHNICITY AND THE INFORMAL SECTOR IN TRINIDAD

For Andrew

Gender, Ethnicity and the Informal Sector in Trinidad

SALLY LLOYD-EVANS
University of Reading

ROBERT B. POTTER
Royal Holloway, University of London

Routledge
Taylor & Francis Group
LONDON AND NEW YORK

First published 2002 by Ashgate Publishing

Reissued 2018 by Routledge
2 Park Square, Milton Park, Abingdon, Oxon OX14 4RN
711 Third Avenue, New York, NY 10017, USA

Routledge is an imprint of the Taylor & Francis Group, an informa business

A Library of Congress record exists under LC control number: 2002025862

ISBN 13: 978-1-138-71835-7 (hbk)
ISBN 13: 978-1-315-19585-8 (ebk)

Contents

List of Figures

List of Tables

Preface

In May 1990, we both travelled to the Annual Conference of the *Caribbean Studies Association*, hosted by Trinidad, to undertake preliminary work for Sally's doctoral research on Trinidad's informal sector. The motivation for this research stemmed directly from Sally's childhood experiences growing-up in Mexico City and an early fascination with the innovative ways people make a living in the so called 'informal economy'. After exploring Port of Spain, and talking to street traders and higglers about their work, we became interested in understanding the ways in which ideas about gender, ethnicity and place shape the opportunities available to different individuals in the informal sector. Back home, Sally's doctoral research proposal developed into an ethnographic study on the working experiences of petty commodity traders, that we hoped would throw some light on the issues which are most salient to individuals and their families in this increasingly important section of the economy. Following an offer by Professor Selwyn Ryan of a Visiting Research Fellowship based at the Institute of Social and Economic Research, University of the West Indies in St Augustine, Sally returned in 1991 to start her field research under Rob's supervision.

This monograph is based on the original doctoral thesis, which has been modified and adapted to incorporate more recent theoretical insights into the informal sector, space, gender and ethnicity. Since the main body of research presented in this monograph was undertaken, the literature on these issues has expanded to provide new ways of looking at how individuals use the labour market to create their own working spaces, and the extent to which these spatial processes are gendered and racialised. As such, this monograph is not an all-encompassing examination of the informal sector in Trinidad, rather it paints a picture of the daily lives experienced by informal petty-commodity traders working in the early- to mid-1990s. Although, the original field research was undertaken in the first half of the 1990s, we believe this monograph will make an important contribution to understanding the social dynamics of informal economies in the Caribbean, and elsewhere.

We would like to thank a number of individuals and organisations for their help with the original fieldwork and the preparation of this monograph. Firstly, Sally and Rob would like to thank the Economic and Social Research Council for funding this doctoral research in Trinidad, along with all colleagues in the Department of Geography, Royal Holloway, University of London. Elizabeth Thomas-Hope and Linda Newson provided very helpful comments on the thesis. Secondly, the research presented in this monograph would not have been possible without the support of so many individuals and agencies in Trinidad and Tobago who gave up their valuable time to assist Sally with her field research. Sincere gratitude goes to Professor Selwyn Ryan and his colleagues at the Institute of Social and Economic Research, University of the West Indies (UWI) at St Augustine, Trinidad; Gwendoline Williams and Vina Jules from the Department of Management; all members of the Women's Studies Unit at UWI; and the traders who kindly talked about their lives and experiences. Also in Trinidad, thanks go to Leslie Bowrin from the Youth Training and Employment Partnership Programme, the Department of Town and Country Planning, the Ministry of Mobilisation and Planning and United Nations ECLAC, for allowing Sally to work with them.

On a more personal note, Sally would like to say a special thank you to the Persad family, the Myers family, Dave Ramsaran, Gwendoline Williams and to her good friend Alyson, for their continued friendship and hospitality during her stay in Trinidad. More recently, thanks to Sophie Bowlby and Cathy McIlwaine for their conceptual input, help with bibliographic material and general support during the writing of this book. Finally, Sally would like to express her eternal gratitude to Andrew and her parents for their unfaltering support and encouragement throughout her doctoral research and beyond. This monograph was partly written when Sally was on maternity leave, following the birth of her daughter Ellie, and she would like to say a special thanks to both Andrew and her Mum for all their help during those hectic days! Both of us, but particularly Rob, would like to thank Kathy Roberts of the Department of Geography, Royal

Holloway for typesetting the final text, and to Sue May for photographically reproducing the figures. Heather Browning of the Department of Geography, University of Reading assisted with some of the cartography.

Sally Lloyd-Evans
and Rob Potter
Summer 2002

1 Gender, Ethnicity and the Informal Sector in Trinidad: An Introduction

> They have simply renounced legality. They go out on the streets to sell whatever they can, they set up their shops, and they build their houses on the hillsides, or on vacant lots. Where there are no jobs, they invent jobs, learning in the process all they were never taught (de Soto, 1989: xix).

Introduction

In 1998, the International Labour Office (ILO) reported that the informal sector accounts for a large proportion of urban employment throughout the developing world. In Africa, informal employment constitutes over 60 per cent of total urban employment and it is estimated that most Asian, Latin American and Caribbean countries exhibit rates which exceed 50 per cent (ILO, 1998: 167). As urban population growth rates greatly exceed employment creation in many developing world cities, labour force growth is also predicted to accelerate rapidly over the next 25 years. A well recognised consequence of the inability of many countries to provide jobs has been the substantial increase in the proportion of the labour force seeking alternative forms of employment outside the boundaries of officially recognised work. The benefits of globalisation which were promised to many developing nations by global institutions, namely formal job creation through foreign direct investment and export-oriented production, have in reality only led to a rise in insecure and low-paid contractual work. In relation to the interdependence of employment and global economic forces, it is structural adjustment which has been most closely associated with formal sector retrenchment and redundancy (Green, 1995; Stewart, 1995), and it is the so called 'informal sector' which many households turn to in order to reduce their vulnerability (see de Soto, 1989; Thomas, 1992, 1995; Scott, 1994). In Latin America, for example, the informal sector grew from 40 per cent in 1980 to 53 per cent in 1990 as a direct result of the debt crisis (Stewart, 1995). It is now well established that in many low-income communities throughout the world, household income is less likely to be derived from regular waged employment than it is through a combination of casual activities, self-employment and multiple occupations.

As a result, the last decade has seen a revived interest by governments and policy-makers in the role of informal economic activity and micro-enterprise as income-generating strategies for poor households in much of the Developing World. Whilst policy initiatives have increasingly looked to the informal sector as a development tool for providing much needed work and employment, there have been relatively few new empirical or theoretical studies of the informal sector which highlight the complex processes which affect the lives of the world's informal workers. Even fewer studies have attempted to deconstruct the ways in which processes of gender and ethnicity shape the work experiences of different communities in different places. This research monograph seeks to make a much needed and timely contribution to the literature by providing a comprehensive analysis of the geography of the informal sector in Trinidad. The study highlights some of the barriers and opportunities facing informal sector workers in a rapidly globalising economy which produces gendered and racialised spaces.

As research studies are snapshots of a given time and place, it is useful to reflect on the context of this research by drawing on the key socio-economic and theoretical debates which have helped to construct the development agenda over the last decade. In 1990, the year the United Nations Development Programme (UNDP) published its first *Human Development Report*, the first named author embarked on a doctoral research project which examined the informal sector in Trinidad, under the supervision of the second author. At that time, much of the developing world was suffering from the effects of global retrenchment, debt and structural adjustment, and the financial crisis which had started in the previous decade. The beginning of the 1990s signalled another turning point for development practice as academics and practitioners started to place greater emphasis on the need to put people first, and to campaign for an empowering development agenda which did not discriminate on the basis of gender, class, ethnicity, nationality or religion. Development activitists, Non-Governmental Organisations (NGOs) and even some global institutions, started to prioritise human development through the pursuit of goals of equity, empowerment, participation, good governance and sustainability. It is in this context of prioritising human needs in a rapidly changing world that the empirical research reported in this book was undertaken. In order to understand the complex processes of equity and empowerment, academics and researchers started to ask questions about the construction of difference and diversity and how different economic or social spaces become both gendered and racialised. Attention was paid to understanding how the interactive processes of gender and ethnicity affect access to resources, power and space.

Despite the sheer magnitude of the informal economy in developing countries and the heightened concern over human needs, recent academic attention has shifted from Africa, Asia and Latin America to focus on the increasingly 'casualised economies' of industrialised nations. Since the early 1990s, interest in gender, race and class has increased rapidly, particularly in terms of studies of labour markets in advanced economies (see Williams and Windebank, 1998, for research on ethnicity and informality in Europe) but there are still few in-depth insights into the informal sector of developing economies which attempt to engage with the interdependent issues of ethnicity and gender. Although the gendering of the informal sector has been well researched, there is an urgent need to understand how the informal sector is racialised and how this affects the ways in which different workers use both 'material' and 'imagined spaces'. Such questions are directly relevant to the politisisation of the sector and the policies which governments and agencies design. It is a central aim of this book, therefore, to attempt to cross some of the academic boundaries between 'First' and 'Third' world issues by drawing upon the strengths of both bodies of literature in the context of the Caribbean, a locality where the labour process has been racialised for centuries. As such, this research takes ideas from contemporary thinking about race, gender and place, but also endeavours to situate the research firmly in policy and poverty alleviation contexts. In order to develop these ideas, this chapter now expands on the interwoven themes of globalisation, informal employment, gender and ethnicity, as well as providing a brief background to Trinidad and the Caribbean region.

Work, Informality and Global Transformations

One of the disturbing features of development in the Third World during the second half of the present century has been the unprecedented growth of population and the labour force. Since 1950, the world's population has grown from 2.5 to 5.3 billion in 1992, with much of this growth having taken place in developing countries (World Bank, 1993). Global economic problems of mounting recession and debt, have had an adverse effect on the poor in developing countries, who have witnessed increasing levels of poverty and declining standards of living. Globally, it has been estimated that over 2 billion people either live in poverty, or at subsistence levels (UNDP, 1992). Furthermore, the income disparity between the rich and poor is widening, with the poorest 20 per cent of world population accounting for a mere 1.4 per cent of global Gross National Product (UNDP, 1992).

The inability of countries to provide employment for a growing labour force constitutes one of the most powerful obstacles to social and economic development for the masses. It has been estimated by the International Labour Organisation (ILO) that between 1985 and 2000, a total of 1,000 million new jobs would have to be created to establish full employment world-wide (ILO, 1988), a task which remains unattainable. Unless there is a fundamental change in the structure of unemployment in developing countries, these targets are unlikely to met. Although the universal consequences of unemployment are undesirable, its effects are more acute in the nations of the so called Third World.

The 1999 Human Development Report (UNDP, 1999) reflects on the decade of 'human development' and concluded that "while globalisation has positive, innovative, dynamic aspects - it also has negative, disruptive, marginalising aspects" (UNDP, 1999: 25). Indeed, as Potter and Lloyd-Evans (1998) have discussed, the 1990s presented a new set of challenges over and above the problems of recession, declining production and structural adjustment which were experienced in the 1970s and 1980s. In this respect, work is becoming one of the key social and political issues of the current century (Pahl, 1988) but the widespread confusion and ambiguity which surround the nature and meaning of work are subject to critical debate. One issue which is widely agreed upon is the need for most households to engage in some form of work. A subject which is less clear, centres upon the definition of the boundary between work and employment. An important area of focus is work undertaken outside the realms of officially accounted employment, a practise which is frequent in developing countries.

Official unemployment and underemployment in developing nations currently stands at over 40 per cent (UNDP, 1998). As a result, a large proportion of the labour force is seeking alternative forms of employment, outside the boundaries of officially defined work, giving rise to what is commonly termed the 'informal sector'. The informal sector refers to an heterogeneous group of activities and employment opportunities, which lie on the margins of the formal, regulated component of the economy, and which fail to conform with conventional definitions of work. In its present form, the informal sector refers to unaccountable and unregistered activities which are found in most countries of the world (see chapter 2). Moonlighting, tax evasion, and 'cash in hand' jobs are familiar activities in many developing countries. Despite difficulties in measuring the exact size of the informal sector, it has been estimated that 50 per cent of the labour force in developing countries work within its boundaries, as opposed to around 5 per cent in developed nations (Thomas, 1992). As Potter and Lloyd-Evans (1998) have discussed in detail, the informal sector is incredibly heterogeneous and provides rather polarised opportunities for workers from different social backgrounds and communities. Although the heterogeneity of the activities undertaken in the informal sector has been well established, less attention has been paid to the diversity of the people who work within it. There is a still a tendency to view informal workers as a homogeneous group of under-skilled and desperate individuals, whose sole reason for seeking informal work is for income-generation. Although the informal sector will always provide a safety-net for poor families who may be channelled into low-paid and insecure jobs, the economy is polarised to such an extent that it also offers other individuals opportunities for self-employment and self-development. Contrary to much of the previous literature, therefore, the informal sector is not just a recepticle or a 'last resort' for unskilled, insecure workers who will undertake any work as a survival strategy. The informal labour market, particularly in the Caribbean context, also provides opportunities for creative entrepreneurship, independence and the building of self-esteem for many workers. Individuals have different motivations to work, which may range from economic considerations through to more personal motives such as a desire for independence or greater self-esteem, and we need to understand the complexity of these decision-making processes. In many circumstances, work obstacles and opportunities are shaped as much by prevailing gendered and socio-spatial processes as they are by macro-economic change.

Social Difference: Gender, Ethnicity and Work

The last four decades have witnessed major economic and social changes on a global scale. These changes have transformed the world's trade and labour markets. One consequence of this economic change has been the rapid feminisation of the labour force in both the formal and informal sectors of many developing countries (Standing, 1999). It is well known that women are more likely to be 'employed' in the informal sector than men, due to a combination of factors which include greater household responsibility, unrecognised or lower levels of skills and training, decreasing household incomes, and in some cases, the desire for greater independence and flexibility (Scott, 1986; 1994).

Recent research on the gendered nature of globalisation has also been important in analysing the ways in which women have transformed and re-defined their gender roles under these new economic and social structures. It is now well understood that gender relations are embedded in all social, economic and cultural processes. In particular, prevailing norms concerning gender roles, identity and social relations are embedded in experiences of work and the labour market. There is now a vast body of literature which analyses the gendering of work in both the developing and developed worlds, which explores the relationships between production and reproduction. Much of this work highlights women's participation in the informal economy of developing countries as an important global trend and there are many excellent studies of women's lives as informal workers (Lawson, 1990; Kanji, 1995; Scott, 1994). In the Caribbean, women's roles as higglers and petty commodity traders have been well documented by Massiah (1993) and Le Franc (1989) amongst others. These studies have all added weight to the notion that the movement of people across space is a highly gendered process.

Much of the recent work on the gendering of labour markets, however, is location specific and there has been little exchange of ideas between research undertaken in the countries of the 'South' with those of the 'North'. This dichotomy between research undertaken on female workers in the so called 'developing' and 'developed' worlds is resulting in a failure of researchers in these two fields to explore each others' ideas and findings which, given the current emphasis on 'interconnectivity', is both unfortunate and surprising. The concept of 'difference', particularly in relation to gender, ethnicity and class, has been well documented in the geographical literature (see Carby, 1983; Westwood and Maynard, 1993) but it has not been given full consideration in development practice and research. Third World feminists such as Mohanty (1991) have been particularly powerful in drawing the attention of western feminists to the importance of recognising difference in terms of class, ethnicity, nationality and religion (see also Kabeer, 1994), but as McIlwaine (1995: 239) argues "whilst Third World women's voices contributed to theoretical orientations within the social sciences, these have not yet been followed through in terms of addressing both gender and race within the formulation of development policies".

Despite the heightened interest in gender issues, however, much of the current research into the gendering of work fails to engage with concepts of race and ethnicity as equally important processes which shape the labour markets of post-colonial societies. One recent exception has been the work by Peake and Trotz (1999) which successfully explores the processes of ethnicity, gender and place in contemporary Guyana. In the main, issues concerning ethnicity, identity and difference are notably absent from many of the established studies of urbanisation in developing cities, despite the prevalence of literature on racialised divisions within the cities of industrialised economies. As Potter and Lloyd-Evans (1998) have argued, race and ethnicity are important components affecting social discrimination and access to basic needs in most developing cities, as they involve implicit processes of racialisation. Residential neighbourhoods and 'communities' are far from socially uniform, as they are usually composed of families drawn from distinct regions or different ethnic or religious backgrounds. In most post-colonial nations, occupational status and social hierarchy are closely interlinked with ethnicity and race, and the informal sector is no exception.

From a different, but not unrelated starting point, much of the current social science literature on ethnicity, race and identity which celebrates difference and challenges the essentialism of much thinking about ethnicity, is firmly embedded in the European and North American experience (Hall, 1992; Bhabha, 1990; Bhavnani and Phoenix, 1994; Gilroy, 1987). A number of these writers have explored the relationships between ethnicity and gender more fully, but there has been little attempt to relate this body of work to different global experiences. In her work on Pakistani female migrants in Britain, Brah (1994) uses the concept of 'racialised gendering' in arguing that the 'feminine identities' expressed and lived out by different women will have distinct racialised aspects and that the racialised identities of Indo-Caribbean women or African-Caribbean women, for example, will be influenced distinctively by gender. This line of thought has major implications for the way we think about individual identities and what is understood about being an 'African-Caribbean woman' or a 'White woman', all of which have a direct effect on labour market behaviour. In relation to employment, working identities partly arise out of, but also influence, employment patterns (Lloyd-Evans and Bowlby, 2000). Thus, in relation to the labour market, racialised and gendered identities are performed and re-formed through activities which are part of actually doing a job, as these experiences are central to identity construction. How do racialised and gendered conceptions of identities influence the structure of the informal labour market and the ideas held by institutions and the different types of work deemed appropriate by Trinidadian workers? Understanding how the processes of 'racialised gendering' influence an individual's labour market behaviour and how they are intrinsically communicated within society takes us to another important set of concepts - those of social capital, place and locality.

Social Capital and the Informal Sector: Place, Locality and Networks

Recent research has shown the significance of social networks, 'social capital' and locality in the operation of labour markets, as they play a crucial role in the economic and status trajectories of both male and female workers (Putnam, 1993; Fernandez-Kelly, 1995; Granovetter, 1973; Portes, 1995). Social capital is a term which refers to the types of values and internal relationships that a particular group or community might have, such as trust, feelings of reciprocity and mutual assistance, and it is through the social networks both internal and external to a group that social capital is created and maintained. It has recently been argued that a greater understanding of social capital, an asset which is extremely important for poor communities, can inform our understanding of poverty and vulnerability at the grassroots level, as well as assist in the quest for empowerment (Moser, 1996). Whilst Evans (1996) examines the institutional value of social capital, which enables low-income communities to engage with the state, others have highlighted the value of building trust and reciprocity through projects such as urban housing, education and health-care (Ostrom, 1996; Heller, 1996; Brown and Ashman, 1996). In particular, concerns over the influence of human capital in enhancing the potential for income generation has given way to a growing recognition of the importance of social capital in the labour market (Portes, 1995; Portes and Sensenbrenner, 1993; Bowlby, Lloyd-Evans and Mohammad, 1996).

In the British and North America context, research has identified a lack of social capital as a key obstacle facing immigrants in their search for stable employment and it has been suggested that social capital is of equal important in the creation of informal enterprises. As increasingly, the new poverty agenda identifies sustainable livelihoods as a key component of development, it is timely to re-address the informal sector in the light of this new conceptual framework, for two main reasons. Firstly, the continued importance of the informal sector in realising the labour power of the poor in times of economic crisis, and the policy attention paid to enhancing informal productivity in the last decade are salient (ILO, 1995). Secondly, the informal sector's dependency on social capital in order to operate effectively has to be appreciated.

As labour power has been identified by some as the "poor's greatest asset" (Moser, 1996: iv), strategies for sustainable livelihoods require improved access to work in times of hardship. As parts of the informal sector are built on local social networks, supported by community loyalty, trust and patronage, it provides a salient starting point from which to study how social capital underpins the living standards of the poor, particularly in relation to productive self-employment and home-based enterprise. As the present monograph will show, the economic viability of small informal enterprises can often be explained by the level of social capital maintained by the operator and the local community. Clearly, different types of social values, thrift or a sense of duty to help neighbours, for example, can assist the economic survival of a group. Values which promote mutual aid, and in particular, aid for members of the same ethnic or social group are seen to be both economic and social assets which can be utilised in times of economic crisis (Moser, 1996; Moser and McIlwaine, 1997). Fernandez-Kelly (1995) has further argued that 'cultural capital', the 'repertory of symbols' used by individuals to communicate and 'make sense' of their experience, are also essential to the identity of communities. Such symbols are highly varied and include words, dress, behaviours, music and religious references. The social and cultural capital of a particular group are mutually interdependent as social capital depends upon members of the group understanding each other's meanings, whilst cultural capital depends upon the relationships for the exchanges through which shared meanings and understandings are developed. In this respect, social capital is of particular importance to informal sector operators who are often dependent on trust, assistance and community loyalty for their livelihoods, but it is important to recognise that the processes of social capital formation are also highly gendered (Lloyd-Evans, 1997) and may be embedded in cultural capital. It is likely that individuals will belong to different networks which influence their access to different jobs, places, credit and knowledge.

Interestingly, the informal sector also illustrates the paradoxical relationship between economic crisis and social capital. On the one hand, whilst informal activity often increases under economic austerity and some activities thrive (Le Franc, 1994), it also stands to suffer most from increased competition, as community networks become strained and vulnerable to breakdown. As Moser (1996) poignantly argues, economic crisis and structural adjustment can exert positive and negative forces on social capital both by strengthening it in times of hardship through reciprocity networks, but also reducing household coping strategies and the ability to 'help out'. Vulnerability is associated with decreasing inter-household reciprocity and the erosion of community level organisations, of which small informal enterprises are an integral part.

The recent decade has also witnessed increasing attention being paid to the informal sector's policy agenda, with governments and institutions promoting strategies which attempt to harness and increase the productivity of enterprises through the implementation of income-generation schemes, credit, training and community-based initiatives (ILO, 1995). The 'formalisation of the informal sector' has gained much support from governments world-wide in a desperate attempt to address the underemployment crisis through self-employment and small business development (Tokman, 1989; Simon and Birch, 1992). As this monograph will argue, much policy research has failed to analyse effectively the ways in which informal workers develop and sustain income-generating activities, particularly under conditions of austerity and economic crisis. Policy solutions which solely focus on enhancing the human capital of low-income workers through education, training and credit often fail as they ignore the interactive and often 'invisible' social processes which govern an individual or household's ability to gain access to particular jobs, business opportunities and successful entrepreneurship.

The research presented in this monograph attempts to explore why some communities and social groups are more successful in developing informal businesses than others. Central to this argument, is the consideration of the role that gender and ethnicity play in the construction and maintenance of social capital. Furthermore, as these processes are often place specific, there is also a need for greater understanding of locally embedded social networks (Hanson and Pratt, 1995). Informal activities are often linked to particular places as they form part of very localised economies, often at the community or street level, and they rely on locally embedded networks, social capital, labour, products and services. Informal activities, particularly visible street trades, help to shape the physical, social and economic spaces of cities. These processes are particularly important in the small island economies of the Caribbean where they are crucial to the maintenance of households across the region.

Work, Informality and the Caribbean: Trinidadian Perspectives

For more than three decades, the problem of large-scale, structural unemployment has been a central concern of informed opinion in the Caribbean. Official unemployment figures for the region have generally been growing since the 1980s, with current figures upwards of 20 per cent for many nations. Not shown within the official estimates is the increasing level of underemployment and informal activity in the Caribbean (Thomas, 1988). As the region is increasingly unable to provide employment for a large proportion of its labour force, a mounting number of workers are turning to the informal sector of the economy to earn a living (Anderson, 1987; Anderson and Witter, 1994). For example, it has been estimated that around 40 per cent of the active labour force in Jamaica, Guyana and Trinidad and Tobago are working in the informal sector.

There has been a general awareness by national governments that the informal sector in the Caribbean is playing an increasing role in providing domestic goods, services and employment since the 1980s (Thomas, 1988; Rampersad, 1991). Unfortunately, the contribution of the informal sector to Caribbean development is unknown due to a lack of empirical research on the subject. Whilst a large body of literature exists on the informal economy in Africa, Asia and Latin America (see for example Wellings and Sutcliffe, 1984; Rogerson, 1988; Tokman, 1989), little attention has been given to the informal sector in the Caribbean. The neglect of this particular topic has been bibliographically documented by Lloyd-Evans and Potter (1992). There is a distinct lack of published empirical and theoretical literature on the informal economy in the small-island states and other territories of the region, with the notable exceptions of informal housing provision, women's work and a few studies of petty commodity production (see Witter and Kirton, 1990; Le Franc, 1994). In particular, the informal provision of low income housing in the Caribbean is an area which has recently attracted attention (Conway, 1981; Potter, 1985, 1992a; Clarke, 1989; Watson and Potter, 1997; Potter and Conway, 1997).

The Caribbean has been struggling under the pressures of debt and structural adjustment, global recession, domestic retrenchment and high unemployment, amounting to 20 per cent in most islands for some decades (McAffe, 1991; Richardson, 1992; UNDP, 1994). The implementation of structural adjustment packages by the International Monetary Fund (IMF) has further restricted public spending across the region, and is leading to a marked increase in unemployment, poverty, and further degradation of the natural and social environments (Pantin, 1989; Le Franc, 1994; Frances, 1995; Green 1995). Following recent International Labour Office (ILO) and IMF initiatives, foreign companies are returning to the Caribbean in order to make use of the cheap labour in the form of Export Processing Zones and government incentive packages (Safa, 1990; Pearson, 1993; ILO, 1995). Policies based on the free trade principle have been backed by the World Bank as a solution to unemployment and the generation of income. The employment of young women in sweatshop conditions in Dominica, Puerto Rico, Jamaica and Barbados has been well-documented by Elson and Pearson (1981) and Safa (1990). National governments have recognised the need to explore small-scale enterprise, mainly found in the informal economy, as a potential solution to social problems attributed to structural adjustment.

Much research has attempted to measure the effects of IMF structural adjustment policies across the globe. Whilst the World Bank and IMF have justified their policies as beneficial to developing countries, others have highlighted their contribution to increased poverty, deprivation and inequality (Cornia, 1990; Le Franc, 1994; Stewart, 1995; Green, 1995). In relation to employment, Structural Adjustment Policies (SAPs) have been associated with formal sector retrenchment and redundancy, which lead to growth in informal employment (De Soto, 1989). The collapse of formal sector employment in Latin America and the Caribbean, along with knock-on effects on opportunities in the informal sector, is of concern when successful job creation is needed to alleviate the worst affects of poverty and deprivation.

Le Franc (1994) questions whether structural adjustment has placed any Caribbean economies on the path to sustainable development. In relation to Jamaica, she argues that the most difficult task is to explore whether there are any identifiable "winners" who can not only function, but expand under structural adjustment (Le Franc, 1994: xi). In Jamaica, entrenchment of the public sector along with the introduction of a liberalised market system has led to some positive changes in employment. Anderson and Witter (1994) state that employment growth has largely been in the informal sector, a trend that Trinidadian statisticians would also support. Despite these advantages, however, many jobs are characterised by low wages, low skills, instability and the lack of worker protection.

As mentioned earlier, recent research has highlighted the plight faced by many women who are unable to secure well-paid employment, and who are often located within the most insecure and low-paid occupations of the informal sector. This research has highlighted the high proportion of women working in the informal sector, although much of this work remains 'invisible' in national statistics (Massiah, 1989, 1993). Within the Caribbean region, the prominence of women in society (Ellis, 1986; Momsen, 1993; Massiah, 1993), and more specifically, the labour force highlights gender as an essential component for research. Female workers undertake a major role in supporting households in the Caribbean, and their contribution in terms of economic productivity is vastly underestimated in the official figures (Antrobus, 1990). It is currently estimated that female-headed households account for 30 per cent of Caribbean households, with women constituting between 30 and 50 per cent of the official labour force of the region, and 40 per cent of the informal, labour force (Momsen, 1993). Massiah (1989) estimates that if home-based work alone was taken into account, it would raise the general participation rates of women by 10 to 20 per cent. Women in the Caribbean constitute at least half the unofficial Caribbean workforce (Ellis, 1986; Senior, 1991), with many operating small informal businesses in the areas of food trading, inter-island trading, and the production and distribution of clothing. Despite its valuable contribution, this body of literature is mainly concerned with women's roles in the informal sector, and little attention has been paid to the relative position of men or to the role of ethnicity, and the relationships between space and work.

Within the Caribbean, the Republic of Trinidad and Tobago is a dual island which maintains a varied pattern of social and economic development. It has witnessed an alarming growth in informal activity in recent years. Trinidad, which is ranked as a middle-income country (UNDP, 1998), has always been viewed as a country with prospects, and is the focus of this book. The twin island of Tobago is not included in this research, as it is a more rural and tourist-based economy, and has a smaller informal sector. The informal sector in Trinidad makes a substantial contribution to employment and income-generating opportunities for low-income groups throughout the country (Phillips, 1985; Rampersad, 1991; Lloyd-Evans and Potter, 1992). Trinidad was fortunate to benefit from oil revenues in the 1960s and 1970s, but equally, was hit by the oil crash in 1983, which threw the economy into rapid recession. The effects of international debt restructuring, a stagnant and dependent economy, escalating unemployment, rising urbanisation and urban primacy, and increasing poverty have all placed Trinidad in a vulnerable position. In terms of urban decay, failed industrialisation and misspent oil wealth, Trinidad is starting to resemble its Latin American neighbours more than other islands in the Lesser Antilles.

Trinidad has witnessed growth in unemployment following a severe economic recession, which resulted in the implementation of an IMF structural adjustment package in 1989 which increased in severity since 1992 (Pantin, 1989). In 1994, Trinidad's per capita GDP was US$3,624 as opposed to US$5,578 in 1982. Since 1983, the official rate of unemployment has increased dramatically from 11.1 per cent of the total labour force to levels of over 20 per cent since 1990, with male unemployment running at 18.2 per cent and female unemployment at 25.3 per cent in 1990 (Central Statistical Office, 1990). There has been some decline since 1991, however, with estimates of around 18 per cent documented for 1995 and 1996. The informal sector in Trinidad makes a substantial contribution to employment and income-generating opportunities for low-income groups throughout the country (Lloyd-Evans and Potter, 1992; Rampersad, 1991). In Trinidad, gender and ethnicity are important forces behind occupational stratification (Ryan, 1991; Ryan and Stewart, 1994), and the sector is subject to a rigid division of labour which often results in restricted work opportunities for women.

The informal sector is one of the least documented areas of the economy in Trinidad and as such, there does not appear to be any general agreement as to the precise definition of the activities included within its confines. In the context of Jamaica, Witter and Kirton (1990) characterise an activity as 'informal' if it violates some law, official regulation or avoids registration, licensing or taxation. In the context of Trinidad, the Central Statistical Office believe it can be divided into three sections constituting: (i) the visible informal sector; (ii) the invisible informal sector or the underground sector; and finally (iii) the domestic sector. In the context of Trinidad, the domestic sector refers to domestic servants, family labour and other unremunerated labour such as women's work in the home.

Due to its colonial heritage, Trinidad is a racially mixed society, which is divided between a large East Indian population (45 per cent of the total in 1990), a slightly higher Afro-Caribbean population (50 per cent in 1990), and a small population of European, Chinese, Syrian and Lebanese (5 per cent). Ethnic diversity is reflected throughout society (Lowenthal, 1972a; Clarke, 1986; Yelvington, 1993), and is witnessed in the spatial distribution of population, employment and settlement. In Trinidad, colour, wealth, education, and culture, dynamically interact as markers of differential social status. The literary scholar C.L.R. James (1963: 83) noted that the living standards of Trinidadians are equated in their group's standing in a 'pluri-defined social totem pole'.

Consequently, an in-depth examination of the informal sector in Trinidad needs to incorporate an analysis of the influence of racialised gendering in occupational choice and constraint, and to interpret how ethnic diversity is spatially defined. As a direct consequence, the significance of place, and more specifically, the importance of peoples' perceptions of different environments, remain important aspects for investigation, which have not been given high priority in the literature on the informal sector in developing countries.

Overall, the combined influence of locality, ethnicity and gender may explain the reasons behind social, and occupational stratification in the informal sector, and identify whether experiences of work differ between groups of workers. An investigation into the factors which are operative in the employment decision-making process, which includes an evaluation of popular attitudes to work, may assist in the development of a number of policy targets to raise employment, and income opportunities, within Trinidad.

Aims and Remit of the Present Monograph

The aims of this book are fourfold. Firstly, it aims to provide a comprehensive geographical insight into the informal economy in Trinidad by examining the social and spatial processes which shape it. Secondly, it explores how the processes of gender and ethnicity (racialised gendering) intertwine to structure both the informal labour market and the opportunities and obstacles which affect the daily lives and careers of informal workers. Thirdly, and in relation to the previous point, this book attempts to examine the kinds of pictures that workers build up about (a) the informal labour market, and (b) themselves and how these ideas help construct conceptions of working identities and 'appropriate work' for different people in the informal labour market and how these decisions are spatially defined and communicated through different social networks. Finally, it explores the ways in which government policy can structure the informal sector through an examination of the policy framework and the role that social capital and social networks play in providing access to resources. Throughout the book, the need to place diversity at the forefront of development theory and practice is highlighted.

The research presented in this monograph was undertaken as part of the first author's doctoral research, which was supervised by the second author. The main field work was undertaken in Trinidad between 1990 and 1992 when the first author was a Visiting Research Fellow at the Institute of Social and Economic Research, University of the West Indies at St Augustine, with subsequent research undertaken during shorter visits throughout the mid-1990s. The often precarious nature of informal activities, their wide range and unaccountability, present problems in terminology, conceptualisation, measurement and research methodology. The question as to how you investigate an activity which is unaccountable to the government, and which is not always visible, and often considered illegal, is not a simple one. In order to overcome this problem, the research was divided into several strands which required the use of both quantitative and qualitative methods.

Firstly, familiarisation with the Trinidadian informal labour market was undertaken alongside the secondary analysis of labour market data and existing literature on employment. Secondly, a quantitative 'reconnaissance' survey was conducted in an attempt to assess the size and nature of informal sector activity across Trinidad, with particular attention paid to assessing the broad macro-geographical orientation and spatial distribution of informal activities. The survey incorporated a series of brief interviews with approximately 800 informal sector participants, with particular attention being paid to the function, location and size of the activity, and the gender and ethnicity of the operator. Details of the structure of the sample, and the criteria, are explained in chapters 5 and 6. This approach provided a basic statistical estimation of the varying importance of activities, and facilitated a basic understanding of the diversity of workers who were employed in the informal sector during this period.

Thirdly, in-depth ethnographic interviews and case studies were undertaken with 60 informal male and female petty commodity traders operating from four distinct locations in Trinidad. The field of ethnography appeared to offer a suitable approach to studying the sensitive issue of informality, and the detailed methodology is discussed in-depth in chapters 7 and 8. As a addition to the main field research, a period of time was spent working with a number of government institutions, and informal sector projects. Here, a series of in-depth interviews and case studies, were undertaken with government officials, and participants in a number of informal sector programmes. This served to highlight the views of the participants involved in schemes designed to assist informal operators, and allowed an assessment of the real needs of the sector from within. An examination of the efficiency and success of a number of schemes was undertaken to provide an evaluation of current government policies concerning informal activities.

In order to address these aims, this book is divided into ten chapters. Following this introductory chapter, chapter 2 provides an in-depth discussion of both theoretical and policy perspectives on the informal sector and prepares the reader for a more detailed discussion of contemporary global issues and work in the Caribbean, which is provided in chapter 3. Chapters 4 to 6 present a definitive empirical overview of employment and the informal sector in Trinidad, based on the fieldwork undertaken. Chapter 4 discusses the employment structure of Trinidad, presents secondary data on labour force figures and occupational stratification, and provides a locally-relevant working definition of informality. Chapters 5 and 6 present the empirical results of research which explores the nature and form of informal activities, and operators, throughout the country. Chapter 5 analyses activities involved in the internal food distribution system, whilst chapter 6 considers activities which may be classed as belonging to the petty commodity and service sectors.

The third section of the monograph, made up of chapters 7 and 8, presents the results of a series of detailed interviews, and case studies, and emphasises the reasons behind occupational stratification in the informal sector in relation to the roles of space, ethnicity and gender. In the concluding chapters 9 and 10, the empirical findings are linked with state policy formation, and tentative suggestions are made for a re-appraisal of the concept of work in Trinidad, which complies with a development agenda which values difference and diversity.

2 Current Perspectives on Informality, Employment and Development

Introduction

The inability of countries to provide sustainable employment for a growing labour force constitutes one of the most powerful obstacles to social and economic development in the new millennium. In the late 1980s, it was estimated by the International Labour Organisation (ILO) that between 1985 and 2000, a total of 1,000 million new jobs would have to be created in order to establish full employment world-wide (ILO, 1988). As Potter and Lloyd-Evans (1998) have highlighted, the global urban population alone had increased from 737 million in 1950 to 2,603 million in 1995 (ILO, 1995). As there are important links between production and employment, social equity and poverty alleviation, the ability of countries to provide sustainable work for their growing populations is crucial. It is people, therefore, who must be the focus of policies which attempt to address vulnerability and poverty.

Escalating urban population growth rates pose particular problems for employment creation in developing cities across the globe, where over 300 million residents live in absolute poverty (UNDP, 1994). Furthermore, global transformations in production, trade and finance have placed a strain on traditional coping mechanisms at the international, regional and household scales. Sustained labour force growth is predicted over the next twenty-five years, with the greatest increase occurring in Africa and the Middle East. By 2015, sub-Saharan Africa will add annually to the world's labour force more than three times as many new workers as countries from the Organisation of Economic Co-operation and Development (OECD), also known as the 'First World club', eastern Europe and the ex-Soviet Union taken together (Turnham, 1993). It is widely speculated that a substantial proportion of these new job seekers will only find work within the informal economies of the developing world.

As we stated in chapter 1, labour market issues have taken a central role in the poverty agenda since the 1950s. This recent history of employment research and practice is also a testament to the various discourses of development which have prevailed over five decades (Hettne, 1994). From early strategies of modernisation and industrialisation through to contemporary thinking about post-colonial development, issues surrounding work and the labour market have remained at the heart of the development debate. Indeed, poverty and inequality, however defined, seem inextricably linked to notions of employability and the availability of secure work. There has been less consensus, however, on the most effective means of providing access to secure livelihoods for the world's vulnerable workers. In particular, the role of the informal sector as a 'tool of development' or as a creator of work has continued to be one of the most widely debated and contentious issues since its 'identification' in the 1950s. Competing views on the nature of the relationships between development, work and informality have been well documented by theorists and policy practitioners alike, and it is the aim of the current chapter to highlight the most influential conceptual frameworks which have sought to analyse the complexities of the informal sector.

Work, Employment and Development: 'Western Perspectives'

Following the promotion of globalisation as a conceptual framework for understanding uneven spatial development between rich and poor nations in the 1990s, there has been a wealth of literature which examines the role of 'Third World workers' in the so-called 'integrated global economy' (Daniels and Lever, 1996). Many excellent studies have drawn attention to the exploitation and manipulation of workers in the Export-Processing Zones (EPZs) and sub-contractual chains of multi-national corporations which have spread across Asia, Latin America and the Caribbean (Chant and McIlwaine, 1995; Pearson, 1994; Afshar and Barrientos, 1999). These studies have not only highlighted the inadequacies of the global economic system, but have successfully encouraged western academics to re-analyse the ways in which global economic processes are affecting the labour markets of developing nations. Unfortunately, deconstruction of the New International Division of Labour (NIDL) has primarily focused on the employment of workers in EPZs and Free Trade Zones, with less attention being paid to the incorporation of informal workers into the global production system. Despite the well-deserved publicity given to the exploitation of workers by increasingly feminised global industries, it is a fact that Export-Processing Zones only account for around 5 per cent of employment across a handful of developing countries. There is still a pressing need to understand the labour market experiences of the majority of low-income workers in the South who engage in other forms of work and employment both within and outside the boundaries of the formal labour market. In fact, the informal sector of the developing world is not merely a marginalised appendage to the 'global economy', it is a major part of the global system on which many millions of workers rely for productive employment, products and services each day.

Looking retrospectively, Ray Pahl argued that work was one of the key social and economic issues of the twentieth century (Pahl, 1988), and the importance of work to the survival, welfare and well-being of low-income households across the globe cannot be overemphasised. However, although the concept of work has been subject to critical debate in a western context, there is still much confusion about its meaning in the developing world, particularly in the light of recent global transformations. There has been much debate over the overlapping concepts of 'work' and 'employment' (see Potter and Lloyd-Evans, 1998). In its narrowest definition, the term employment is given to work undertaken in return for a wage or other remuneration. Attempts to measure employment rates, however, have often only included employment in the formal economy which is accounted in national statistics, thereby omitting other forms of employment undertaken in the informal economy or the household (Massiah, 1993) Unemployment in the Third World is often viewed as a symptom of unequal and inadequate development, but attempting to identify the 'unemployed' remains a highly controversial task.

Firstly, difficulties arise as attempts to measure categories of employment are often constructed around western concepts of work (Pahl, 1988). Western theories of urban economic structure and labour force segregation have often failed to adequately analyse and explain the structure of the urban labour force in developing countries, particularly in relation to the increasing informalisation of work, which we will discuss later in this chapter. Work undertaken outside the realms of officially accounted employment is prevalent throughout the urban and rural economies of developing countries (ILO, 1995; UNCHS, 1996). Much productive work is undertaken outside the confines of the formal waged economy, indeed many household productive and reproductive activities are unremunerated. Informal activity, self-employment, casual work and home-based production have provided an alternative to formal employment for decades. It is important, therefore, to expand western notions of work to include a wider range of social and economic activities which, due to their unregulated nature, often have the greatest effect on urban areas.

Secondly, there is the problem of definition (Gilbert and Gugler, 1992). The ILO defines the 'unemployed' as those who are without work but actively seeking it (Hussmann, 1990). It is widely argued that the true unemployed are not amongst the urban poor. As far back as 1968, Myrdal argued that unemployment is a luxury few can afford (Myrdal, 1968). The 'luxury unemployment thesis' (Udall and Sinclair, 1982) argues that due to the absence of social security, only educated professionals, such as white collar workers, public sector executives, or possibly new entrants to the labour market who are still able to rely on family support, constitute the unemployed in most developing countries. As a result, Udall and Sinclair (1982) argue that the unemployment figures published by official agencies are meaningless and inappropriate as they fail to provide a clear picture of the true structure of employment in developing economies.

Low participation rates in the formal economy, along with measured unemployment at under 10 per cent for many countries, result in a substantial proportion of the working population being unaccounted for. This is often due to the unsuitability of the criteria used for inclusion and exclusion of individuals from the official labour force, which largely exclude informal employment and household work. As Turnham (1993) argues, unrecorded production absorbs as much labour time as all combined activities in the recorded sectors of the economy. Goldschmidt-Clermont (1990) estimate that household work accounts for between 30-50 per cent of GDP in many developing nations. Household activities, which are often undertaken by women and children, include household enterprise, house construction and maintenance, housework and child-care, and urban food production (Drakakis-Smith, 1990). The failure to include these activities as 'productive employment' often results in unrealistically low female participation rates, and provides a distorted view of the relative importance of formal employment in many developing countries.

Due to the inadequacy of the term 'unemployment', it is now widely recognised by researchers and academics that 'underemployment' provides a better indication of the employment problem. Gilbert and Gugler (1992) define underemployment as the under-utilisation of labour in three distinct forms. The first, and most common form, occurs where workers are so numerous that many are less than fully employed, or work less hours than they would like. Street trading often provides a good example. Secondly, underemployment can be related to fluctuations in economic activities during the day, week or month when there is no work. Thirdly, there is 'hidden underemployment' where people are employed even when there is insufficient work to keep them fully occupied. According to the ILO, 'visible underemployment' refers to those who have worked less than the normal duration, 'disguised underemployment' to workers whose skills have been under-utilised, whilst 'potential underemployment' accounts for those whose productivity is inadequate (Hussman, 1990; ILO, 1995). A large proportion of the underemployed are seen to constitute the informal sector which often provides part-time, casual and unproductive jobs for the urban poor. As the next section will show, however, the informal sector is not just a haven for marginalised workers, it is also a provider of productive employment opportunities, albeit one that is associated with certain difficulties and problems.

The Informal Sector and Development Paradigms

Theorising about the informal sector has to a large extent followed the major paradigms in development theory and practice. It was in the light of growing underemployment and the lack of 'modern jobs' that theoretical debates began to focus on the structure of Third World economies after the Second World War. Interest in the existence of a 'traditional', or as it was often referred to 'marginal', employment sector gained momentum in the 1950s and 1960s, with the rise of modernisation theory. The modernisation school of thought argued that developing countries should follow the path of developed nations, by pursuing the goals of industrialisation, and modernisation of their economies (Lewis, 1954; Rostow, 1960; Myrdal, 1957, 1968). Within this framework, the 'backward economic sector', which incorporated a large pool of casual labour, was considered a hindrance to economic development and it was widely predicted that this 'traditional' sector would be eradicated once prosperity increased. Structural problems, such as unemployment and underemployment, were seen as temporary obstacles which would be overcome by industrial development (Hirshmann, 1958).

One non-western phenomenon, characteristic of most situations of underdevelopment, which had caught the attention of pioneers in development theory, was the 'dualistic' nature of underdeveloped economies. Dualism referred to the co-existence of an 'advanced', or 'modern', sector with a 'backward', or 'traditional' sector. Supporters of this approach highlighted the traditional economic sector as the major barrier to development. This set the background to one of the most influential theories of development in the 1950s, provided in Lewis' work on Third World economies which was characterised by an 'unlimited supply of labour' (Lewis, 1954). Lewis combined his knowledge of the West Indian experience with classical economic theory, to outline an economic situation where unemployment was high, and the ability to absorb the increased labour force had been exhausted. Lewis' solution to the problem was industrialisation by invitation, a model which was pursued in the West Indies during the 1960s.

The heyday of the dualistic approach was the 1970s, when growing criticisms of marginality (Quijano, 1974) focused attention upon the problems of employment and economic structure. It had become clear that programmes advocating modernisation, and capitalisation, had not raised labour absorption in the industrial sectors. The dualist interpretation was quickly attributed to the employment structure, which was seen to constitute a modern, efficient, formal employment sector and a traditional, unproductive haven for the underemployed.

Development in the 1970s, was heavily dominated by another perspective, the dependency approach, which originated from the Latin American debate on underdevelopment. Dependency provided an alternative intellectual perspective on development, which was rooted in the Third World (Cardoso and Faletto, 1969). Originally from the Marxist tradition, the theory provided an assault upon conventional ideology based on the relationship between international trade and development, and contained an elaboration of an alternative framework, the centre-periphery model (Dos Santos, 1970; Frank, 1967; Quijano, 1974). Dependency focused on the unequal and dependent relationship which existed between the developed, and developing, nations. Furthermore, Cardoso (1976) argued that this dependent relationship generated a process of underdevelopment.

From a dependency perspective, the informal sector can be seen as dependent on, and exploited by, the formal economy. Santos (1979) originally developed a model where two sectors of the economy, the upper and lower circuits, were inextricably linked. He argued that the informal sector provided low cost goods and services to both sectors, and as such helped to keep formal wages low. Criticisms of the dependency approach focus on the theory's limited explanatory value (Leys, 1977), and on its failure to recognise the importance of developing countries' own power group, the local elites.

The late 1970s witnessed a move from dependence to interdependence, through the globalisation of development theory. The oil crisis in 1973 demonstrated the vulnerability of western industrialism, and highlighted the power of Transnational Corporations (TNCs) in the international economy. Development theory began to focus upon the interdependence between nations, based on the existence of an hierarchical world order. Corbridge (1986) argued that a handful of strong states had emerged, states which were dominated by TNCs. The World Systems Approach recognised a complex system of core western nations, and Third World peripheral states (Wallerstein, 1974).

Within the World Systems Approach, the informal sector is seen as a contributor to the accumulation of wealth of core states via TNCs. Here, masses of informal sector workers, often women, are employed in small informal workshops producing goods for export to the West. The increasing amount of poor, informal, waged-labourers in developing countries, represents one of the greatest disadvantages to promoting informal sector employment. It has been argued by Safa (1990), that the existence of a large informal sector attracts foreign companies to take advantage of cheap labour in the Caribbean.

Structuralism, linked to the world systems approach, emphasises that there are both external, and internal, constraints on Third World economic development. Structuralist solutions to development focus upon eradicating poverty through a basic needs approach, where diversified employment opportunities play a major role. Encouragement of the informal sector, where peoples' purposeful and intelligent energies are used for productive purposes, is now widely seen as a component of successful development policies. Recently, Non-Governmental Organisations (NGOs) have taken a major role in supporting informal employment and self-reliance through the promotion of fair-trade policies, co-operatives and credit unions. In many regions, the state has responded to these initiatives by attempting to 'formalise the informal sector', an agenda which has provoked a controversial debate over the role of the informal sector as an employment provider (see chapter 9). Within this debate, some of the original arguments concerning the concept of informality have re-surfaced in the academic and policy literature.

The Development of the Concept of the Informal Sector

Within development studies, there exists a large body of literature which attempts to define and explain the presence of the informal sector (ILO, 1972; Bromley and Gerry, 1979; Tokman, 1989; De Soto, 1989; Thomas, 1992, 1995). Despite this contribution, investigations into the nature of informal sector activity have often been obscured by theoretical debate over its definition. As Portes, Castells and Benton (1989: 1) comment "the informal sector has come to constitute a major structural feature of society, and yet the ideological and political debate surrounding its development has obscured comprehension of its character".

Despite its widespread recognition as a 'new concept', following Keith Hart's work in the 1970s, the existence of informal sector activity had been documented since the 1950s. Prior to the 1960s, there had been a number of studies dealing with irregular economic activities (Lewis, 1955; Simpson, 1954). Beggars, hawkers, and small-scale operators were commonplace in the growing Third World cities of that time. In a study of street begging in Kingston, Jamaica, Simpson (1954) identified street workers as social failures. Following Oscar Lewis' (1966) *Culture of Poverty*, negative views were projected of informal operators.

As previously discussed, perspectives on informal sector development closely followed the path of development theory, with many discussions of the informal sector taking the dualist school of thought as their point of departure (Lewis, 1954; Reynolds, 1969; Quijano, 1974). The modern sector was identified as a dynamic contributor to the economy, and as a provider of a well-organised labour structure, characterised by large industry, the public sector and other regulated businesses. By contrast, the backward sector referred to those activities which were unregulated by government, inefficient, small-scale and unproductive.

Lloyd (1979) referred to the sector as that of the 'lumpenproletariat', consisting of workers who had rejected the dominant values of society and had turned to crime, prostitution and begging. Also coined as the 'marginal economy', the sector was seen to include a vast range of economic activities which were poorly organised, difficult to enumerate and invisible in the official census (Breman, 1976). Although dualism has been widely criticised for its failure to recognise the linkages which exist between sectors, its merits lie in drawing greater attention to the existence of an informal employment sector.

Another major influence in the study of informality has been the International Labour Organisation (ILO). In 1964, the ILO adopted the Employment Policy Convention (No. 122) which encouraged governments to follow a goal of active full employment. The ILO's *World Employment Programme* at the 1967 *International Labour Conference*, suggested that a number of country-based pilot studies should be carried out. The first country mission was Colombia in 1970, which was followed by Sri Lanka in 1971 and Kenya in 1972. These studies questioned the applicability of the concept of unemployment, as defined in developed nations, to developing countries, where there is no social security system. The mission to Kenya changed the focus from unemployment to the employment of the 'working poor' (ILO, 1972: 9), and the sector was coined 'informal' by Hart in 1973.

What is the Informal Sector? The Definition of Informal Activity

Within the academic literature, there have been numerous attempts to establish criteria for the recognition of informal activities. A number of early studies, commonly referred to under the title the "enterprise approach", attempted to define the informal sector through a list of characteristics which distinguished between informal and formal activity (ILO, 1972; Weeks, 1975; Davies, 1979). Davies (1979) argued that informal sector activities are characterised by their ease of entry, small-scale, intensive use of labour, and family ownership. By contrast, formal sector activities required formally trained workers for their large-scale, capital intensive, corporate businesses. Santos (1979), Breman (1976) and McGee (1979), amongst others, criticised this approach for its failure to recognise the numerous discrepancies. For example, many informal businesses have their own entry requirements. Recent work by Tokman (1989), and Rogerson and Hart (1989), provides further evidence to suggest that the structure of informal enterprises does not always differ from its formal counterparts.

Other researchers have examined the idea that the fundamental characteristic of informal employment is based on self-employment (Singer, 1970; Hart, 1973; Scott, 1979; 1986b). Scott (1979), advocated that no clear-cut dichotomy exists between waged and non-waged labour, as there are a number of intermediate forms of operation which exist between waged work and true self-employment. Increasingly, waged labour is becoming a common activity in the informal sector, particularly in the form of contractual arrangements with corporate firms.

Following the self-employment approach, a popular approach focused upon the mode of production as the decisive factor in identifying informality (Davies, 1979; Moser, 1978; 1984). It was argued that the formal sector differs from the informal sector, because it represents a different mode of production. Davies (1979) argues that the means of production in the informal sector are non-capital intensive, and are owned by those who operate them. In the formal sector, the means of production are capital intensive, and privately owned by a small elite class.

Moser (1978) argued that the informal sector is a subordinate mode of production, exploited by capitalism. Based on both the Marxist concept of 'petty commodity production', and on the theory of unequal exchange, the radical school of thought has re-defined the informal sector as a 'reserve army of labour' (Castells, 1977; Connolly, 1985). Economic surplus generated in the informal sector is transferred to the formal sector through two major mechanisms. Firstly, the informal sector lacks access to the basic resources of production, which are monopolised by the formal sector and secondly, the informal sector is forced into a position whereby it must pay higher prices for its purchases, but can only ask lower prices for its outputs. Therefore, the informal sector is limited by its relationship to the formal sector, and the sector as a whole is said to be 'involuting'.

The informal sector is seen to be exploited by the capitalist economy in a "help the poor without threatening the rich" strategy (Bromley, 1978: 1036), and which eradicates the need for the state to provide jobs for its labour force. Castells (1977) argues that the informal sector experience is similar to Third World informal housing settlements, which provide a cheap, easy solution to the housing crisis. Safa (1981, 1986) and Scott (1986a) have documented the fact that unregulated activities play a critical role in subsidising the costs of TNC operations in the Third World, particularly in their use of cheap female labour.

As previously documented, the search for a more widely accepted approach has focused upon the identification of linkages between the informal and formal sectors (Santos, 1979; Sethuraman, 1976, 1978). Following this line of thought, the concept of an informal-formal continuum, along which all economic activities would take their place, has gained support. Sethuraman (1981) placed many small-scale informal enterprises, such as hawking and petty commodity production, at one end of the continuum, and suggested that formal enterprises, such as TNCs, would be placed at the other end. He also suggested that as an informal activity grew, it would occupy another position along the hierarchy.

Following the existing literature, the present authors have devised an approach which is useful in categorising informal activities (Potter and Lloyd-Evans, 1998). This classification stems from an economic perspective (Thomas, 1992), and is based on production, motivation and market involvement, where informal activity is classified according to four categories of production: the household sector, informal sector, irregular sector and criminal sector.

Firstly, there is the existence of a **subsistence sector**, where goods and services are produced by the household solely for its consumption. The well-known activities of housework, the use of unpaid family labour and reproduction would fall into this category (Moser 1984, Chant, 1987). Small surpluses may well be sold in a local market, but the prime motive of production is subsistence, rather than profit.

The second category consists of **small-scale producers and retailers**, who primarily produce or sell for the acquisition of a wage. They are often self-employed, and have established their own business in order to provide themselves with work. Typical workers in this category are street traders, artisans, food sellers and some home-based producers. Many small family enterprises would also fall into this sector. According to Sethuraman (1981), and Tokman (1989), an operator's motive for entering the sector is an important consideration for determining the degree of informality of a business.

A third category is one which is increasingly forgotten, but accounts for a large proportion of the informal sector, particularly in Latin America (De Soto, 1989). The main occupants of this sector could be called the **petty capitalists**, as their main aim for establishing an informal business is the extraction of profits, which may be greater than in the formal sector. The avoidance of taxes, appliance with employment legislation such as minimum wages, hours and conditions, attract many successful entrepreneurs to the informal sector. Many petty capitalists will employ waged labour, often at low wages in sweatshops in order to produce goods at low costs. These businesses demonstrate that large profits can be made within an informal unit, and support the argument that the informal sector is not conclusively made up of the 'casual poor' (Bromley and Gerry, 1979).

A large proportion of petty capitalist businesses will be contracted to large formal sector firms, and it is within this type of business that the greatest exploitation is found. Workers, many of whom are women, have no protection and are truly exploited by the informal system. Many women are forced to take low-paid informal occupations as their lack of education and skill, combined with reproductive responsibilities, restricts them from the formal economy (Redclift and Sinclair, 1991; Momsen and Kinnard, 1992). In a similar manner, many large enterprises will employ out-workers to undertake menial tasks in their homes. The clothing and electronic industries are prime examples of this type of 'informal' employment, and have been well documented by a number of authors (Gerry 1979; Moser, 1984; Brydon and Chant, 1989; Safa, 1990; Stitcher and Parpart, 1990).

A fourth category within this classification refers to those activities which are **criminal** and socially undesirable. Criminal activities such as drug smuggling, theft, extortion, prostitution and protection are all part of the informal sector, and are not to be treated in the same light as previous categories. They belong to the underground and black economy, and are not given great consideration in this monograph, for reasons which are outlined subsequently.

This integrated approach reflects the recent changes in attitudes towards the informal sector. No longer seen as an homogeneous group of activities, the informal sector is now being encouraged and supported. Recent literature has recognised the need to support informality, without attempting to rigidly define its boundaries (Tokman, 1989). According to Portes, Castells and Benton (1989) the informal economy is a commonsense notion, the moving social boundaries of which cannot be frozen by a strict definition.

This view is adapted in the present research. It stresses the need to understand the informal sector in terms of a process which engages workers in the labour market in a range of different social and geographical contexts. Groups of young workers are now entering a casual-labour market in many regions of the world. The informal sector is ambiguous, in that it encompasses wealth and poverty, productivity and inefficiency, exploitation and liberation. The informal sector represents a process of income generation, which is essentially characterised by a lack of regulation by government institutions. Portes, Castells and Benton (1989: 12) expand this notion by adding that it operates "in a legal and social environment in which similar activities are regulated". In the present context, this is taken as essentially a good working definition which needs no further deliberation. Rather, attention needs to focus upon the socio-spatial dynamics of the informal sector in the current economic climate, and in particular the ways in which its participants are engaged in a gendered labour process.

Recent Perspectives on Informality: Globalisation and Feminisation of Labour

Recent academic and policy attention has focused on the reasons why processes of informalisation are spreading across industrialised nations as well as in the Developing World (ILO, 1996; Williams and Windebank, 1998). In this respect, researchers are currently asking the same sets of questions which were raised during the ILO's employment missions in Africa and Asia in the 1960s - who works in the informal sector and for what reasons, how is it structured, and is it just a marginal or survival economy? Detailed answers to these questions largely remain elusive due to the paucity of accurate quantitative and qualitative data on the expansion of informal economic activities at both the national and regional scales (ILO, 1996). As Williams and Windebank (1998) have asserted, micro-level studies appear to be the only way of reflecting changes in the labour markets of many developing countries. A further obstacle to understanding the dynamics of the sector has been the lack of exchange of ideas and literature between researchers in the 'North' and 'South'. These academic divisions do little to advance a global understanding of informality.

From a western orientation, 'informalisation' theorists have sought to explain the growth of the Third World informal sector in terms of recent changes in the operation of the New International Division of Labour and global production. The 'informalisation thesis' explains the expansion of informality across the globe as a condition of economic recession and deregulation which leads to the increased marginalisation of low-waged labour from formal work (Amin, 1996). Although there is evidence to suggest that the increase in sub-contracting and homeworking practices by multi-national firms has often increased informal employment in parts of Latin America and south-east Asia, this type of work only accounts for a relatively small part of the informal sector. Whilst processes of informalisation have increased their presence in most nations, such labour market processes are not 'new' in countries of the South where informal markets have provided employment and production opportunities for many decades. Leading on from this perspective, there is a danger that the particular dynamics of the informal sector in developing countries will become increasingly misunderstood or merely seen as another 'outcome' of the uneven global economy. Furthermore, supporters of the 'modernisation' school of thought still claim that the informal sector will diminish as the economies of developing countries modernise (ILO, 1996). This position fails to acknowledge the fact that the informal economies of the Asian NICs still play an important role in their economic success (Cheng and Gereffi, 1994). Elsewhere in Latin America and the Caribbean, the process of labour formalisation through similar export-processing strategies have paralleled growth in the informal sectors.

Therefore, despite the widespread recognition of the diverse activities encompassed by the informal sector in the developing world, there is still an western orthodoxy which maintains that the informal sector exists as a survival strategy for marginalised and poor populations (see Williams and Windebank, 1998; Maldonado, 1995). Although the informal sector does provide a 'safety net' for marginalised job seekers, the sector encompasses a heterogeneous labour market with its own hierarchy of socio-spatial divisions of labour (Castells and Portes, 1989; Rakowski, 1994; Thomas, 1995). As Chapters 7 and 8 will show, the informal sector is a space for successful entrepreneurship and provides income earning opportunities for all income groups (Hart, 1990; Lautier, 1990). Like its formal counterpart, however, the informal sector maintains its own division of labour which restricts access to the means of production for different social groups. As Williams and Windebank (1998) have convincingly argued in respect of the informal sector in advanced industrialised nations, there is a pressing need to understand the social and spatial configurations of informal work and analyse the prevailing economic, institutional and environmental conditions which shape local specifities. Research has highlighted the fact that neither the informal or formal sectors can be homogeneously characterised by positive or negative characteristics. However, there already exists a valuable body of literature which suggests that job opportunities and characteristics, working conditions and wage differentials are more likely to be influenced by gender.

There have been many debates over the gendering of the informal sector and in particular, the extent to which the informal sector is a 'female sector' (Scott, 1979; 1994). Studies have shown that increasing numbers of women are undertaking informal work across the developing world, particularly if unpaid labour and household production are included in its definition (Massiah, 1993). The extent to which women are channelled into informality, either as a result of their exclusion from the formal labour market or due to their reproductive responsibilities (Chant, 1991), is less well understood. Although there are studies which show that women are more likely to undertake survival strategies, such as homeworking under recent conditions of economic austerity, other literature argues that the informal sector provides a flexible and independent form of working which can empower female workers. Therefore, the issue of whether the informal sector is a feminised sector is highly complex. Although, on aggregate, more men than women work in the informal economy overall, there is evidence to suggest that an increasing proportion of women are entering the sector in most countries.

In her research on informal employment in Lima, Peru, Scott (1986, 1991, 1994) has convincingly argued that the informal-formal sector model is fundamentally gender-blind. For Scott, the problem lies in the fact that a key feature of the paradigm is a single 'axis of segmentation' of the labour market, which is based on specific sectoral characteristics. The association of formal employment with high-paid, skilled, protected and stable jobs, and its informal counterpart with low-paid, exploitative and casual work, is seen to be a misrepresentation of the different jobs undertaken by men and women in developing economies. According to Scott, a gender-focused analysis highlights the existence of a further 'axis of segmentation' which segregates the opportunities open to men and women in a rigid gender division of labour. In this context, the negative characteristics associated with informal employment are likely to be found in jobs undertaken by women, regardless of whether the job is deemed to be part of the informal or formal economy. Conversely, men's work is generally found to be characterised by 'formal' type qualities, such as higher pay and security, both within and outside the confines of the informal sector.

This school of thought has provoked considerable debate over the marginalisation of female workers in the lower echelons of the labour market, particularly in activities which are traditionally linked to the household such as cooking, cleaning, child-care and dress-making (Roldan, 1985). Ideologically, while some women regard such activities as an extension of their household duties or as 'helping out' rather than productive work, the same activities represent business opportunities for others (Miraftab, 1996). Understanding these differences and dimensions is central to analysing the dynamics of the informal labour process. Whilst there is no doubt over the existence of such a gendered division of labour in the informal sector, where women's labour power can be constrained by their reproductive activities, such divisions are also influenced by other factors such as spatiality, ethnicity and generation. In the Caribbean, young dynamic female entrepreneurs are challenging traditional stereo-typical roles by breaking into 'working spaces' previously dominated by men (see chapter 8). With a few exceptions, issues relating to locality and space have not been given adequate attention in the development literature.

The Gendering of Urban Spaces: Informality and 'Blurred Boundaries'

There are well established linkages between space and poverty (Amis, 1995), which highlight women's exclusion from production and income generation as one explanatory factor for their disadvantaged position in many societies. There is also increasing evidence to show that men and women's conceptions, experiences and use of space differ (Bowlby, 1990; McDowell, 1993; McDowell and Sharp, 1997; England, 1991; Hanson and Pratt, 1995), and the links between the 'social' and the 'spatial' have been well researched by feminist geographers in the context of the industrialised cities of Europe and North America (Moore, 1988; Bondi, 1990; England, 1991; McDowell, 1993). Much of the feminist work which seeks to explain gendered spatial inequalities has criticised dualist categories of 'public' and 'private' as they oversimplify the realities of women and men's working lives (Vaiou, 1994; McDowell, 1993; Milroy and Wismer, 1994), for as Radcliffe (1993: 103), poignantly argues, "the reality of women's lives go beyond simple dichotomies". The ways in which women experience space and negotiate the boundaries between public and private in order to develop coping strategies have received much attention by western feminists but there is still a lack of similar research in the developing world (but see Davidson 1996; Wills, 1996; McIlwaine, 1996; Radcliffe, 1995; Peake and Trotz, 1999; Lawson and Klak, 1990). Indeed, dichotomies between 'public' and 'private' are even less easily differentiated in the developing world as they are in Europe or North America. In fact, the informal sector provides an excellent window for examining the ways in which women and men move between the spaces of public/private and reproduction/production (see Lawson and Klak, 1990, for Latin American examples).

In the context of the informal sector, women's association with the 'private sphere', the household and reproduction, can be linked to traditional notions of their identity as carers and 'helpers' rather than producers in their own right, whilst men's identity is constructed through public images and productive roles. Through their identities as marginalised or excluded 'others', the lives of female informal sector participants are often reflected in spatial seclusion and boundary negotiation (McIlwaine, 1996). Women may exhibit more restricted and disadvantageous use of spaces, particularly in cities, which will reflect on their labour market opportunities. In her research in Oaxaca, Mexico, Wills (1996) challenges the validity of the public/private dichotomy by analysing how women's location within urban space affects the construction of the boundaries between these spaces, and asks whether the increasing feminisation of the labour market in Latin America has led to new identity formation for female workers.

This fluidity is well summed up by Massey (1994) who argues that public and private are not clearly divided spaces, instead they comprise a 'multiplicity of spaces' where lines of division may or may not be crossed. Notions of 'multiplicity' are useful in thinking about the informal sector, and the ways in which it encompasses different social groups within cities. It is now well established that participation in the 'public' sphere is central to the survival of poor households, but there is a need to investigate the existence of 'intermediary' spaces', perhaps within the community, which are accessible to women from the household (Milroy and Wismer, 1994. As Stitcher (1990) poignantly argues, movement into public spaces cannot result in increased power and liberty for women if men won't allow it. Within cities, therefore, there are both 'visible' and 'invisible' boundaries, and arenas of conflict, which female workers must negotiate in order to gain access to markets, technology, knowledge and information, finance and customers.

The structure of the informal labour market, characterised by its blurring of 'economic' boundaries and non-compliance with institutional and spatial norms, makes it an ideal focus for understanding the ways in which different workers use particular localities for survival and how places are conditioned by prevailing gendered and racialised processes. As the informal sector is 'governed' less by the state and formal institutions and more by socio-spatial processes, we might argue that notions of ethnic and gendered identity are central to the embeddedness of certain social groups within its confines. Furthermore, we need to understand the role that social capital plays in developing and maintaining distinct 'gendered' or 'racialised' informal networks in the labour market. Although post-colonial discourses have thrown some light on the importance of appreciating 'difference' in countries of the South, there is still a lack of empirical research on racialised gendering and its influence on labour market access. Nowhere is this more apparent than in the Commonwealth Caribbean, where informality is a way of life for many.

Conclusions

As this chapter has attempted to show, there are key economic, social, environmental and institutional conditions which shape the informal sector in different places. As with individuals, different places also have their own identities, a factor which adds a layer of complexity to the interplay between gender, ethnicity and space. In the context of development policy, there is a need to conceptualise these differences and relate them to practical grassroots objectives. In societies like the Caribbean, where the informal sector is deeply embedded in society as a 'way of life', social and spatial factors may shape the informal sector as much as the macro-economic framework. Despite the large body of literature on the informal sector, there is an apparent lack of empirical research on this topic in the small island economies of the Commonwealth Caribbean, at a time when most islands are facing the consequences of recession. Of particular importance in Trinidad and elsewhere in the Caribbean are issues of racialisation, which are deeply ingrained in society as a result of the region's historical legacy. The next chapter provides some insight into the path of 'development' followed in the Commonwealth Caribbean, and examines in some detail the economic and social development of Trinidad from an historical perspective.

3 Perspectives on Caribbean Development

The Caribbean Region

This chapter initially aims to provide a general overview of the development of the Caribbean region, and then focuses specifically on Trinidad. Following a brief introduction, the chapter examines the history of the Caribbean, with particular reference to colonialism, slavery and the plantation economy. In continuation, the chapter presents an analysis of the importance of labour and work in the Caribbean, a region which has been part of the international division of labour since the 1500s. This is followed by a brief examination of the current economic and social problems faced by the region, such as economic dependency, poverty and debt.

The region known as the Caribbean, or more familiarly as the West Indies, consists of a vast array of small island states. The term 'West Indies', is roughly synonymous with the islands of the 'Antilles', also referred to as the British Caribbean, under which countries like Jamaica and Trinidad fall. Today, the label 'West Indian' is more often used to refer to a specific culture, rather than a place of origin. The Caribbean comprises twenty-eight nations and has a total population of around 35 million people (Richardson, 1992). The arc of the region, displayed in Figure 3.1, stretches from Belize in central America and the Bahamas located to the east of Florida, to the Greater Antilles (Jamaica, Belize, Haiti, Dominican Republic and Puerto-Rico) to the smaller Leeward and Windward chains through Trinidad and Tobago to Guyana, Suriname and Cayenne on the coast of South America.

The term 'Commonwealth Caribbean' refers to those islands which have been, or are presently, British colonies. Following the break-up of the unsuccessful Federation of the West Indies in 1962, Antigua, Bahamas, Barbados, Dominica and Grenada have all become independent states within the Commonwealth, and Guyana and Trinidad and Tobago are now Republics. St Christopher/Nevis, St Lucia, and St Vincent and the Grenadines are self-governing constitutional monarchies which are individually associated with the United Kingdom for external affairs and defence. These islands along with Antigua, Grenada, Dominica and Montserrat have formed themselves into the Organisation of Eastern Caribbean States (OECS), which is currently working successfully towards the goals of economic and political unity. Belize and the British Virgin Islands also work closely with the group. The remaining British Caribbean

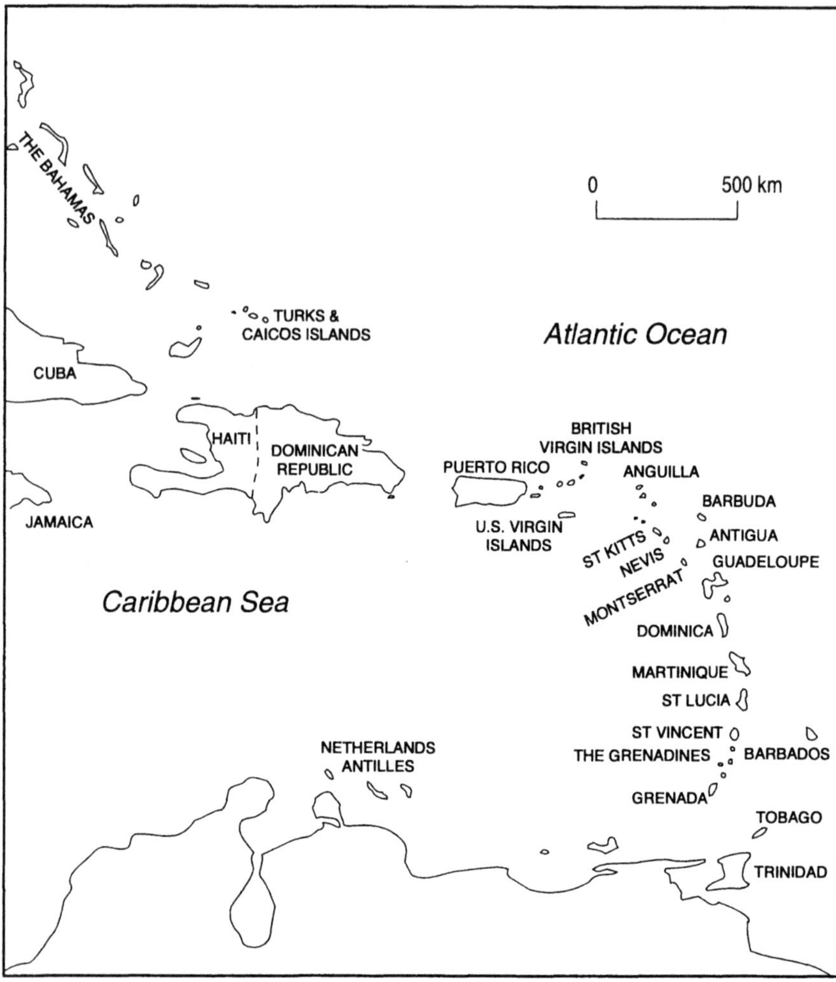

Figure 3.1 The Commonwealth Caribbean

includes Montserrat, Anguilla, British Virgin Islands, Turks and Caicos and the Cayman islands, which are still governed by the United Kingdom. Bermuda is still a British colony, but has few contacts with other Caribbean islands in terms of trade and economic relations.

There are many perceptions as to what represents 'Caribbean', in both the geographical, and cultural dimensions. The region is broadly defined according to both its geographical location, and its cultural assimilation. For instance, the island chains of the Greater and Lesser Antilles are located in the same 'region' as the Guianas on the north-east coast of Central America, and Belize, due to cultural and historical ties. These boundaries, which are ill-defined, have led to difficulties in studying the region as a whole due to the cultural and economic diversity displayed within. As such, Lowenthal (1972a: xiii) talks of the "unevenness and differences of these societies, their insularities and common bonds", an apt description of the complexities which present themselves in the Caribbean.

The precise manner of the development of the Caribbean region defies easy academic explanation. Demas (1965) and Worrell (1987) note that small island size, undiversified economies and inherited economic dependency are characteristic of the region. Although most of the islands are politically independent, they are still subject, in varying degrees, to external economic and military domination. Despite dependent linkages with foreign powers, the region is full of local complexities, for which an understanding cannot simply be found in its colonial relationship with Europe. Whilst many of the islands retain common scars of colonialism and slavery, they also represent distinct countries in their own right. More specifically, each nation is a micro state which is dependent on an intricate set of linkages operating within the country, the region and the international forum. Unfortunately, a typical western view of the Caribbean as a far away tropical paradise still remains. The publication of a quarterly lifestyle magazine *Caribbean World* represents a good example of the imagery which is associated with the region. To many outsiders, the islands epitomise fantasy, sunshine and enjoyment.

Despite individual distinctiveness, one factor which the islands of the Caribbean share is a common heritage, a binding historical past, which has shaped their economies and societies in such a way that has not been seen elsewhere. No other region of the world has been subject to the length of external domination which has been experienced in the Caribbean. The last 500 years has witnessed Caribbean domination by other nations in the global search for power and wealth. This unique region has been subjected to centuries of imposed power, as the sovereignty of islands was shifted from the hands of one conquering power to another. This domination has led from slavery, through to the importation of Western models of development involving industrialisation and modernisation (Lewis, 1955) and more recently, economic restructuring agreements with the International Monetary Fund (IMF) (Thomas, 1988; Lundy, 1999). Foreign cultures, languages, and races have been superimposed onto the original population of Caribs and Arawaks. Today, the islands are inhabited by a mixture of peoples, few of whom are related to their ancient ancestors.

The nature of Caribbean development, past and present, is a subject that is gaining in academic interest. Although the literature on the Caribbean is not as extensive as the coverage on other developing continents, there is a growing body of work which seeks to explore the complexities of the region (Thomas, 1988; Potter, 1989; Deere *et al*, 1990; McAffe, 1991; Richardson, 1992; Momsen, 1993; Klak, 1998; Potter, 2000). For researchers who advocate that the dependency school of thought has largely been abandoned in the light of the New World Order (Wallerstein, 1974), the countries of the Caribbean bear witness to the fact that a strain of dependent development still exists (Frank, 1967; Quijano, 1974). Wallerstein's (1974) development of a European centered world economy driven by a capitalist division of labour is also relevant to the Caribbean situation. Similarly, geographical theory has attempted to seek explanation for the existence of core and peripheral areas, unequal exchange and inequality (Taylor, 1986). That is not to say that the functioning and development of the region is attributable to dependency alone, but that it is still an important consideration when exploring the history of development in the Caribbean (Potter, 1989).

It has been argued by many authors (Rivera, 1987; Thomas, 1988) that development still eludes the Caribbean. As McAffe observes "in few regions can the maldistribution of power and wealth be seen more clearly than in the lands that Columbus first sighted, those of the Caribbean" (McAffe, 1991: 3). As a whole, the region is rich in resources, labour and culture and yet poverty is increasing. Unemployment is rapidly escalating, amounting to 30 per cent in most islands, purchasing power is falling, and there is a marked inequitable distribution of income (UNDP, 1992).

A decline in the prices of Caribbean exports, sugar and fruit, has lead to further local retrenchment of the economy. The lack of investment in domestic agriculture has resulted in increased imports of essential items, at a greater cost due to widespread currency devaluations, inflation and social unrest. Many islands, including Jamaica, Barbados and Trinidad, have attempted to graft light and heavy industry onto a colonial agricultural framework, but with limited success. Following Lewis' (1955) theory of *industrialisation by invitation*, national governments were encouraged to attract investment by foreign companies in light manufacturing plants. Operation Beehive in Barbados, launched in 1969, is a good example of a strategy built on the sale of cheap labour (Potter, 1981; Clayton and Potter, 1996). Trinidad, on the other hand, followed a more ambitious industrial programme by attempting to develop an efficient petroleum based economy, as will be discussed.

The region faced an external debt of US$21 billion in the 1980s. Caribbean economies have been overseen by foreign consortia of the IMF, World Bank, and the Inter American Development Bank, through a series of structural adjustment packages, the effect of which has been decreased public spending, poverty and debt (Deere *et al*, 1990; Potter, 2000). Jamaica, the Dominican Republic, and Trinidad and Tobago, paid out a combined US$1.3 billion more in debt and interest charges between 1986 and 1988, than they received in grants and loans (Girvan *et al*, 1990). Recently, there has been a decrease in the demand for Caribbean products as American and European quotas have curtailed imports of Caribbean products, a process which has repercussions for the poor (Mitchell, 1989).

The Caribbean region has approximately 35 million residents (Richardson, 1992). Ethnically, the region is dominated by a two-thirds majority of black African descendants which represent the legacy of the slave trade. In addition, there are minority ethnic groups, although their extent greatly differs from island to island. It is not surprising to find substantial groups of other races in some islands, for example, East Indians constitute nearly half the population of Trinidad. There is a similar pattern of linguistics as Spanish, French, English and local dialects are all spoken in different islands, which is a direct result of colonial history.

Columbus' Islands: Dependent Linkages or Transition to Independence?

The Caribbean has been regarded as an appendage of the European-oriented world economy since the heralded arrival of Columbus in 1492. The islands were settled and conquered firstly by Spain, and then by Britain, in a period which ranged from 1624 to the early 1800s with the earliest European conquests being the Leeward Isles, and St Kitts in 1624, Barbados in 1627, Jamaica in 1655, and Trinidad and Tobago in 1797 (Lucas, 1890). Prior to Columbus's journey, an aboriginal people incorporating Carib and Arawak Amerindian tribes had already inhabited the region for several thousand years (Richardson, 1992). The sixteenth and seventeenth centuries saw the Caribbean perform the role of a Spanish transit zone between the mainland and South America, a route used for the extraction of gold (Sauer, 1966).

The Caribbean was not firmly attached to the European economy until the mid 17th century, when the islands became its main supplier of tropical produce, such as sugar cane and spices. In the early eighteenth century, most of the smaller islands were constantly swapping hands between the powers of the Spaniards, French, English and the Dutch. Writing in 1890, Lucas, an historian, stated that the islands were merely used as 'stepping stones' in the history of global trade. This was a movement which marked the start of the division of labour on a global scale, a process which affords a central theme within this chapter.

A Brief History of the Caribbean: The Transformation of a Landscape

As previously mentioned, the Caribbean was first colonised by the Spanish voyage of discovery in search for gold. The Spaniards found the islands to be a prime starting point for their search for gold in Latin America. Ferdinand of Spain referred to the importance of importing black slaves because "all these be getting gold for me" (Sauer, 1966: 206). The Spanish had little interest in settlement or trade in the region, and only settled on the largest islands. By the year 1511, the Spanish fleet had arrived at the last island of the region, Trinidad (Conway, 1984).

On arrival in the Caribbean, the Spanish found the native population to consist of tribes of Arawak and Carib Indians who were highly susceptible to European diseases. The existence of Amerindian tribes is well documented by Newson (1976), Rouse (1986) and Watts (1987). Historians are uncertain of the factors surrounding the demise of the indigenous Indians, but it is widely suggested that it was a combination of disease, food shortages and slaughter. The weakness of the indigenous people in the first few years of contact, combined with abstraction of cultivators from their plots in order to work for the Spanish resulted in years of disease, food shortages and death (Thomas, 1988). The diminishing indigenous population marked the first stage of environmental and cultural devastation in the region. The widespread importation of black slaves, which ensued the 'discovery', was based on the apparent weakness of the indigenous Indians, and the need to replace them with a more resilient labour force (Williams, 1970; Wallerstein, 1974). As Spanish agricultural staples did not fair well in the region due to the climate, Columbus brought in animals and sugar cane, the latter becoming almost synonymous with the Caribbean.

Although the Spanish dominated the large islands of the Greater Antilles, now known as Cuba and Hispaniola, they never actively colonised the Lesser Antilles, with the exception of maintaining a small administrative presence in Trinidad. It was the 1600s which saw the capture of many smaller islands by the other European nations. The advent of North European settlement did not begin until 1624, when a small number of English and French families arrived in St Kitts. British and French objectives differed from the Spanish, in that they wanted the islands for trading purposes and colonisation (Brereton, 1979, 1981). Colonisation was a gradual process, which started with the cultivation of crops such as tobacco, cotton and cocoa, and later sugar cane. This marked the beginning of the Anglo-French domination of the islands, which soon spread to Barbados in 1627 and Guadeloupe in 1635 (Lucas, 1890), and to Trinidad in 1802 (Conway, 1984). Sugar cane came to Barbados from Brazil in 1640, and spread to other islands during that decade. At the same time, a further influx of African slaves brought in to work in the fields began to change the population of the islands (Watts, 1987), a movement which was to have long-lasting consequences for the region.

The conquest of many of the islands by the British, Dutch and French had only served to enhance the transformation of the Caribbean islands. Many islands were turned into monocrop economies, as sugar cane cultivation on small islands competed heavily with local food crops and forest. The islands became absorbed in an expanding European commodity exchange over which it had no control. The growing demand for sugar cane in Europe gave little regard for the widespread social devastation which was taking place. The most spectacular documented case of environmental and social devastation in Caribbean history was the French burning of the forest and scrub of the entire island of St Croix "to make the islands more healthy" (Dirks, 1987: 16).

The legacy that has been left by the colonial powers is one of sugar cane domination, an industry which is still important in providing employment and foreign exchange. During slavery, the production of local subsistence crops had been limited, a problem which has been carried into the present agricultural system. In 1973, Norman Girvan observed that Caribbean nations produce what they do not need, and import most of what they consume (Girvan, 1973). Many countries, including Trinidad and Tobago, still have to import over 70 per cent of their food requirements (UNDP, 1992). Small-scale agriculture has never been able to compete with export agriculture in terms of fertile land provision, or wages. Bananas are the second most important export crop of the region with large multinational corporations, Geest Industries of Britain and United Brands of USA, holding a monopoly over exports. Geest buys the entire crop from Dominica, St Lucia, St Vincent and Grenada in agreement with the Windward Island Banana Growers Association (WINBAN) which represents 16,000 to 20,000 small-scale producers. This type of international domination places the small-scale farmer in direct response to external constraints. According to Beckford (1972), the plantations always had command over labour and technology, excluding agricultural advancement to the small-scale farmer.

The Search for Employment: The Global Importance of Labour Provision in the Caribbean

Columbus' voyage of "discovery" also represented a spatial expansion of political and economic control (Wolf, 1982). The Caribbean has been part of the international system of trade for four centuries, a process which is best exemplified through the region's integration in the international division of labour. The effects of slavery, emigration and foreign investment are widespread. The region's external focus has been a direct result of its historical introduction into trade since the 1400s. As a result, the plantation economy, the most influential and well-documented aspect of Caribbean history, represents one of the most important contributors to understanding the existence of modern Caribbean society. The concept of plantation agriculture in the region has been well-documented by a number of academics including Beckford (1972), and Sheridan (1973). Sheridan (1973) states that the nature of the plantation makes it a global and not a regional enterprise, as factors of production from the entire globe are united. In this respect, the Caribbean production unit consisted of sugar cane originally from the Asian continent; labour from the West Indies, Africa and India; buildings, materials and livestock from North America; and capital, technology and management from western Europe.

Lewis (1955) argues that the plantation was a pioneer of the global division of labour and capital transfers. Many present-day global companies operate a system which is an extension of the concept of the plantation. In other words, production takes place in a country where labour is cheap and abundant, whilst the other factors of production are imported and profit is extracted to the metropole. When the country in question ceases to be the most favoured and profitable location, the factors of production are simply moved elsewhere.

In his famous thesis on the global importance of plantation agriculture, Eric Williams (1962), the late Prime Minister of Trinidad and Tobago, indicated that it was the capital accumulated in the plantation which partially financed the Industrial Revolution in the United Kingdom in the 1700s. The plantation combined factory and field at an early date, and was 'industrial' prior to the rise of industry in Europe (Mintz, 1985). Geertz (1963), in his analysis of the plantation system, identified the concept as an attempt to bring the islands' crops into the modern world but to leave behind their people, an attitude which could also be used to describe the current use of labour in the region's Export Processing Zones (Safa, 1990).

The term 'plantation' describes a variety of land units which have the common link of displaying several distinct characteristics (Beckford, 1972). Firstly, plantation land was considered to be a factor of production because capital accumulation was considered to be the prime goal of the plantation. Secondly, overall control was centralised by the owner who made a substantial investment in technology, as the process was highly mechanised. Labour was imported from elsewhere, and coerced to work on the plantation, either through slavery, or through schemes such as indentured labour. The plantation produced solely for the international markets and, in this respect, has instigated the production of metro-capital under a Caribbean setting.

The immense influence of the plantation as the dominant unit of production is displayed throughout the region in terms of settlement patterns (Potter, 2000). It was the plantation which acted as the socio-economic unit of the countryside and not the village. An early production unit was approximately 200-300 acres so that the cane could be quickly processed and cultivated intensively. Today many rural communities, such as Caroni in Trinidad, are still present on the old plantation sites. Rojas (1989) and Potter (1995) refer to the Caribbean settlement pattern as *plantopolis*, a pattern which was initially influenced by the plantations, and a primate city which has developed over time into the current Caribbean metropolis (Conway, 1989; Potter, 1989, 2000). Initially, towns acted as colonial-administrative centres, and not as industrial cores (Clarke, 1974; Potter, 1993a). Today, the region is characterised by high urbanisation, currently estimated at over 50-60 per cent, and urban primacy where a large proportion of country's population reside in the capital (see Potter *et al*, 1998; Potter, 2000). In Trinidad, over 60 per cent of the country's population live in Greater Port of Spain (Conway, 1989).

Although much speculation has occurred concerning the historical influence of the old colonial powers in the region, little consideration is given to the counter effect of the Caribbean on the metropoles. It is argued by Mintz (1985), that labour regimes on the plantations conformed with a strict division of labour which was later to be used in the Industrial Revolution in the United Kingdom. He argues that this model of labour utilisation was first established in the Caribbean where it would later be adapted in the UK. It is further argued that the extraction of wealth from the colonies was essential for investment in the Industrial Revolution, which is heralded as the start of the UK's development. Sugar provided by the Caribbean was also instrumental in providing an important dietary supplement to the working classes who toiled in British factories.

A legacy which has remained from the Caribbean plantation, has been the continued inclusion of Caribbean workers in the international division of labour. The Caribbean has been witness to the continued sale of its labour force in the international market in the last 500 years. Although this process has taken a number of different forms, work and employment have remained central to the transformation of Caribbean society. Lowenthal (1972a) argues that two 'agencies' exert influence on the social and economic development of the region. Firstly, there is emigration from the region in search of work (Thomas-Hope, 1992); and secondly, there has been the more recent movement of foreign companies, culture and goods into the region in search of cheap labour (Safa, 1990). Both processes tend to leave the Caribbean people dependent on the outside world. The Caribbean appears to be dominated by its ability to provide labour, both at home and abroad.

Migration has played a dominant role in the demographic development of the region. The flow of slaves into the Caribbean varied, with 300,000 entering Jamaica, Barbados and the Leeward Islands in the 17th Century, and 1.4 million in the following century (Curtin, 1969). The Windward Isles received an additional 140,000 slaves, and Trinidad and Tobago and Guyana a further 50,000. The abolition of slavery, between 1834 and 1838 led to the implementation of indentureship in order to continue a good supply of labour for the plantations. Since the abolition of slavery, there have been many subsequent migrations both within the region, and internationally. Jamaica and Barbados provided large numbers of labourers for the building of the Panama Canal (Richardson, 1992). The discovery of oil in Trinidad and Tobago in the early 1900s attracted large numbers of workers from other islands during the period 1931-1946. This movement has resulted in the racial and ethnic diversity shown by the region as a whole (Lowenthal, 1972a).

Patterns of migration in the 20th century may be seen as a reversal of the pattern developed by the plantation economy. Prior to independence in the 1960s, there was a mass exodus of Caribbean workers to Europe, in search of work, as part of a replacement population scheme. Large numbers of West Indians emigrated to Britain to take up vacancies in the National Health Service, and the transport and the public sectors (Peach, 1984). This started a pattern of continuing seasonal and permanent emigration from the Caribbean, yet again in response to the demand for labour. The situation has changed little in recent years with the onset of migration to the USA and Canada which has only recently been slowed (Thomas-Hope, 1992). It is estimated by McAffe (1991), that 20 per cent of Caribbean born people currently live in the United States.

Migration is a way of life in the Caribbean, and its prominence has had repercussions on both the islands and the recipient countries. Continued migration in search of work has altered Caribbean household structure, resulting in many children growing up with absent fathers as portrayed in the novel *My Mother who Fathered Me* (Clarke, 1954). The absence of male workers has also led to a high female participation rate in the labour force, with high numbers of women working in the informal sector. It is currently estimated that female-headed households account for 30 per cent of Caribbean households, with women constituting between 30 and 50 per cent of the official labour force of the region, and 40 per cent of the informal, labour force (Momsen, 1993). Massiah (1989) estimates that if home-based work alone was taken into account, it would raise the general participation rates of women by 10 to 20 per cent.

Work is an important determinant of wealth and status in the Caribbean, and it accords a measure of independence and social respect. Caribbean workers, particularly women, will undertake most types of work, a factor which places importance on the role of the informal sector. The current phase of the Caribbean role in the international division of labour has been witnessed in the last 10 years. Global and foreign companies are returning to the Caribbean in order to make use of the cheap labour in the form of Export Processing Zones and government incentive packages (Safa, 1990; Pearson, 1993) Policies based on the free trade principle are currently backed by the World Bank as a solution to unemployment and the generation of income. The employment of young women in sweatshop conditions in Dominica, Puerto Rico, and Barbados has been well-documented by Elson and Pearson (1981), Elson (1983) and Safa (1990).

International trading arrangements have returned some of the existing European control to the United States, which is now the major influence in the region in terms of trade, military power and aid. American interest in the Caribbean has been growing since the 1980s. The Caribbean is often cited as being in the 'backyard of the US', a fact which is supported by heightened political and economic interest. There have been a number of new aid, trade and military policies adopted to strengthen involvement in the region (Deere *et al*, 1990). The Caribbean Basin Initiative (CBI) represents one of the US attempts to assist in the development of the region. The CBI attempted to solve the region's economic problems by integrating the region more closely to US markets. It was hoped that by giving the region increased duty-free access to the US market, Caribbean exports would increase. There has also been an increased military presence, particularly following the political unrest in Grenada in 1983, the attempted coup in Trinidad in 1990, and the violent elections in Jamaica in 1992.

Today, the Caribbean is a geographical receptacle for material and cultural stimuli from outside the region (Richardson, 1992), in the form of crops, animals, people, technology and food. This does not exclude the fact, however, that the region has developed a distinct identity of its own, one based on the amalgamation of tradition and modernity. Imported and local influences have been subtly combined in the different islands, to the extent that the Caribbean is a melting pot of culture, ethnicity, economic development and technology, where direct contrasts lie side by side. It is not uncommon to see a Catholic church next to a Mosque; a modern glass building next to a shack; a donkey and cart following a petrol tanker. The ensuing reliance on food imports has been further consolidated by new consumer preferences for foreign food and products. In many islands, local produce is seen to be of an inferior quality and the preference for 'Kentucky Fried Chicken' over traditional meals has lead to further consumer imports. The globalisation of American culture has far reaching implications for the Caribbean in terms of its future development (Potter, 1993a, 1993b, 2000).

Economic and Social Development in Trinidad: Overview

As one of the largest islands in the southern Caribbean in terms of territory (4,828 square km), population (1.2 million) and natural resources, Trinidad has always been viewed as a country with prospects. Years of alternating poverty and prosperity have made their mark on the population and government of this small ex-colony. Trinidad was fortunate to benefit from large oil revenues in the 1970s, but found itself suffering from diminishing returns, and debt in the 1980s. In recent decades, Trinidadians appear to have lived from boom to recession, altering their lifestyles to match both their incomes and government expenditure.

In comparison to other islands in the Caribbean, Trinidad appears to be more developed in terms of its social and economic structure. Unlike the other islands of the Lesser Antilles, it largely abandoned its agricultural base during the oil years and has never fully returned to it. Instead, it has constantly attempted to promote industry and the service sector. The capital, Port of Spain, is becoming more typical of a small Latin American city than other capitals in the Lesser Antilles in terms of infrastructural development and urban morphology (Conway, 1984, 1989; Potter, 1985, 1993b). Communications and infrastructure have generally improved, but with this advancement has come another strain of problems associated with urban development. Uncontrolled urbanisation, vast rural-urban disparities, escalating unemployment and an increase in crime have all accompanied the limited gains that Trinidad had made during the oil boom (Conway, 1989).

Trinidad's development, although largely uncontrolled, has often served to place the country outside the bounds of countries that are perceived to have severe development problems. Instead, it is seen as being somewhere between developed and underdeveloped, and consequently is viewed by outsiders as undeserving of assistance. Yet, an in-depth look into the workings of the country shows that beneath the reasonable level of real GDP, which in 1989 was US$6,266 per capita, there is a large population in both the rural and urban areas which exists from hand to mouth, and lives in squalor. The obvious wealth of a small sector, consisting of the middle and upper classes, hides the apparent poverty. Furthermore, it could be argued that many Trinidadians, especially those living in certain areas of Port of Spain, have a poorer quality of life than their counterparts in Barbados and Grenada, due to the problems of pollution and crime, which are associated with city life.

Trinidad's current economic climate is a true reflection of its historical background, which still possesses remnants of European rule. The country was a colony under Spanish and British rule for many centuries, and it has only been responsible for its own development for a short time. For a surprisingly short period, 1958-1962, the twin-island state of Trinidad and Tobago was a member of the autonomous Federation of the West Indies. It was in 1961, when Jamaica left this experiment, that Trinidad's then Prime Minister Eric Williams remarked that 'one from ten leaves none' and led Trinidad and Tobago to independence in 1962. In 1976, the country adopted a new constitution, under which it became a republic replacing the Queen and her Governor General with a President chosen by Parliament, although operative control was still vested in the Prime Minister.

The geography of Trinidad represents a diverse pattern of physical and social development. As shown in Figure 3.2, the country's physical boundaries extend from a tropical rain forest in the northern mountain range, through to the undulating plains of Caroni's cane fields, to the flat southern coastline dominated by oil exploration. The typical Caribbean image of paradise, endless beaches and palm trees does not apply to Trinidad, and the island has its own distinct and unique identity. This physical diversity is also mirrored by a pattern of widely divergent social and demographic characteristics.

Due to its colonial heritage, several cultures and religions exist within a

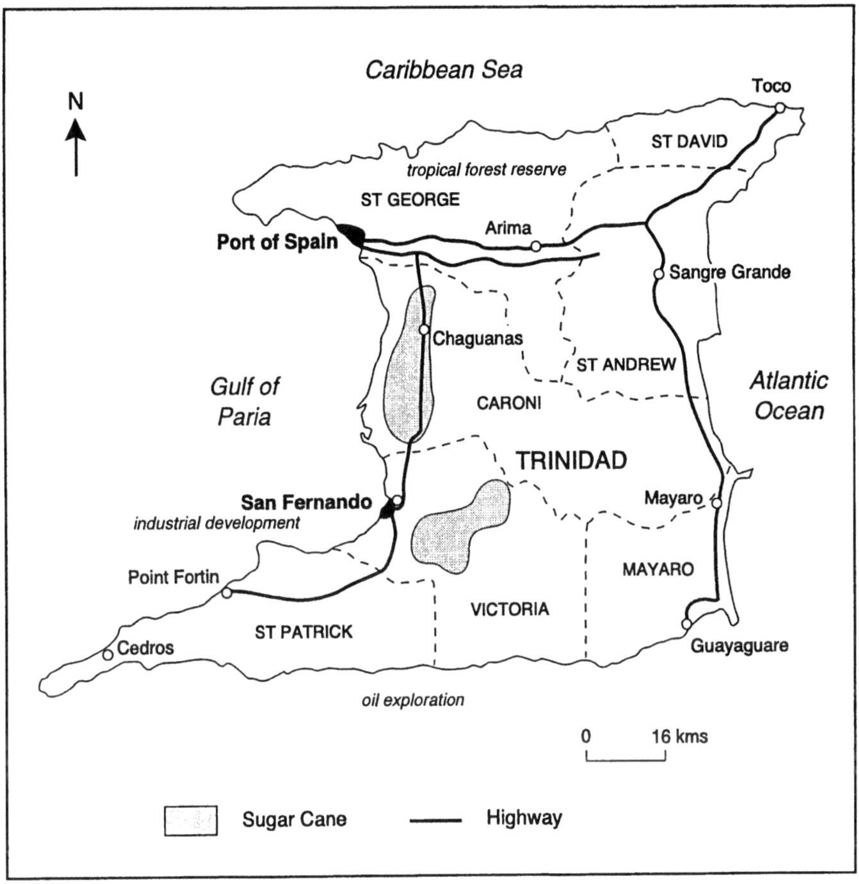

Figure 3.2 Trinidad's Spatial Pattern of Social and Physical Development

limited space. Although the national anthem suggests harmony, a degree of plurality is reflected across society in terms of culture, employment and development (Lowenthal, 1972a; Clarke, 1986; Conway, 1989). Trinidad celebrates a host of festivals from Catholic to Hindu and Muslim, as religion is merged within a West Indian identity (Yelvington, 1993). All societal groups are Trinidadian first and foremost, but their indigenous culture plays an important part in the formation of the geography of the island.

The social and physical development of Trinidad has been preconditioned by a number of external influences over which it has had little control. The historical evolution of the country, a progression maintained solely for the purpose of colonial domination and the abstraction of wealth, is responsible for the amalgamation of a number of distinct economic systems, cultures and religions, which have served to shape the geography of the country into its present form. Historically, the society has exhibited a rigid, racially determined socio-economic structure which was geographically expressed (Braithwaite, 1953).

Each major economic and social transformation in Trinidad had important repercussions for the geography of the country, particularly in terms of the spatial distribution of population, employment and settlement. In particular, the island's unique colonial heritage was influential in ascribing a strict social hierarchy to the mixture of races which found themselves living together in a small island. A past history of colonial domination has designated a major role to the forces of culture, religion and ethnicity in determining an individual's place in society. This fundamental factor has resulted in a distinct spatial and regional distribution of the population according to class, occupation and ethnicity.

Recently, in the short period of time since independence in 1962, the country has experienced rapid economic growth followed by an unforseeable deep recession. These economic and societal changes have been mirrored on the ground by a transformation of the country's demographic, cultural and physical patterns of growth. Independence represented an important milestone for the development of Trinidad as the colonial chains, which had once preconditioned the country's development, were abandoned in the light of a national based control. Despite the prevailing fact that the Caribbean maintains its role as a dependent part of the world system, controlled by the metropoles, Trinidad has attempted to break from this relationship through its internal development and national growth strategies (Thomas, 1988). Although Trinidad is still subject to a large degree of outside influence, the arrival of independence at the same time as the oil boom, gave the government an opportunity to re-evaluate the economic and social goals of the island (Carrington, 1967; Conway, 1984; Auty, 1989).

The Early Years: From Conquest to Colony

The Legacy of Trinidad's Colonial Past: Plantation Economy, White Domination and Social Segregation

The twin islands of Trinidad and Tobago have experienced a range of colonial conquests since their 'discovery' by Spain in 1498. It was not until the late decades of the eighteenth century that Spain decided to develop Trinidad in a pattern similar to other colonial outposts in the region (Borde, 1992). The tool of development was the infamous 'plantation economy' (Beckford, 1975), which had swept through the non-Hispanic islands. This was based upon the intensive monocultural production of sugar. The New World plantation system combined African slave labour with European management, finance and technology. In order to capitalise on this system, the Spanish brought across African slaves from the mainland to provide labour, the native population of Trinidad being too small to utilise in the fields.

The highly-organised basis of the plantation helped to revolutionise agriculture in the Caribbean. By the 1760s, both Britain and France owned profitable sugar islands, and Trinidad was greatly sought after for its potential. The Spanish wanted to develop Trinidad into a main sugar producer, but advancement was still hindered by the lack of labour, capital and expertise. Consequently, in 1783, they turned to French planters from other Caribbean islands by granting foreign catholics the privilege of settling in Spanish colonies under the Cedula de Pobulacion. This influx of French farmers, and their slaves, was to have a long lasting influence on the geographical and social evolution of Trinidad.

The settlement of the French in Trinidad in the 1780s and 1790s created a new society, as aspects of both French and Spanish culture were superimposed onto an African heritage. Many of the French became absorbed into the landowning class, and they contributed to the economy by promoting plantation agriculture and slavery. Trinidad's rapidly-growing prosperity attracted the British, who captured the island in 1797. In 1802, Trinidad became the first British Crown Colony, and in 1814 Tobago became a British colony of the Windward Island group (Williams, 1970). Trinidad and Tobago were not joined administratively until 1889. The British invasion brought a new period of political and social reform with the influx of English speakers and the Protestant faith. Within a decade, a small elite English minority ruled over a predominantly French and African population, with the French farmers occupying a middle strata in the society. Trinidad was an experimental colony for the British, in that it was the first territory to experience Crown Colony rule.

As Trinidad's economic structure was slow to expand and change, so was the country's social structure prohibited in its progression forward. As a nineteenth century colony, Trinidad maintained a strict social hierarchy based on status and occupation in which ethnicity, or more precisely skin colour, ascribed placement within the former categories. The administrative and elite classes consisted of whites, either from the mother country or other Caribbean colonies. Beneath this small elite group there was a middle class which consisted of the merchants and the 'Creole planters', often from the French islands, who were responsible for managing the land. There also existed a divergent group of "free coloureds" who had also come to populate the island. Unsurprisingly, the 'underclass' consisted of black labourers, traditionally African slaves, brought in to work the plantations (Braithwaite, 1953; Brereton, 1993). The Africans were of varied ethnic and religious groups from the west coast of Africa (Warner-Lewis, 1991).

The plantation served to keep the majority of the population subservient to their masters, and trapped within their own poverty. Men, women and children were forced to work long hours for a meagre wage or, more commonly, a voucher for the plantation shop (Brereton, 1979). The black population was prevented from attaining social mobility by its lack of access to opportunity through education or employment training. Their lives were segregated from the white population by exclusion to institutions such as the 'country club' and the many 'white' sectors of the island. Their confinement to the plantation estates, where they lived, allowed their colonial masters the opportunity to rule the island without much resistance.

By the early nineteenth century, Trinidadian society was led by the white upper class Spanish, English and French descendants. After the emancipation of slavery in 1834, when black labour was hard to retain on the sugar plantations, a number of other sources of potential labour were tapped. Portuguese labourers were brought in from Madeira and settlers from China were integrated in a system which was repeated across the globe (Bentley and Henry, 1969; Johnson, 1987). Lastly, and most importantly, in 1845, there began a stream of indentured labourers from India (Ramesar, 1976).

As a result of extensive colonisation, the late 1800s witnessed a growing population which consisted of an amalgamation of many cultures. There existed a predominant strain of descendants of black slaves imported from West Africa by the Spanish and British. Add to this the colonial landowning classes, French Creoles, and a small Lebanese, Chinese and Syrian community, and there emerges a picture of a multi-racial Trinidad whose economy has been shaped and dominated by this colonial pattern ever since (Wood, 1968; Johnson, 1987).

Despite the emergence of a 'westernised' Afro-Creole middle class, plantation agriculture continued to play a major role in shaping society, as it perpetuated the existence of an agro-proletariat in the imported and indentured East Indian population. The abolition of slavery in 1842 freed many workers who settled beyond the plantations' peripheries, either as tenant farmers or as non-agricultural labourers. This sudden 'independence' for the black population was enhanced by the arrival of indentured East Indians who were imported to work on the plantations. Interestingly, the influx of indentured East Indian labour in the late nineteenth century placed the black population in a higher social bracket, as the Indians, perceived as 'coolies', were treated with contempt and mistrust, a problem faced by most immigrant populations (Vertovec, 1992). Whilst the East Indians continued to work on the plantations, a large proportion of the black workforce had abandoned their agricultural base for a more urban lifestyle with the advent of the oil industry. In the early years of indenture, East Indians were separate from the rest of society (Roberts and Braithwaite, 1967; Bell, 1970; Abdullah, 1991).

This movement served to attach a stigma to much of the Indian population, based on the supposed rurality and backwardness associated with agriculture, by those of African descent who saw themselves as modern, more urban and upwardly mobile. The stigma associated with agriculture is still very apparent in Trinidad, as it is in many developing countries, where the adoption of an urban lifestyle is considered paramount to development. This in turn has produced a devastating effect on the production of food for local consumption, and the decline of a sound agricultural base which is needed to fend off food imports from the developed world.

By the start of the twentieth century, the colonial state was still concerned with the export of primary products and 'cash crops' such as sugar, coffee and cocoa, which typically undermined domestic food production. Although the export-oriented economy encouraged other commercial activity, particularly foreign trading, it discouraged industrialisation due to the fear that it could undermine the primary economic base. It was not until the advent of the Second World War that concern over Trinidad's development was raised. Despite the country's contribution to the world economy, in terms of oil and sugar exports, the country gained very little in return. As with many other colonies, poverty and other obstacles to advancement were the reward for years of hard labour.

Discontentment amongst workers in the more important sectors of the economy began to mount, and by the late 1930s their dissatisfaction resulted in rioting (Nicholls, 1971; Craig, 1982). In the twentieth century, the gradual movement away from the plantation economy did not increase the possibility for change in the status, or occupation, for the majority of the islanders. According to Robinson (1971: 60), the techniques used for creating an elite in the plantation days were simply reciprocated in the present century under the 'aid to industries legislation'. In this instance, the only changing variable is the nature of the operation, which has substituted the offer of land to an elite class with industrial incentives to foreign entrepreneurs. This proved to be a similar constraint to social mobility for the indigenous population as the plantation society had been. The unavailability of employment in the professional sector provided an obstruction for well educated locals to improve their occupational status.

It was also at this time that plans were made for the controlled development of both the country's export agriculture, and oil sectors. The onset of the war was a turning point for Trinidad, as greater attention was focused on this colony in terms of infrastructural development, and it started its journey towards industrialisation.

Post War Trinidad: Sugar, Oil and Colonial Rule

Trinidad and Tobago was greatly affected by the war, as were many other outposts of the British Empire. Prior to this event, the famous 'Butler-led' riots of 1937-1938 had swept through the British Caribbean, due to poverty and hardship amongst a large proportion of the population. These violent uprisings against unfair British control led to the establishment of the famous Moyne Commission (Williams, 1970). This Commission sought to investigate the social and economic conditions which existed in Barbados, British Guiana, Jamaica, Trinidad and Tobago and other colonies. It had been reported that the islands were suffering at the hands of poverty and injustice, which the population were no longer willing to tolerate peacefully. The Commission had barely commenced its work when the investigation was hampered by the outbreak of war in 1939.

At that time, Trinidad was experiencing the adverse effects of a growing population (473,000 in 1939), with a birth rate of 31 per 1,000 population (Conway, 1984). In order to provide increasing amounts of goods and services, agriculture became the economic focus, mainly in terms of sugar, cocoa, coffee, citrus fruits and ground provisions. The outbreak of war led to much suffering in Trinidad, as the country followed a typical pattern of colonialisation characterised by its dependency on imports. It was only the 1941 blockade, which stopped trade across the Atlantic that lead to an effort to decrease Trinidad's reliance on imported food (Carrington, 1967). The Government's initiatives to encourage agriculture were formatted in slogans such as "Grow more food, man must live" (Carrington, 1971). A marked improvement in the status of farming tempted a small population back to the land. The vast sugar cultivators, such as Tate and Lyle, were forced to devote large areas of land to vegetables, under a system of controlled prices.

At the same time, an American-British lend-lease agreement led to the American occupation of the island in 1941, which lasted until 1967. This military decision perpetuated the start of a strong American influence, which is clearly visible in the economy and society of Trinidad today. In contrast to the domestic production initiative, vast American expenditure provided the purchasing power and tastes for the expansion of new markets overseas, which were tapped after the war. Immediately following the war, levels of consumption and production returned to their pre-war patterns, once again increasing the dependence on imported goods. Trinidad soon found itself prey to a mounting balance of payments deficit, and a falling standard of living.

By 1946, oil, which had been discovered in 1907, began to dominate the economy in terms of output and investment. In the same year, oil revenues accounted for a massive 75 per cent of total export earnings. Unfortunately for the domestic economy, its highly capital-intensive production led to little improvement in employment, generating jobs for only 3 per cent of the labour force, whilst the agricultural sector still employed 25 per cent of the workforce. The vast plains of central Trinidad were devoted to the extensive production of sugar cane, an area which still employed 30 per cent of the active population, and accounted for 10 per cent of the country's exports. Trinidad's economy was inherently dependent on oil and sugar.

In 1946, Trinidad did not own a single share in the extraction and production of its own petroleum. The large multinationals Texaco and Shell were accumulating wealth at the expense of the government. In addition, all oil refining, except a limited amount for local consumption, was carried out abroad. The origin of control in the sugar plantations was hardly different. A 1953 *Economic Survey of Colonial Territories* published by the Colonial Office stated that two-thirds of the sugar cane produced in Trinidad came from estates owned by foreign companies such as Tate and Lyle, with the remainder coming from small peasant farmers. The dependent relationship with the colonial powers was reiterated throughout other sectors of the economy, including finance where three commercial banks, Barclays, The Royal Bank of Canada and The Canadian Bank of Commerce held 75 per cent of their total assets abroad (Carrington, 1967).

Trinidad's economic reliance on petroleum and sugar continued to a point where together they provided 85 per cent of foreign exchange in 1950. At the same time, another major structural weakness of the economy was becoming visibly apparent, the inability of the economy to absorb the growing labour force. The task of providing jobs, denied by the oil sector, became a burden to the weaker sectors of the economy. Mounting import bills, reliance on the international market, and devaluation against the dollar in 1952, forced Trinidad to float two loans for the development of its infrastructure. As a consequence, the public debt rose by 43 per cent and Trinidad started its journey along the trail of debt, unable to shake off its dependency on its colonial master and the international market.

Lloyd Braithwaite's work *Social Stratification in Trinidad* (1953), outlined the racially constraining nature of status and occupation which still prevailed in the island after the Second World War. The population of the country had reached 750,000 by 1956 due to an enormous increase of 17 per cent over the previous six years (Central Statistical Office, 1986), but there was still marked disparity between social groups. In the late 1950s, the national income was distributed in an uneven manner with the top 5 per cent of households controlling 22.5 per cent of the country's wealth. In direct contrast, the lowest 20 per cent of income earners held only 3.4 per cent (Ahiram, 1966: 105). At this time, urban incomes were almost twice as high as rural ones, and with the marked rural-urban division of the population according to ethnicity, the result was a hierarchy of wealth according to race. Cross (1972) states that prior to independence in 1962, the annual per capita income of whites was £1,250, of Afro-Caribbean's £260, and of East Indians £195. Independence in 1962 brought no immediate relief for the population, a third of whom were described as living in real poverty (Henry, 1975: 18). Despite the end of British rule, the rigid social hierarchy proved hard to break, and there were still clear signs of racial discrimination within employment (Camejo, 1971; Harewood, 1971).

Economic Development in Trinidad since 1950

The Oil Years: From Windfall to Industrialisation

Although oil was discovered in Trinidad as early as 1907, it was not until the 1950s that the country greatly expanded the extraction of this resource. The period from 1951-1957 was the golden age of oil operations in Trinidad (Scotland, 1983). Crude oil production reached a substantial level of 79,000 barrels per day in 1956, as opposed to a previous figure of 60,000 barrels per day. International oil prices rose due to the Suez Crisis, and the future looked brighter for this small colony (Carrington, 1971).

Prior to 1950, there had been little in the way of manufacturing, with the exception of a few national industries such as rum production, and textiles. However, the 1950s saw the enforcement of Arthur Lewis's scenario of '*industrialisation by invitation*' (1955). Along with many other developing countries, the adoption of the western-oriented modernisation theory of development had gripped the West Indies, and industrialisation was seen to lead to full employment, high rates of economic growth and social development. Echoes of the industrialisation package travelled throughout the developing world, remnants of which are clearly visible today.

Lewis (1955) stated that in order to develop a manufacturing sector in a small country, it is necessary to attract metropole business which brings capital, technology, organisation and market influence. In exchange for creating employment opportunities and generating foreign exchange, the metropoles would be eligible for an incentive package which included release from income tax, infrastructural support and regional co-operation. The colonial powers were surprisingly unreceptive to the idea until Dr Eric Williams became Prime Minister in 1956, and pushed forward his strategy of industrialisation by invitation based on the *Theory of Unlimited Supplies of Labour* (Hirschmann, 1958). Williams believed that the development of industry would stimulate the economy to such as extent that all unutilised and underemployed labour would eventually be absorbed into a growing workforce. He also identified this scenario as one which would eradicate the need for an informal sector, a sector which was seen as contributing to the under-development of the country.

Over the next thirteen years, the annual output of the manufacturing sector was to rise by $100 million, although its overall success was limited. In 1953, a total of 23 pioneer industries had contributed to only 7 per cent of the GDP in manufacturing. The annual average rate of growth achieved between 1951-1961 was 8.7 per cent, an impressive figure for a developing nation. Unfortunately, much of the benefit was lost to foreign investors, whilst the situation at home was still hampered by unemployment. It has been estimated by Carrington (1971), that between 1950 and 1963 there was a total increase in the labour force of 100,000 of which the pioneer industries only absorbed 7,000. During the same period, oil and sugar industries lost 3,800 jobs due to mechanisation. Despite the claims of industrialists, the newly-developed manufacturing sector could not be relied upon for job generation. Best (1980), in his analysis of the programme, points to the problems encountered by continued metropole ownership of the means of production which further entrenches a traditional economic relationship. This line of thought was not adopted by Eric Williams, who accelerated the move towards industrialisation following independence in 1962, in the hope that Trinidad would leave underdevelopment behind in its colonial shadow.

Williams' Model for Development: Nationalisation and State Intervention

Prior to independence and until 1971, Williams and his party the Peoples' National Movement (PNM) concentrated on the stimulation of industry in the pursuit of national development. Williams wanted to move Trinidad away from dependency to become a modern entity within the region. One of the highest priorities was given to the administration of planning and development, and the extensive nationalisation of industry. Central to his plans for national development were the development of Tobago, improvement of the sugar and garment industries, the expansion of poultry farming, and the administration of a national survey of housing which never really came to fruition (Government of Trinidad and Tobago, 1978).

A vast number of workers had abandoned agriculture in the hope of gaining a higher paid job in the industrial sector, an expectation which was short-lived. This change in employment started a drift of population from the rural to the urban areas in search of higher paid industrial jobs which did not exist (Conway, 1986). In addition, the country was experiencing an upsurge in the growth of the population which was averaging 3 per cent per annum. Government spending on infrastructure and services during the oil boom reached a staggering TT$13 million in 1956, but had declined to a deficit in 1971. By the same year, foreign borrowing had already reached TT$25.5 million. Following a similar trend, the balance of payments deficit on visible trade grew from $TT12 million in 1956 to

TT$249 million in 1971.

Alongside the industrialisation programme, a series of Five Year Plans was adopted between 1959 and 1978. The first plan (1959-63) emphasised the need for improvement of public services and infrastructure which further drew upon public sector revenues. The second plan (1964-68), further depleted the country's financial reserves in order to run the essential services of the Trinidad and Tobago Electric Co (T&TEC), the Water and Sewerage Authority (WASA) and the Trinidad and Tobago Telephone Co (TELCO). Despite severe economic problems, it was a time when marked improvements in the standard of living of the population were made as many communities were supplied with electricity, water and telephones. Williams gave full priority to education, with the result that a vast amount of money was spent on providing free education for children throughout the country, an achievement to which many developing countries still have not aspired.

The third plan, launched in 1969, was proposed at a time when it was clear that the industrialisation model had failed. Black power movements and Caribbean independence provoked an echo throughout the region. The Trinidadian lifestyle, already a blend of many cultures, became prey to the marketing companies of North America (Potter, 1993a). The inflationary effects of oil price increases had led to the demand and payment of higher wages. Wage rates had rapidly increased by 25 per cent in 1961, and had continued to rise by 10 per cent per annum until 1965 (Seers, 1969). Williams saw a middle path which involved a partnership between government and foreign investors, in the pursuit of economic and social objectives for the 'people's sector'. A case was also made for the expansion of the state sector, so that it was involved in the running of the economy at all levels. Trinidad quickly adhered to state intervention, as the government invested its oil wealth in enterprises throughout the economy.

In the 1970s, the PNM highlighted industrial growth as the way forward. The Point Lisas industrial estate, in the South, was earmarked as the new 'growth pole' to please the planning authorities, whose national framework document advocated decentralisation and regional industrial development (Government of Trinidad and Tobago, 1978). The plan also specified the development of other national industries, including the Point Lisas Development Company, Federal Chemicals, the Iron and Steel Company of Trinidad and Tobago (ISCOTT) and Fertilizers of Trinidad and Tobago (FERNTIN). Unfortunately, these companies finally came into being during a recession, and subsequently, they have not attained their potential targets. Ultimately, many of these operations, particularly ISCOTT, have been continually subsidised by the Government, and have been detrimental to the remainder of the economy.

Scotland (1983), summarises the Government's policy by highlighting the achievements made by Williams in administering increased tax relief and welfare benefits to the majority of the population, subsidisation of the cost of living, increased aid to CARICOM, and increased expenditure in infrastructure and education. A 1972 White Paper on *Public Sector Participation* in industry stated that the government was to be at the focus of the national economy. It argued that the public sector has an important role to play in building institutions to strengthen the economy, to protect the national interest and to ensure the development of national income (Government of Trinidad and Tobago, Third Five Year Plan, 1969).

The widespread involvement of the State in economic activity represents a strong feature of the existing economy. The State enterprise sector had grown to the extent that in 1986, there were 46 wholly-owned companies operating in Trinidad and Tobago. These enterprises are represented in every sector of the economy: oil, gas, petrochemicals, asphalt, airlines, banking, tourism, sugar, insurance and agriculture. In many cases, the Government has acquired private companies merely to save redundancies, thereby propping up companies with Treasury funds. This has contributed to a general malaise in the economy, which is often associated with state control.

In order to play a central role in all aspects of the economy, the government set up a number of well known institutions, including the National Housing Authority, the Agricultural Development Bank, the Industrial Development Corporation and most importantly, the National Petroleum Company (NP). Despite many criticisms of the policies implemented by Williams and his Government, the country did make rapid gains in the development of infrastructure, health care, and most importantly education, which have served as an invaluable base for future improvements.

The Current Years: Restructuring for Economic Independence

Debt and Development - Achieving the Balance

After more than twenty-five years of political independence and responsibility for national economic development, the economic structure of Trinidad and Tobago has evolved in a manner which has showed limited gains from recent change, notably in infrastructure. Despite recent economic problems, the standard of living in Trinidad still ranks amongst the highest in the Caribbean region. In addition, the economy of Trinidad managed to sustain an average annual growth rate of 3.1 per cent from 1965-1973. Between 1973-1983 it grew at an accelerated annual rate of 5.8 per cent (Central Statistical Office, 1988a).

The oil boom years of 1974-1982 saw the establishment of a reasonable infrastructural base due to increased government expenditure, but the debate still continues as to where the majority of the oil wealth flowed. In comparison with other smaller islands in the region, Trinidad has essential infrastructure such as seaports, airports, electricity generation and water production, telecommunications and road transport. Despite this, its capacity to serve many rural areas is well below its potential.

According to the Government, the development gains of the country are evident in terms of broader indicators. Trinidad and Tobago has an adult literacy rate of 97.2 per cent, although in many rural areas it would appear that this estimate is too high. Similarly, official figures state that 97 per cent of urban dwellings, and 77 per cent of rural dwellings, have access to safe water (Government of Trinidad and Tobago, 1991). Notwithstanding the positive features of development, such indicators must be viewed with caution. Beneath the perceived development lies a country in the grip of many structural problems, both economic and social, with a large proportion of the population living well below the levels stated by Government. In contrast to the achieved levels of development talked of by officials in terms of education and infrastructure, Trinidad still retains many characteristics of underdevelopment including poverty, unemployment, dependency on a single commodity, poor housing and uncontrolled urban development. Continued underdevelopment can partly be attributed to a number of structural economic problems which the country faces.

One of the most obvious, and persistent weaknesses, of the economy is the continued dependence on a single commodity, petroleum, with little successful economic diversification. This dependency is a major source of economic dislocation as the economy is forced to adjust to fluctuating demand conditions, the monetary policies of industrialised countries, and supply trends in major oil producing countries. Following the oil price hikes in the 1970s, the ratio of petroleum exports to GDP rose to a peak of 38 per cent in 1980, when oil revenue constituted 64.8 per cent of government's current revenue. In 1981, the price of petroleum fell on the international market which led to a further contraction of 16 per cent in 1983.

In 1989, the petroleum sector still contributed 28 per cent of GDP at market prices, despite the adverse effects of low oil prices and a reduction in production levels. Further decline in contribution to GDP is critical to the well being of the economy. In 1985, the sector contributed 70 per cent of GDP and although the reduction in reliance on oil is welcome, it is far from satisfactory. The fact remains that the country is still acutely dependent on petroleum exports for obtaining foreign reserves to finance expenditure on goods and services. The experience of Trinidad appears to be consistent with the characteristic dependence of the other oil exporting countries in the developing world.

To finance their mounting balance of payments problem the Government used national savings, as well as borrowing both locally and abroad. Almost overnight, Government expenditure on services declined along with the contraction of the non-oil sectors. Increased balance of payment problems resulted in the devaluation of the currency in 1985. The restriction in spending and consumption saw a number of small businesses going bankrupt. In 1986, GDP contracted for the fourth year in a row and official unemployment rose to 17 per cent. It was in this year that the Peoples National Movement was finally removed from office after thirty years of rule, and the National Alliance for Reconstruction (NAR), was voted in. In his first budget speech of January 1987, the new Prime Minister, A.N. Robinson, warned that a number of budgetary measures were necessary in order to avoid the country going to the International Monetary Fund (IMF). Although Robinson promised to administer a more 'people-oriented' model of development, by concentrating on job and housing provision, his plans were severely restricted by the onset of widespread recession.

Further contraction of the economy occurred in 1987, when unemployment escalated to 20 per cent and the country found itself on its way to the IMF (Pantin, 1989). Rapid increases in prices during the period 1974-82 had been accompanied by a rapid escalation of wages, salaries and fringe benefits. It is noticeable that after 1983, the effect of the downturn of the economy began to moderate the rate of increase in wages. Eventually, increases in the wages of the petroleum sector put upward pressure on all levels of the economy. In an attempt to bring expenditure in line with revenue, the Government sought to reduce the cost of living allowance to all public sector workers in 1987, and instigated a wage cut of 10 per cent in 1988. The national currency was also devalued again in the same year.

In November 1988, Trinidad signed its first agreement with the IMF under the compensatory financing facility for Standard Drawing Rights (SDR) of US$88 million. In January of the following year, it signed a further Stand-by-Agreement for SDR US$99 million, which came with the conditionalities of a structural adjustment package. This further led the country to negotiate for a World Bank Structural Adjustment Loan (Pantin, 1989). The reason for the arrangements with the IMF was the country's inability to repay US$1.8 billion due between 1988 and 1991. The government alone had borrowed US$285 million to finance several projects, including the industrial developments of the electricity plant TRINGEN II, and the Natural Gas Liquids Plant (SELC). It had also taken an International Development Bank loan for improving primary schools. In light of the impeding exhaustion of foreign exchange reserves, and the debt servicing difficulties, it was apparent that the country's external debt needed to be restructured in order to support necessary supplies of foreign exchange.

The IMF provides borrowing facilities as long as the borrower agrees to implement a series of policy measures. The Trinidadian government was instructed to alter its economic and social policies. Firstly, the government has been required to limit its public spending, which has had an adverse affect on the provision of social services. In addition, taxes have been kept low to encourage productivity in industry, thereby restricting the governments' revenue, and interest rates are determined by 'market forces'. In continuation with the IMF's free market strategy, import controls, previously adopted by Trinidad, have to be removed in order to promote free competition. As a result, foreign imports, including clothes and luxury food items, have flooded the market at the expense of local goods since 1992. Trinidad has reacted by promoting a 'buy local' advertising campaign to dissuade customers from purchasing foreign goods on the shelves of the supermarkets.

According to the IMF, incentives should also be given to the private sector to increase investment in both national and foreign industry. Direct incentives include a decrease in corporation taxes, and indirect incentives involving a reduction in public spending. Finally, and most importantly to countries hit by growing unemployment, is the retrenchment of local industries as a result of government stagnation. In the case of Trinidad, where there is major public sector control of the economy, this will lead to job losses and wage cuts. Public sector workers have already faced a 10 per cent wage cut as a result of these measures.

Subsequently, Trinidad has become increasingly burdened by the repayment of loans that it does not need, whilst the economy struggles to survive under the new policy objectives maintained from outside. In 1987, Trinidad was struggling to service an external debt of US$397 million, a payment used to support public sector enterprise.

Oil prices also weakened at the end of 1987, and prospects for repayment were not good. Total imports alone constituted approximately 42 per cent of GDP in 1988. Debt service in 1987 was predicted to be US$ 470 million (Farrell, 1989). In 1989 debt service accounted for 54 per cent of GDP. Pantin (1989) argues that Trinidad has walked into a 'Valley of Debt' which it will be unable to leave. He argues that Trinidad could have followed an alternative path by attempting to resist help from outside, and solve the matter internally by following a 'sacrifice option'. This would be based on the development of a new industrial policy to decrease dependency on oil, and concentration on job creation schemes based on small enterprise. This, combined with a policy of restricted spending, could reflate the economy and keep the country out of the hands of the IMF.

In addition to immediate problems, current borrowing will depend on the petroleum sector for repayment. Any downward fluctuation of the market will have disastrous consequences, such as those experienced in the Latin American oil producing countries in 1983. In analysing the current situation, the only promising result has been the restriction of the government's ability to continue throwing money at inefficient national industries. This is the only perceived advantage, as in the main, little thought has been given to poverty, unequal income distribution, unemployment and social costs, which have risen as a result of the transformation of the economy. By seeking help from the IMF, Trinidad has become entrenched in a situation of mounting debt and social discontentment, whilst the economy has experienced few benefits from the loans.

By 1990, the Trinidadian economy was in crisis, as visible unemployment reached 22 per cent (Central Statistical Office, 1991). The Government was forced to introduce a system of Value Added Tax at 15 per cent in order to avoid a further devaluation of the currency, which not surprisingly led to further disenchantment and suffering. The Trinidadian economy has been constantly hindered by a number of structural weaknesses, both in the national and international markets. Despite the severity of economic problems faced by Trinidad, none is singularly more important than persistent unemployment, and special mention must be made here of the intractability of the problem. Since 1983, the official rate of unemployment has increased dramatically. The rate of unemployment, which averaged 11.1 per cent of the total labour force in 1983, climbed to an average of 22 per cent at the beginning of the 1990s. Despite financial and economic prosperity, Trinidad has for many decades been unable to supply work for its labour force. The increasing role now being played by the IMF, in dictating the terms of government in Trinidad, is enhancing the employment crisis.

Culture, Ethnicity and Social Differentiation in Trinidad

Lowenthal (1972a), in his work on the cultural and societal complexities of the Caribbean region defines Trinidad as a plural society, where position is derived from a combination of occupational status, income differential and ethnicity. This view is further reinforced by Cross and Heuman (1968), and Beckford (1972), who stated that within Trinidad, social class identity is not based on physiological criteria, as in North America, but on a combination of the three factors stated above. The country has a remarkable heterogeneity of population as a result of slavery, indentured labour and immigration. The population consists of people of African descent, East-Indians, Syrian and Lebanese, Chinese and Europeans. Although ethnicity has played a major role in the social hierarchy of the past, increasing importance is being placed on occupation as providing status in present day society. Yelvington (1993) writes of a commodification of ethnicity which in turn determines allocation in the division of labour. It is important to note the spatial importance attached to colour and ethnicity in Trinidad, especially when considering rural-urban differentials within the island (Wood, 1968).

The importance of the agricultural base to the East Indian population is shown in central and southern Trinidad, where over 50 per cent of the population are of Indian descent. This is in marked contrast to the north of the country, where over 50 per cent of the population of the north-west and north-east are of African descent. This includes the capital, Port of Spain, in the calculation. Interestingly, the south-eastern quarter of the island, known as Mayaro District, and other areas surrounding the oil refineries, are also predominantly African. In contrast, south-western Trinidad, which incorporates the port of Cedros, is densely settled by East Indians. These patterns of settlement reflect the African control of the oil industry and the domination of the East Indians in the agricultural plains of Trinidad (Vertovec, 1992). The heavy dominance of East Indians in Cedros, which serves as a fishing area, is also notorious for its smuggling operations from the Venezuelan mainland.

As an extension of this theme, there are also notable variations in the distribution of the population between rural and urban areas according to racial descent (Clarke, 1986). East Indian association with agricultural pursuits has been documented by Richardson (1975), Ramesar (1976) and Ryan (1991a). Table 3.1 shows the distribution of rural and urban populations in Trinidad according to race. The statistics indicate that although there is an equal distribution of those of African descent between rural and urban areas, there is a large proportion of East Indians living in rural areas. This is a factor which is important when considering the unequal provision of rural services and opportunities.

The distribution of wealth and poverty in Trinidad also reveals a degree of ethnic disparity. Escalating poverty and hardship reached a tense climax in 1970 with the Black Power movement, which sought to bring to an end the damage effected by the country's colonial past by ending white elitism and foreign dependence. The movement, which is well documented by Hintzen (1981), took the form of riots, public sector strikes and demonstrations. It did not achieve its desired effect, but rather, ended in a situation of chaos, which was ensued by a national State of Emergency. Appeasement offered by Prime Minister Eric Williams was given in the form of the 'Development and Environmental Works Division' (DEWD), a programme which marked the start of increased public funding in Trinidad. The programme provided funds for casual employment in various infrastructural projects, including road construction, but the results were disappointing as the projects were predominantly urban based, and mainly involved with the employment of black labour. Susan Craig (1982), argues that as little attention was given to the predominantly Indian areas, the programme was another result of the racially dominated political policies operative within the country.

Urbanisation and the Growth of Major Cities

Urban growth is a major force in the Caribbean (Clarke, 1974; Potter, 2000), and Port of Spain and San Fernando are no exceptions. Potter (1992b) notes that the Caribbean is one of the most highly urbanised regions of the world, with over 50 per cent of the population residing in urban areas. According to Michael Anthony (1988), Trinidad alone has a total of 48 towns and villages, with 60 per cent of the national population residing in urban areas in 1990 (UNDP, 1992). Between 1960 and 1980,

Table 3.1 The Racial Distribution of Population in Trinidad by Urban and Rural Areas

Racial Group	Percentage of total population by area:	
	Urban	Rural
African	49	51
Indian	17	83
White	65	35
Chinese	67	33
Mixed	51	49

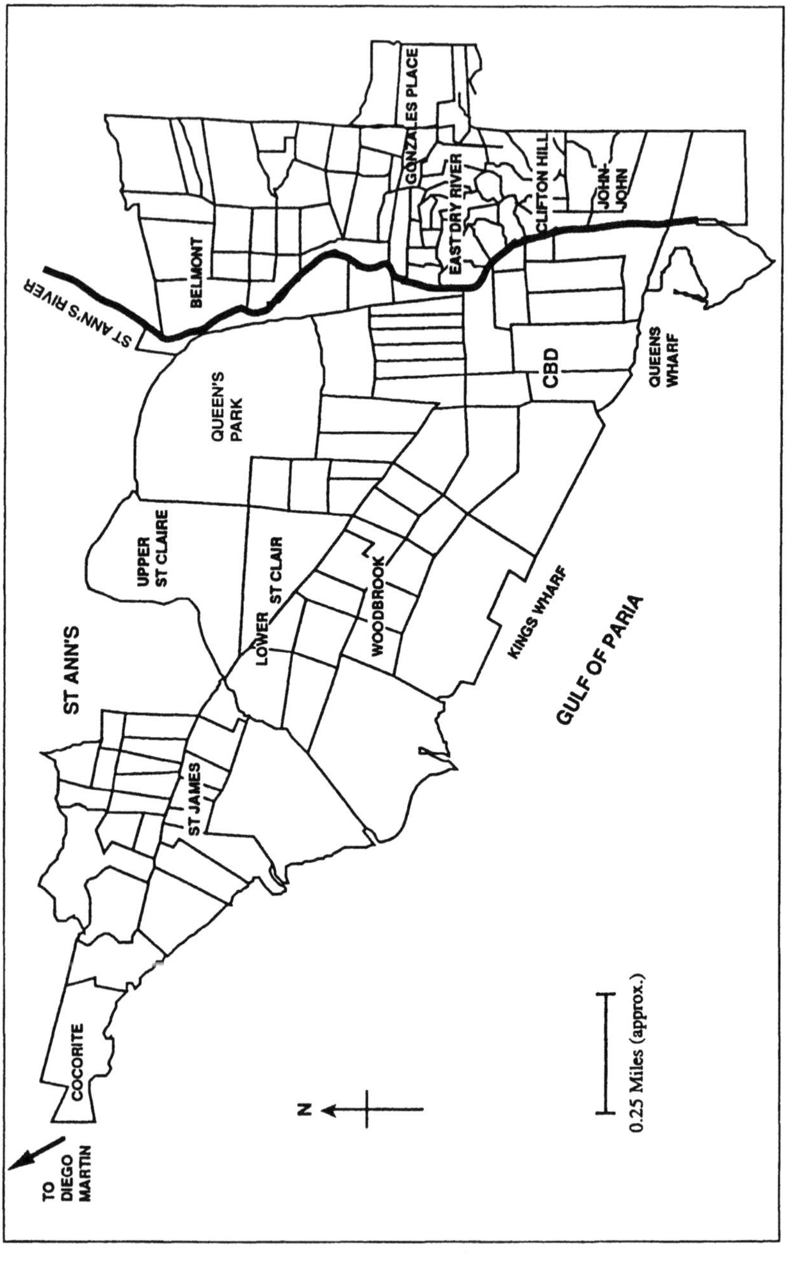

Figure 3.3 Port of Spain: Location Map

Trinidad's urban population grew by 42 per cent (Hope, 1986). In 1992, the combined population of Port of Spain, and the surrounding county of St George was over 500,000 (Statistical Digest, 1992, Central Statistical Office). The size of the urbanised population in Trinidad is constantly growing, but population distribution between settlements has changed historically. The early settlement pattern in Trinidad was a direct consequence of colonial rule which enabled the powers to extract wealth from the island. The capital, Port of Spain, developed by the Spanish in 1584 (Lucas, 1890), was later used by the British as a port of call, for merchant ships, and as an administrative centre.

Hence, Port of Spain's development was both planned and restricted to facilitate colonial rule. Elsewhere in the country, settlement patterns were primarily a direct result of the location of the plantations, with a large proportion of small settlements in Trinidad given over to sugar cane and subsequently, as a response to the petroleum industry. In the 1800s, settlements in the rural districts of Caroni, Nariva, and Victoria, developed around the plantations, in a pattern which conforms to Rojas's notion of plantopolis (Rojas, 1989). Villages such as Couva, Princes Town and Debe firstly provided homes for the plantation slaves, and later became homes for East Indian indentured labour in the 1850s. Local towns and villages grew up around the plantations, and this development increased with the abolition of slavery when many of the Afro-Caribbean workers left the fields to find other work. Many of the freed workers from the northern cocoa plantations settled in the hills surrounding Port of Spain, but in addition to this influx, migrants from elsewhere in the country were attracted to the capital from the mid-1800s (Conway, 1984).

East Indian indentured labourers developed their own settlements in the south of the country, for the purpose of enjoying their own culture and belief systems. The late 1880s marked another transformation in Trinidad, when the building of an extensive rail system to aid the extraction and transportation of cane opened up many inaccessible regions to the population in the east (Anthony, 1975). The mining and refining of oil in the early twentieth century contributed to a counter-flow of population to the south, a process which aided the growth of Trinidad's second city San Fernando (Clarke, 1986). The 'North' and 'South' still retain separate identities, with the north being predominantly urban and Afro-Caribbean in culture, and the south undertaking a more agricultural and industrial role with strong East Indian profile. However, a common linkage between both regions is the growth of the country's main cities, San Fernando and Port of Spain.

According to Conway (1989), it was the oil boom that first prompted urban growth in San Fernando and St Patrick in the south of the country, and rural-urban migration which lead to Port of Spain's expansion in the 1920s. By 1931, the pace of urban growth was accelerating, and between 1946 and 1960, Greater Port of Spain extended its boundaries to Diego Martin in the west and Tacarigua in the east. The Eastern Main Road made gains from the rural districts of St Andrew, as workers left their agricultural base. St Patrick county in the south experienced net gains due to nearby oil exploration, but many other rural regions experienced great losses (Conway, 1984). Between 1960 and 1980 census figures show that St George grew rapidly as a service and residential sector. The 1970 Census shows that in the 1960s, Port of Spain began to lose population to the growing corridor in St George along the Eastern Main Road. This trend of suburbanisation continued as Trinidad's population was becoming accustomed to a more urban lifestyle. Today, St George is one of the most densely populated regions of the country. Subsequently, this area has become visibly important in terms of informality in terms of trading and petty commodity production, as will be explored in subsequent chapters.

Port of Spain, which has been the island's capital since 1774, has been subject to centuries of accelerating growth. The structure of the city has been described by Conway (1981) as a history of sectoral expansion. The original site of the city was constricted to the north by a mountain range, and to the south by the sea, so its growth occurred in a linear fashion, as indicated in Figure 3.3. Over 60 per cent of Trinidad's population now reside within the boundaries of Greater Port of Spain (Government of Trinidad and Tobago, 1989). A high-density low-income residential area has developed from the central city to the eastern periphery, incorporating the districts of East Dry River, John John and Clifton Hill (see Potter and O'Flaherty, 1995).

It has been estimated by Conway (1984) that over 50 per cent of the capital's housing is structurally poor, much of which is concentrated in unplanned settlements due to rapid population growth. By contrast, middle and upper-income residential settlements, including Ellerslie Park, St Ann's, West Moorings and Diego Martin are concentrated to the west of the city, with a rapidly extending sub-system of urban development which is extending eastwards to Arima. Meanwhile, this concentrated settlement had placed many pressures on the ability of the city to house and service its population.

4 Work, Employment and the Informal Sector in Trinidad: An Overview

For more than three decades, the problem of large-scale, structural unemployment has been a central concern of informed opinion in the Caribbean as indeed, elsewhere in the developing world. According to Farrell (1978), Caribbean unemployment has largely been attributed to a shortage of capital, to the malfunctioning of the labour market, excessive rates of population growth, the importation of inappropriate technologies, and the effects of colonisation. More specifically, Trinidad has recently witnessed a growth in unemployment following a severe economic recession, which resulted in the implementation of an IMF structural adjustment package. The inability of the country to provide work for a growing labour force has culminated in a rapid growth of informal sector activity.

An increase in economic polarisation, and the emergence of government tolerance of the informal sector, led to an increase in informal activity in the 1990s. Much research has attempted to measure the effects of IMF structural adjustment policies across the globe. Whilst the World Bank and IMF have justified their policies as beneficial to developing countries, others have highlighted their contribution to increased poverty, deprivation and inequality in the Caribbean (Cornia, 1987; Le Franc, 1994; Stewart, 1995; Green, 1995). In relation to employment, Structural Adjustment Policies (SAPs) have been associated with formal sector retrenchment and redundancy, which leads to growth in informal employment (de Soto, 1989). The collapse of formal sector employment in Latin America and the Caribbean, along with knock-on effects on opportunities in the informal sector, is a major problem when successful job creation is needed to alleviate the worst affects of poverty and deprivation. In Jamaica, Anderson and Witter (1994) stated that employment growth has largely been in the informal sector, a trend that Trinidadian statisticians would also support. These new opportunities, however, are characterised by low wages, low skills, instability and a lack of worker protection.

As elsewhere in the region, the early 1990s marked a period of great socio-economic transition for Trinidad due to the implementation of structural adjustment. At this time, the geography of the informal sector was constantly changing according to macro-economic trends which were largely dictated from outside the country. These growth trends incorporated inducement towards the informalisation of a range of activities. Prior to 1992, when a substantial proportion of this research for this monograph was undertaken, increasing poverty had led to a growth in the market for low-cost informal goods and services, and widespread restrictions on foreign imports had encouraged the development of a black market for specialist goods imported goods in the late 1980s. However, in 1992, Trinidadians' witnessed the full effect of a structural adjustment package which largely served to increase the vulnerability of a substantial proportion of the population. Like other Caribbean neighbours, the Trinidadian government was required to implement a number of changes. Firstly, it had to limit its public spending, which has had an adverse affect on the provision of social services. In addition, taxes have been kept low to encourage productivity in industry, thereby restricting the governments' revenue, and interest rates are determined by 'market forces'. In continuation with the IMF's free market strategy, import controls previously adopted by Trinidad to protect domestic industries had to be removed in order to promote free trade. As a result, foreign imports, including clothes and luxury food items, have flooded the market at the expense of local goods since 1992, thus threatening the competitive edge of many informal traders. Secondly, the Government was forced to introduce a system of Value Added Tax at 15 per cent in order to avoid a further devaluation of the currency, and was encouraged to begin a privatisation programme which has recently seen the sale of national service utilities. In 1994, Trinidad's per capita GDP was US$3,624 as opposed to US$5,578 in 1982, a fact which illustrates the nature of social and economic decline experienced in recent years. In 2000, GDP per capita stood at US$6,186.

During the early 1990s, therefore, state institutions in Trinidad recognised that the informal sector was an important provider of work and a contributor to the social, economic and political development of the country. Despite this awareness, the government, along with the International Labour Organisation (ILO) and the United Nations Economic Commission for Latin America and the Caribbean (UNECLAC), established the fact that little was known of the true nature of the informal sector in Trinidad. The Central Statistical Office (CSO), and the local planning units, confirmed the present author's awareness of the lack of documented empirical research and published academic literature on this subject (see also Lloyd-Evans and Potter, 1992).

As a result of this omission, this chapter has three main objectives. Firstly, through secondary data sources, it documents current employment trends and analyses the composition of the informal sector in relation to the labour market. Secondly, the chapter identifies sectors and characteristics specific to the informal sector of Trinidad, derived from field research and interviews held with local government officials. Thirdly, a broad classification of informal workers is presented and socio-spatial patterns of informalisation are highlighted.

The following profile of the informal sector emerges from an analysis of data derived from two sources. Firstly, statistical and documentary evidence was gathered from interviews held with a number of governmental and institutional departments, including the Central Statistical Office, the Social Sectors Planning Unit, the United Nations ECLAC and the ILO. In addition, reference was also made to pertinent reports and the 1990 census materials. Secondly, the author's own interpretation of the informal sector was facilitated by a series of preliminary observations, and the use of field diaries, incorporated as part of the reconnaissance field work.

Labour Market Trends and Unemployment in Trinidad

Trinidad appears to have been plagued by structural unemployment since its independence in 1962. A *Times* survey in 1966 (25 January 1966), indicated that unemployment was already becoming a problem for the country. During the 1960s, its causes were identified as a rapidly increasing labour force, which coincided with the introduction of capital intensive production, most markedly in the petroleum sector. These were seen to be mere teething problems for a newly independent country, and unemployment was tackled in a number of ways. Firstly, a family planning programme was introduced in combination with a policy which suggested that unskilled workers could emigrate to North America and Britain. More saliently, it was seen that the real solution lay with economic diversification and a decreased dependence on oil, neither of which have been achieved to date. Throughout the boom years of the 1970s, the increased growth of output, detailed in the previous chapter, was still not paralleled by a reduction in unemployment.

At the time of this research, data from the 1990 census which is shown in Table 4.1, indicated a steady decline in the size of the working labour force since the 1980s. Of the eligible labour force (persons of 15 years and over) of 835,8000 in 1990, the actual labour force was estimated to be 461,300. This figure included 366,000 persons who were employed and 95,200 who were officially unemployed. The unemployment rate in the third quarter of 1990 was 20.6 per cent, with male unemployment running at 18.2 per cent and female unemployment at 25.3 per cent. The official unemployment rate remained in the region of 20 per cent in the early 1990s, although it has undergone a recent decrease to around 12 per cent in 2000. Changes in the economy of Trinidad in recent decades have also brought about changes in the formal employment market. An evaluation of the changing structure of formal employment highlights sectors which have the potential to utilise informal activity. It is also essential to recognise those categories which are important to irregular workers,

Table 4.1 Labour Force by Sex and Employment Status in Trinidad and Tobago, 1990 (thousands)

Labour Availability	Year			
	1987	1988	1989	1990
Eligible population (aged 15+)	752.2	822.3	833.9	835.8
Labour force	478.8	476.8	469.1	461.3
Employment	372.3	371.6	365.7	366.0
Unemployment	106.6	105.1	103.4	95.2
Unemployment rate (per cent)	22.2	22.0	20.1	20.6
Male unemployment	20.7	21.2	19.3	18.2
Female unemployment	25.2	23.0	21.8	25.3

Source: Labour Force Bulletin of Trinidad and Tobago, Central Statistical Office, various issues.

namely the self-employed or 'own account', and unpaid workers.

Employment Structure and Underlying Trends in Occupations

The *Annual Labour Market Information Study of the Social Sectors Unit* (Ministry of Mobilisation and Planning, 1990), provides figures on the occupational structure of employment in Trinidad between 1989 and 1990. An analysis of this data reveals a number of current trends within the officially accounted economy.

What is referred to as the 'Community, Social and Personal Services' sector, provided the largest share of jobs (24.4 per cent) in the economy in 1989. Government workers, especially females, were largely concentrated in this sector. In 1989, the sector accounted for 72.1 per cent of all female public sector workers. More importantly, about 18 per cent of the total workers in this sector are classified either as 'Own Account Workers', 'Unpaid Workers', 'Employers' or 'Learner/Apprentices', many of whom are deemed to be part of the informal sector. It is also an important source of employment for youths (defined as persons between the ages of 15 and 24) both male and female. Over one-quarter of the nation's youths found employment within this sector, a factor which may be associated with the unskilled nature and low-wages associated with these occupations.

The 'Wholesale and Retail Trade, Restaurant and Hotel' sector was the second largest source of employment in the third quarter of 1990 at 12 per cent. Interestingly, about 30.15 per cent of workers operating under the headings of 'Employer', 'Own Account', 'Unpaid Worker' and 'Learner/Apprentice' were in this sector, thereby, indicating that this component is also an absorber of informal activity. Once again, this sector is an important employer of females, currently at 31 per cent of the total working population. The concentration of women, youths and irregular workers in both sectors is linked to the insecurity, low wages, unsociable hours and low status ascribed to many jobs. Furthermore, female domination is possibly linked to a gendered division of labour which places women in the traditional roles of carer and provider.

The third largest source of employment was in the 'Other Agriculture, Forestry, Hunting and Fishing' sector (8.5 per cent). A substantial proportion of workers, 26.4 per cent, fell under the 'Own Account', 'Unpaid Worker' and the 'Learner/Apprentice' sectors. As expected, it was also a more important source of employment for males than females, and for youths aged 15 to 19. Within Trinidad, many of these occupations are likely to be informally based. The 'Other Manufacturing Sector' (excluding sugar and oil) and the construction sectors are also important sectors of employment for males. The manufacturing sector provided jobs for 10 per cent of the employed population in 1990. The construction industry accounted for 21.8 per cent of males in 1989, but these figures have been declining rapidly due to recession. Employment in the sector has been facing a downward trend since 1987 in line with the reduction of

Government expenditure on public services.

Employment prospects in the four remaining sectors, 'Sugar', 'Petroleum and Gas', 'Electricity and Water', and 'Transport, Storage and Communication', are limited in their importance. Collectively, these sectors only provided 12.9 per cent of total jobs.

Classification of Workers by Skill and Profession

Within the census data, workers are also categorised by their skill or profession. For example, workers in the 'Other Manufacturing Sector' may also be classified as a 'Tradesmen', according to their specific occupation. Current underlying trends in employment within Trinidad appear to lean towards more craft-oriented occupations. Slightly less than one fifth (18.6 per cent) of all persons with jobs in 1989 were classified as either 'Craftsmen', 'Tradesmen' or 'Production Process Workers'. In 1989, approximately 54.9 per cent of this group had at most primary school education, with no formal training in relation to job training opportunities. Of these, 38.5 per cent had no training at all. There are notable gender variations here, with males being five times more likely to be in this category than females.

Most 'Craftsmen' are found in the 'Other Manufacturing Sector' and the 'Community, Social and Personal Services Sector'. Together these sectors accounted for more than three fifths of all craftsmen in 1989. It is interesting to note that these sectors also provide a large number of irregular job opportunities. Unfortunately, the figures also reveal the low levels of skills and education held by craftsmen in Trinidad. The lack of training may be an important target for possible future assistance for the informal sector.

Another important pattern is the occupational stratification of the workforce according to gender. Many occupations, particularly those associated with manual labour and machinery, are seen to be exclusively male. This is in direct contrast to the high female participation in the service and caring professions of the 'Community, Social and Personal Services Sector', and the 'Wholesale and Retail Trade, Restaurant and Hotel Sector'. Females were also greatly over-represented in 'Clerical and Related Occupations'. More than two-thirds of all young working females were in these occupations in 1989.

A further analysis of the labour force figures, shown in Table 4.2, indicates that high numbers of female workers are only found in a few employment sectors; 'Community, Social and Personal Services', 'Wholesale and Retail Trade, Restaurant and Hotel', and 'Other Manufacturing Sectors'. A prime aim of the reconnaissance surveys, presented in chapters 5 and 6, was the investigation of gender stratification in informal occupations.

Table 4.2 Distribution of Workers by Occupational Category and Gender, 1989

Occupational Category	Male	Female	Total
Sugar	11,800	1,000	12,800
Other agriculture	29,700	8,100	37,800
Petroleum and gas	15,500	1,200	16,800
Other mining	500	0	500
Other manufacturing (excluding oil)	26,400	10,100	36,500
Electricity and water	6,700	600	7,300
Construction	34,800	3,200	38,000
Wholesale, retail, restaurant and hotel	31,600	29,700	61,000
Transport and communication	22,600	4,400	27,000
Finance, insurance and business	12,000	11,000	23,000
Community, social and personal services	55,100	49,300	104,400

Source: Labour Force Bulletin of Trinidad and Tobago, Central Statistical Office, 1989.

An Estimation of the Informal Sector in Trinidad

From an examination of the 1989 labour force figures shown in Table 4.1, we calculate that only 34.5 per cent of the total eligible labour force was formally employed. A more important trend is the increase in the proportion of the eligible working population, nearly half, who are not included in the official labour force. Table 4.3 provides a representation of the size of the non-institutionalised population, aged 15 years and over, and the components of the Labour Force over the period 1988-1990. It is important to note that 45 per cent of the total non-institutional population, 15 years and over, was counted as not officially working in 1990. This provides evidence to suggest that a substantial proportion of the unaccounted labour force were seeking work in the informal economy.

A substantial proportion of the official labour force is still in the 'Own Account', 'Unpaid Workers' or 'Unemployed' categories, all of which are deemed to contribute to the informal sector. If these figures are added to the 45 per cent of the population who are already excluded from the labour force figures, then it could be deduced that the informal sector is providing jobs for up to 60 per cent of the eligible working population.

Taking into account that a proportion of this group may be in education, early retirement or may choose not to work, it is not unrealistic to suggest that the informal sector accounts for at least 50 per cent of the total labour force in Trinidad and Tobago. These figures serve to highlight the plight of those who are forced to earn a living by irregular means. The Trinidadian Government uses the 'Own Account' category to obtain a preliminary base figure of the size of the informal sector. This will still only be a partial estimation as there will be many workers who escape enumeration in the official figures. This method analyses the occurrence of Own Account workers, omitting professionals and university graduates, to provide an indicator of informal activity.

This category provided employment for 15.9 per cent of the total number of persons employed in 1989, and 18.8 per cent in 1990. With the exception of 'Own Account' workers, the number of persons officially employed in Trinidad declined significantly during 1990. The 'Own Account' workers registered a 16.0 per cent growth rate between 1989 and 1990. This growth may largely be attributable to the growing informal sector, which has had to absorb workers from a range of other employment sectors.

Official labour force participation also differs greatly according to gender. The participation rate for males over 15 years old is between 60 and 70 per cent, although women only account for 30 to 40 per cent of the official figures. For example, the 'Wholesale and Retail Trade, Restaurant and Hotel Sector' was a source of employment for one fifth of all male 'Own Account' workers, but provided jobs for one half (53.9 per cent) of 'Own Account' females. This further supports the arguments which identify high female activity rates in the informal sector. Stitcher

Table 4.3 Percentage Distribution of Population According to Employment Status in Trinidad, 1989

Employment Status	1988	1989	1990
	(percentage of total workforce)		
Officially employed	45	44	44
Officially unemployed	13	12	11
Unaccounted	42	44	45

(1990: 11) advocates that "women's labour force participation is increasing, even while their formal, paid employment, and their incomes from such employment, may be stagnating or declining". Further analysis of statistics on 'Own Account' workers, highlights the concentration of women in the service sectors. Furthermore, the 'Other Agriculture Sector' and 'Wholesale and Retail Trade, Restaurant and Hotel Sector' also include a substantial amount of 'unpaid workers' who are female (4,500 in each sector), a factor which indicates that such businesses may be family concerns.

The Informal Sector in Trinidad: Geographical Perspectives

The informal sector is one of the least documented areas of the economy in Trinidad and as such, there does not appear to be any general agreement as to the precise definition of the activities included within its confines. It has been referred to by many different terms, including the 'subsistence sector', 'underground sector', 'invisible sector', 'underground economy', and 'black economy'. Each of these terms highlight certain characteristics of the sector, but none appear to cover the same ground. In one of the few documents concerning informal activity, the Director of the Central Statistical Office, advocates the setting up of an informal register, but until an agreed methodology can be established, the task remains elusive (Rampersad, 1991).

As documented in chapter 1, it is necessary to define a basic working definition, or set of constructs, which enable the reader to more fully visualise the nature of informal sector activity in Trinidad. According to the Central Statistical Office (CSO), and other official bodies in Trinidad, the informal sector can be defined as that section of the economy which is not recorded in the official statistics, and/or not legal and/or not taxed. The CSO also believe it can be further divided into three divisions constituting (i) the visible informal sector, (ii) the invisible informal sector or the underground sector (which covers the illicit and socially devalued activities discussed later in this chapter) and finally, (iii) the domestic sector. In the context of Trinidad, the domestic sector refers to domestic servants, family labour and other unremunerated labour, such as women's work in the home. From their research in Jamaica, Witter and Kirton (1990) characterise an activity as 'informal' if it violates some law, official regulation or generally accepted standards of business behaviour. It is well established, however, that this formal/informal dichotomy is socially determined and is subject to change over time.

Following the considerations provided in chapter 1, the definition of the informal sector adopted here is those activities which generally operate under the evasion of at least one government law or regulation. This broad definition facilitates a greater understanding of the nature of the sector than a narrower one. For the purpose of this research, the informal sector is seen as incorporating those activities which are not carried out under the rules imposed by political powers. Furthermore, the informal sector includes irregular activity for self consumption and/or for persons directly associated with an agent. From the undertaking of field reconnaissance, observations and diaries, the author has constructed a more precise evaluation of those activities which make-up the informal sector in Trinidad.

Informal Activities in Trinidad: An Overview

Within the context of Trinidad, it is possible to broadly divide informal activities into categories according to whether they belong to the primary, secondary of tertiary economic sectors. Primary and secondary activities include farming, market gardening, building construction, artisanal craft production, leather and clothing production, and food and alcohol-related industry. Tertiary enterprises, and distributive trades, include transport provision, petty trading, street hawking, catering, domestic and restaurant services, agents and dealers. Popular activities in Trinidad include the selling of coconut water, roti and soft-drinks along the road-sides. Other informal service providers include musicians, launderers, barbers, photographers, vehicle repair and other maintenance workers, brokerage and middlemen.

The often referred to 'underground economy' is that part of the informal sector which is seen to be strictly illegal and hazardous to society. The dangerous nature of such activities made further examination of this sector unwise in the present work. Illegal services include stolen goods, drug trafficking, prostitution, smuggling, bribery, political corruption and protection rackets. Transfer activities include petty theft, speculation, embezzlement and gambling. Due to its proximity to the South American mainland, Trinidad is particularly susceptible to the smuggling of drugs and other illegal goods. Goods are easily smuggled through the unprotected port of Cedros, located on the South Western tip of Trinidad, and can then be transported up through the islands of the Caribbean to North America. Advice was given as to the dangerous nature of such activities and understandably, no further investigations were made apart from a more detailed look into the small-scale smuggling of consumer goods which will be expanded upon in chapter 9.

The informal sector in Trinidad comprises a heterogeneous array of activities many of which have no similarity to others within the grouping. In order to understand the various components of the informal sector, a comprehensive typology of informal activities in Trinidad is shown in Table 4.4.

The contents of Table 4.4 have been grouped into four broad categories, according to their economic function (see Thomas, 1992). These are retailing, small-scale production, service oriented, and formal businesses which utilise informal methods. Within each section, further

Table 4.4 Functional Typology of Informal Sector Operations in Trinidad

A. RETAILING

1. Processed Food Trading

(i) Doubles and other Indian snacks
(ii) Channa, nuts and sweets
(iii) Beverages
(iv) 'Snow-cone' (ice cream)
(v) Spices, Peppered-Mango
(vi) Herbs, Sea Moss, local products
(vii) Roti and hot food
(viii) Hot-corn

2. Unprocessed Produce Trading

(i) General fruit
(ii) Mangoes
(iii) Water melons
(iv) Coconut water
(v) Vegetables
(vi) Fish
(vii) Poultry and Halal meat
(viii) Sweetcorn

3. Commodity Trading

(i) Clothes
(ii) Shoes and leather
(iii) Crafts and artefacts
(iv) Jewellery and trinkets
(v) Household items
(vi) Newspapers
(vii) Suitcase trading
(viii) Electrical and mechanical items
(ix) Imported goods

B. SMALL-SCALE PRODUCTION

1. Food and Fresh Produce

(i) Fruit processing and preservation
(ii) Vegetable and nut processing
(iii) Bread and cake producers
(iv) Catering for functions
(v) Home-production of hot food
(vi) Market gardening
(vii) Small-scale farming

2. Petty Commodity

(i) Garments
(ii) Tie-dye, printing and art
(iii) Crafts
(iv) Jewellery and trinkets
(v) Shoes and leather
(vi) Hardware/household
(vii) Electrical/mechanical

3. Specialised Production

(i) Cottage industries
(ii) Carnival
(iii) Music, ie steel pans

C. SERVICE-ORIENTED

1. Daily Service Providers

(i) Laundry
(ii) Domestic
(iii) Shoe repair
(iv) Hardware repair
(v) Motor vehicle servicing
(vi) Construction
(vii) Maintenance
(viii) Taxi-driving (Maxi's)
(ix) Gardening
(x) Beauty services/hairdressing
(xi) Odd jobs, ie car cleaning

2. Specialised Services

(i) Tourist guides
(ii) Car-park attendants
(iii) Car, home rentals
(iv) Residential lodgings
(v) Secretarial, clerical
(vi) Legal, medical
(vii) Distribution/storage
(viii) Begging
(ix) Informing/protection
(x) Party (fete) organisers
(xi) Carnival organisers
(xii) Bottle collecting/recycling

Table 4.4 continued

D. GOODS AND SERVICES PRODUCED WITHIN THE FORMAL SECTOR, USING INFORMAL MEANS

1. Goods and Services	*2. Irregularities in Income Distribution*
(i) Unlicensed production/retailing	(i) Illegal importation
(ii) Production using unlawful methods	(ii) Official corruption
(iii) Use of irregular capital, ie stealing	(iii) Irregular loans/credit
(iv) Practising without licence, ie medical	(iv) Fraudulent book-keeping
(v) Counterfeiting and falsification	(v) Tax evasion

differentiation is also made between product type. Section A, retailing, lists a wide range of retailing activities, commonly found throughout Trinidad, under three sub-categories: processed food trading, unprocessed food trading, and commodity trading. The trading of goods and services is a prime informal sector occupation in Trinidad. Processed food traders, such as Doubles vendors (a popular snack made with channa) can frequently be found in most areas of Trinidad. Another important group, unprocessed produce traders, are widely responsible for the internal distribution of food and fresh produce. Vendors selling the familiar products of coconut water, doubles and fresh fruit can be found on most streets. The third category in Section A, commodity traders, constitute an important group of retailers trading in clothes, electrical items and trinkets, who are visible in most urban areas.

Section B contains occupations which are associated with small-scale production. Here differentiation is made between the production of food, 'petty commodity' production and specialised industries. Within Trinidad, small-scale farming and market gardening play an important role in the national provision of food. Petty commodity production embraces the popular occupations of artisanal craft production and clothes-making. The category of specialised production refers to the contribution of the informal sector to local arts, such as steel pan and Carnival.

Section C contains a vast selection of the many types of informal services offered in Trinidad. These include daily services, such as laundry and vehicle repair, and specialised services relating to tourism and business. Other less visible informal services include the organisation of fetes and carnival, which are important earners of income in Trinidad. Finally, Section D incorporates those formal sector activities which have strong connections with the informal sector. In this category are the many illegal operations which function throughout Trinidadian society, and elsewhere in the developing world. These include, amongst others, licence and tax evasion, smuggling, and irregularities in income distribution.

As a continuation from the development of a broad typology of informal occupations, it is also possible to distinguish between the many types of informal sector worker who make their living from the same occupation. The informal sector is ambiguous, in that it encompasses wealth and poverty, productivity and inefficiency, exploitation and liberation. As discussed in chapter 2, debates still focus on whether the sector is a haven for structurally marginalised workers or productive entrepreneurs (Portes and Walton, 1981; Portes *et al*, 1991). As informality is becoming increasingly widespread in Trinidad, its participants emanate from a wide range of social groups, and they enter the informal sector for different reasons. The difficulty, however, does not lie with identifying these different groups, but rather in providing an explanation for their motivation to work informally.

Socio-spatial Geography of the Informal Sector in Trinidad: An Overview

There are several characteristics of informalisation in Trinidad which warrant greater attention, but there are four which are most visible. Briefly summarised, these include the heterogeneity of activities undertaken by the informal sector, the socio-spatial division of labour, the nature of formal-informal sector interaction and the spatial geography of the sector.

Heterogeneity of informal enterprises - Primarily, the informal sector in Trinidad undertakes two economic and social roles which need distinction. On a nation-wide level, the informal sector provides a number of important functions which are crucial to the running of the country. It operates an efficient and flexible method of distribution of labour, products and capital. Furthermore, it provides a range of low-cost services to the entire population. The operation of a large number of informal taxis and 'maxi-taxis' (mini-buses) along a vast number of routes, provides a frequent and cheap transport service. With the decline in the service of the nationalised bus service, it is an important method of travel, particularly in Port of Spain.

Taxi-drivers provide a good example of a national service which is provided only on an informal basis. Drivers own their vehicles, and either operate individually or as part of a co-operative. They need to register with the government in order to gain the recognised H plate, but are otherwise not subject to legislation regarding incomes or safety of vehicles. Many taxis are old American cars which were bought by their drivers in the boom period of the 1970s. During the recession, many workers lost their livelihoods and have utilised their cars in order to make a living. Incomes are low due to the high competition, but it is one of the only jobs open to those near retirement age. Discussions, held with drivers on daily trips to Port of Spain, revealed stories of successful workers in the oil industry who had been forced to seek a living on the streets by driving their once prized possession, a large American car.

The informal sector is also an outlet for popular culture which is enjoyed by the entire population. Carnival itself is an informal event which raises large amounts of money for its organisers. Carnival costumes are made by informal sector workers, and many pre-carnival fetes (parties) witness the articulation of capital, often to the wealthier members of society. The famous steel-pans are also made in informal workshops.

The national importance of the sector is also paralleled by its role in the neighbourhood or local economy. Many informal operations are undertaken on a local level to provide jobs, goods and services to the neighbourhood. The sector acts as a survival system, particularly for the poorest communities in the south of the island, and Eastern Port of Spain. Local communities are often self-sufficient in clothing provision, food, mechanical and electrical services. Many communities, such as Diego

Martin, a western suburb of Port of Spain, have a thriving local informal sector offering a wide-range of services.

At a time when governmental spending has decreased, and the private sector is diminishing, a local economy allows settlements to retain and support their population. Furthermore, the intricate social capital and kinship/friendship networks that develop provide a well-needed informal source of capital and assistance. In many cases, exchange and bartering are more commonly used than money. Profits can often be maximised with a minimum return, an important consideration in low-income communities.

Socio-spatial division of labour - A second observation is that the informal sector performs a number of differing roles in its provision of work. Drawing on the existing literature (Thomas, 1992, 1995) and fieldwork observations, it is possible to identify four main sectors of informal activity which attract different groups of workers, as highlighted in Figure 4.1 (see also Potter and Lloyd-Evans, 1998). These can be classified as (i) subsistence operators (ii) small-scale entrepreneurs (iii) petty capitalists, and (iv) criminal operators.

The first group, 'subsistence operators', engage in informal activity in order to provide goods and services for household consumption. The well-known activities of housework, the use of family unpaid labour and reproduction, often fall into this category. In Trinidad, a good example of subsistence workers are the small farmers who grow food for consumption, and sell their surpluses to provide other necessities. The second category consists of small-scale entrepreneurs and small family businesses in both the production and retailing sectors of the economy, who primarily work informally for the acquisition of a wage. They are often self-employed, and have established their business in order to provide themselves with a livelihood. Typical workers in this category are street traders such as the familiar female 'higgler', artisans, and some home-based producers (Le Franc, 1989). Within this category, there are also workers who engage in informal enterprise to subsidise a formal wage or household income. Many households in Trinidad receive both informal and formal incomes, depending on the current economic climate and the employment status of its members. For example, some operators may be 'recessional workers', as they participate in informal work in times of hardship, but discard their jobs when household income levels have risen. Many street traders, clothing producers and daily service providers utilise the sector for this purpose. Typical enterprises include artisanal and leather production, food retailing and repair services.

According to Sethuraman (1981) and Tokman (1989), an operator's motive for entering the sector is an important consideration for determining the degree of informality of a business. The creativity and entreprenuerial spirit of many informal workers have been channelled into the development of small, productive retail and service enterprises which make use of tax avoidance and other legislation. It is important to note that self-enhancement and an improved standard of living are the main motives of this group, who hope that a small business will assist in their social mobility.

A third category is one which is increasingly forgotten, but which does account for a growing number of businesses in the new global economy. The main occupants of this sector could be called 'petty capitalists' as their main aim for establishing an informal business is the extraction of profits, which may be greater that in the formal sector (de Soto, 1989). The avoidance of taxes, labour legislation, safety laws and minimum wages, attracts many businesses to adopt an informal strategy. Petty capitalists will frequently employ waged labour, often at low wages in sweatshops in order to produce goods at low cost. These businesses are evidence of the fact that large profits can be made within an informal unit, and support the argument that the informal sector is inextricably linked to the international economy. A large proportion of petty capitalist businesses will be sub-contracted to larger formal sector firms, and it is within this type of enterprise that the greatest exploitation if found. The clothing and electronic industries are prime examples of this type of 'informal employment' but this sector is relatively small in Trinidad in comparison with its Latin American neighbours.

A fourth category of informality refers an expanding group of 'criminal operators' who participate in undesirable activities such as drug dealing, smuggling, theft, extortion and protection, which are becoming increasingly important in global capital accumulation. The international drug trade, for example, is a major employer of small-scale operators and is deemed responsible for increasing violence and crime in Jamaica and Trinidad. Government officials believe that much of the wealth circulating in more legitimate informal businesses in these islands stems from the profits of the drug industry.

Once the motive for engaging in informal sector work has been established, further identification can be made of the specific market roles undertaken by different groups. Regardless of product specialisation, operators may also be classified according to their role within the sector. This classification also considers the interaction of people, goods and capital between the informal and formal sectors of Trinidad.

Formal-informal sector interaction - Individuals and households also participate in the informal sector at different levels, based on their role in each of three levels of the economic process: production and supply, distribution, and retail. Firstly, there is the commercial sector, which incorporates large businesses, imports and other formal supplies. Secondly, there is a small-business sector, which includes a variety of local producers, many of whom operate in the informal sector. Lastly, there is a category of workers who provide small amounts of goods and services through subsistence units, home-based production and unwaged labour. It is recognised, however, that this classification is not exclusive, as much interaction takes place between the three categories denoted. For example, many home-based producers will also supply the commercial sector.

From the production base, there are many distribution routes which may be taken to reach the customer. As expected, a large proportion of the commercial supply will be transported directly to the formal stores and supermarkets, such as 'Hi-Lo'. In addition, a selection of goods will be distributed to wholesale warehouses and formally organised markets, such as Port of Spain's Central Market for fresh produce. Here, goods may either be sold direct to the consumer or, as is more likely, to a middle-person working within the informal distribution sector, or an informal trader.

A prime example of the interactive nature of the formal and informal distribution networks is illustrated by the role undertaken by the female higgler. The higgler buys produce from formal markets and informal suppliers, and will either sell the goods on the streets or in a market or to another informal trader to retail elsewhere. Within the informal environment, goods may pass many hands before being sold to the customer by a street hawker. Small businesses will utilise similar distribution links to the commercial sector although, many workers will often undertake both the production and retail processes themselves. The informal network is one of the prime methods of distribution available in Trinidad, as will be discussed in chapter 5.

Workers in the final, subsistence category may often be forced to retail their own products due to the small quantities involved. Many subsistence farmers sell their limited surplus from a stall located outside their property, this being staffed by their children. There is also unlikely to be another person involved in the retail of small items sold to supplement household incomes, such as flowers, needlework and confectionery. Larger amounts may be sold to a higgler or middle-person for distribution. However, many home-based producers work for commercial businesses and their goods will be distributed formally.

Spatial geography of the informal sector - Finally, it is important to understand the spatial geography of informal activity in Trinidad, and there are several recognisable patterns of spatial organisation of informal activity in Trinidad which are worth noting. These include the prominence of petty commodity/street trading, the concentration of retail services along the country's main transport routes, the importance of the west-east urban corridor, and the spatial differentiation of occupations.

Street trading, a long tradition in the Caribbean, is prolific throughout the urban centres of Trinidad. Many different products are sold in this manner, from fresh fruit and vegetables to imported electrical goods. Street retailing is popular with customers as it facilitates 'the lime' (a Caribbean pastime of hanging-out with friends). A Sunday visit to the coconut seller, situated on the Savannah in Port of Spain, is a local custom.

The most popular locations for street vending include downtown Port of Spain, San Fernando, the Eastern Main Road, and Arima, although it is still popular in smaller locations. Also visible in Trinidad are the large numbers of fresh produce, and hot-food traders along the main transport routes and smaller rural centres, such as Toco in the north. The highway sale of fruit and vegetables is a profitable occupation with a large customer threshold. Stalls are open all hours and provide a convenient way of purchasing fresh fruit. Informal agriculture also acts as an important source of rural enterprise.

The marked concentration of informal enterprises engaging in productive, service and retail functions located along the west-east corridor, which extends from Port of Spain to Arima, is one of the most interesting features in Trinidad. This conurbation commands a hinterland of over 320 square kilometres and a population of 600,000 (National Census, 1990). The region, which coincides with the county of St. George, extends through a system of close knit communities which stretch from Caranage in the West to Arima in the East. This is further reinforced by the major road system known as the east-west corridor. Two parallel East-West arterials, the Western and Eastern Main Roads, and the more recently built Churchill Roosevelt Highway, connect these communities with each other, and with the capital. Informal activity is also prolific along the Southern Highway.

The final spatial observation concerns a noticeable division of labour based on ethnicity and gender. Specific locations appear to attract workers, either by choice or constraint, of similar ethnicity and/or gender. In San Fernando, and the south of the country, many informal occupations are undertaken by workers of East Indian descent. By contrast, occupations in Port of Spain and some northern settlements are mainly undertaken by workers of Afro-Caribbean descent. These occupations are further subject to a gender division of labour In a stratified society such as Trinidad, gender and ethnicity assume important roles which need clarification.

Conclusions: Informalisation as a Trinidadian Work Ethic

The informal 'doubles' (a local Indian snack) or 'coconut' vendor has become synonymous with Trinidad. Ask a local to visually describe Port of Spain and he/she will probably talk of the congestion of the informal maxi-taxis, street vendors and rum shacks. Informality is a way of life for many people in Trinidad, a life-style which has been pre-conditioned by colonial, economic and social traditions. Many Trinidadians favour the independence given by self-employment, an occupation which provides both the flexibility needed to work unregulated hours, and which allows participation in social activities such as Carnival, Cricket and 'the lime'.

Trinidad is not an island of formal, nine to five, employment.

Economic informality has been widespread for many years. The formal sector, has for the most part, been dependent upon its relationship to the world market and restricted to colonial and state-run enterprises. Traditionally, the street hawker or higgler has provided local goods for the people (Katzin, 1959). In this respect, the economy is shaped by government supported activity on one hand, and small productive informal enterprises on the other. It is not surprising that, in addition to the severe repercussions of recession, associated with informality, the informal sector is growing in favourability amongst many social groups. It is also suggested that in the present economic and political climate any move towards a type of work which is more locally tuned to the needs of the Caribbean, and less linked to the international economy, may gain momentum in support. The informal sector can be seen as an entrepreneurial environment for the Caribbean, which brings together bonds of popular solidarity, creativity and flexibility.

Other less favourable causes of informality include the current economic crisis, lack of formalised employment and the absence of better work opportunities. Equal concern centres on the inability of certain social groups to gain access to formal employment due to a number of constraints. Following in the footsteps of its past, Trinidad places great emphasis on formal education, much of which is still externally-based. Furthermore, traditional societal values still confine certain groups to specific occupations based on ethnicity, class and gender. Household and reproductive roles also act as major influences on job allocation. As work in Trinidad adopts a variety of roles and guises, it is important to distinguish between them.

Within this chapter, a number of key characteristics of the Trinidadian informal sector have been identified which have not previously been documented. As elsewhere, the informal sector is heterogeneous in both its activity and workforce. It is socially important to the country as it provides an outlet for popular culture, art and music. Economically, it acts as a distribution network for a number of essential products and services, including food and transport. Furthermore, it is more Trinidadian in nature than the formal sector, which is still internationally-oriented. Its accessibility to many social groups has led to informality being adopted as a way of life for workers from different locations and backgrounds. Despite its widespread applicability, however, it remains highly stratified according to a number of social factors.

It is therefore imperative that a greater understanding on the informal sector is developed. Approaches which conceptualise the people working within the informal sector in a stereotypical manner also need to be explored. For example, details on whether the sector is comprised of the most poorly paid and unskilled workers, or ambitious entrepreneurs, is just one such consideration. It is suggested here that an examination of whether informality is a uniform social phenomenon, or one which is more strongly influenced by ethnicity, gender and space, is also vital. It is taken for granted that ethnicity and gender are underlying factors in all social affairs in Trinidad, but identification needs to be made of the specific influence of the processes of racialised gendering in the informal employment process. Within this context, spatial ramifications also need some recognition, as they are important to the future development of social infrastructure in Trinidad.

The informal sector in Trinidad is currently surrounded by misconception and erroneous stereotyping. With the heightened institutional interest in the dynamics of a type of employment market which is more flexible, research into its true identity is paramount. At a national level, information on the informal sector needs to be established to study the distribution of basic needs, incomes and services, in order to form a comprehensive policy of development.

If it is established that a wide cross section of labour in developing countries trade 'informally', then observations need to be made not only concerning the extent of their informality, but their distribution networks and access to markets. This is an important factor both for the business and the individual. As the informal sector operates widely throughout the economy in Trinidad, there is a need to look closely at the markets in which people operate, their access to good jobs, and the occurrence of informality across society.

Many of these ideas are pursued in the two chapters which follow. These present an analytical appraisal of the data collected in a nation-wide reconnaissance survey which aimed to examine two of the most important components of the informal sector, namely the food distribution and petty commodity sectors.

5 Informal Sector Food Production, Distribution and Retailing

This chapter presents some of the main findings of the reconnaissance survey designed to examine the overall nature and scale of the informal sector in Trinidad. Following the need to gain knowledge on the nationwide operation of informality in Trinidad, as noted in chapter 1 a basic survey was devised to identify important informal occupations, and determine the characteristics of their operators. The aim was to carry out a brief, but extensive survey which would also highlight those activities justifying further examination, and to focus on issues of ethnicity, gender and spatial location. The results of the reconnaissance survey identified two important areas of informal activity, the informal food distribution system and non-food petty commodity production, retailing and associated services. This chapter investigates the findings of the survey in relation to the internal food distribution system in Trinidad, whilst chapter 6 examines the role of petty commodity production.

Food production, distribution and retailing is an important activity in providing incomes in developing countries. Although literature exists on the rural production and supply of food, with frequent reference made to farming and subsistence production (Pedersen, 1992), little attention has been given to urban food production and the rural-urban distribution system. Although petty commodity trading as an activity has been covered in detail (McGee, 1979; Holm, 1992), overall coverage of the distribution of basic foodstuffs is limited (Drakakis-Smith, 1992). Drakakis-Smith (1992) argues that although individual aspects of the internal food system, such as the hawking of cooked food and the operation of wholesale and retail markets, have been widely debated, few researchers have covered the full range of food-related activities.

In summary, there is a notable lack of research which takes an holistic approach to food systems in developing countries, focusing on patterns of supply, distribution and consumption. The result is "a massive and persistent misunderstanding of the petty-commodity sector, its complexities and the food needs of the poor" (Drakakis-Smith, 1992: 260). As the informal sector plays a major role in the food sector of many developing countries, it remains a prime focus point for examination in a world-wide context, and especially within the Caribbean.

The importance of food production, distribution and retailing should not be underestimated in the Caribbean, a region which has for centuries been unable to feed its population. In 1989, Trinidad imported food amounting to US$914.4 million, with years of hard labour and wealth having been ploughed into plantation agriculture at the expense of the domestic food market. Trinidad has been forced into importing essential food-stuffs to feed a nation which is unable to grow what it consumes (Deere *et al*, 1991). Recent changes in tastes have served to increase the dependency of the country on the international market for the provision of food, as Trinidadians develop a preference for western convenience foods.

In this light, the internal food distribution system plays an ever-increasing role in trying to supplement the government's efforts to provide sufficient food for the nation. Due to the extensive cultivation of sugar on the plains of the Caroni region, Trinidad's largest fertile area, there is little of either good land or capital for investment in domestic agriculture. Centuries of agricultural neglect have resulted in a present-day situation where there are only two main sources of fresh food supply in Trinidad. In contrast to popular belief, a vast amount of fresh produce is imported into the island, both legally by the government or private companies, and illegally by informal sector traders. The other supplier is not the commercial farmer, but the small-scale, own-account farmer who is a fundamental source of produce for a large proportion of the population. Despite the fact that there are a limited number of producers, there are by contrast a larger number of retailers and market mechanisms which distribute the produce to the customer. When observing the internal food distribution system in Trinidad, it is not surprising to discover that the informal sector plays a large role in the supply of food, and exerts an even greater influence in its distribution. Linkages between official food supplies, illegal imports and the many types of informal retailing establishments, also serve to illustrate the integrative nature of the informal and formal sectors.

The economic situation in Trinidad, characterised by restrictions implemented by the International Monetary Fund (IMF), debt and domestic recession, resulted in increasing difficulty for the government in affording expensive food imports, which use up valuable foreign reserves needed to service debt repayments. This fragile situation was further hampered by the IMF's structural adjustment package, implemented in 1990, which forced Trinidad to open its markets to imports previously banned. Trinidad had protected its domestic industry and foreign reserves from outside competition by only allowing necessary imports, such as basic foodstuffs and materials for industry, into the country. Raw materials for the construction and petroleum industries, and vegetables and wheat for domestic consumption are common examples of popular imports. The free market operation advocated by the IMF in 1991, has resulted in the importing of clothes and luxury food items, such as wine and confectionery. The recent changes in Trinidadian lifestyle and taste, which occurred during the oil boom, have placed a preference on foreign goods over domestic supplies due to the belief that foreign is better. This change in consumer habits is placing increasing competition on the already struggling domestic food market, and on the people who rely on the domestic sector to earn a living.

In order to assess the importance of the internal food distribution system, in terms of indigenous trade and economic contribution, it is necessary to examine the process further. The aims of this chapter are three-fold. Firstly, it provides a brief synopsis of the domestic agricultural sector in Trinidad, paying specific attention to the growing role of the informal sector. Secondly, the true nature of the informal food distribution sector is analysed through the presentation of results from the reconnaissance survey. Here, attention will be paid to establishing the various types of informal food production and retailing operations in Trinidad, concentrating on their size, function and geographical distribution. Furthermore, the chapter also identifies the ethnicity and gender of those workers who operate the activities. Finally, the importance of the informal sector, in rural-urban interaction, is established by analysing the distribution of activities along the three main transport arteries of Trinidad.

Food Production, Distribution and Retailing in Trinidad: The Role of the Informal Sector

There are a number of regions which are important in the production of fresh produce in Trinidad. The eastern coast, particularly the area surrounding the settlement of Mayaro (refer back to Figure 3.1), is important for coconut production which is still undertaken on large estates. As the southern region of the country is dominated by industry, agricultural production is undertaken by households on the small-scale. Although a large area of central Trinidad is covered by sugar cane, this land is more fertile and more favourable for small-scale production than the south.

There are also several areas in the north of the country, where land is generally fertile and the climate is favourable, which give rise to both urban and rural small-scale production. Firstly, there is an area to the north-east of the island known as Toco (see Figure 3.1). Here, fertile soil allows the cultivation of vegetables, ground provisions and fruit such as mangoes, bananas and pineapples, by local farmers and households. A large proportion of this produce is brought for sale in, and distributed from, the eastern market town of Arima, often by female higglers. Similarly, the north-western tropical forest is also favourable for the growth of similar products, and small-scale cultivation takes place on the old cocoa estates near Maracas Bay. From here, produce is transported to Port of Spain's Central Market where it is distributed to all parts of Trinidad. It is worth noting that Central Market is also the main receiver of imported produce in

Trinidad. Informal traders will travel to the Central Market to buy imported goods at a fixed government price in order to distribute them to other parts of the island. In this respect, the informal trader is also one of the main channels of distribution for the formal sector. The precise operation of Central Market will be discussed in chapters 7 and 8, which examine the role of informal trading in detail.

Although the rural regions of Trinidad are more important in terms of total agricultural production, urban household production is on the increase. Despite the fact that land is scarce in Port of Spain, many households try to cultivate mango or lime trees and vegetables to supplement their diet, and to retail if possible. A good location for production is Diego Martin, a suburban low-middle income residential area, which is situated in a fertile valley. Household cultivation on the surrounding slopes is widespread and forms a further supplement to the incomes of the locals who sell their produce to traders.

Despite a localised production system, retailing is undertaken on a national scale, as most of the produce farmed is not sold in the zone of production. A large proportion of goods are transported to a local market, and sold to a middle-person who will then sell to individual or family traders. Alternatively, a farmer may decide to retail the produce directly on the street or in a market. Direct retailing is more usual for a family business, which has a reasonable amount of produce for sale, as some members of the family can establish a regular retailing location whilst others cultivate the land. This extended system is more commonly practised in the central plains of Trinidad which have been settled by families of East Indian descent. However, a general observation is that many rural producers abstain from selling their produce directly to the consumer, particularly if this involves travelling to Port of Spain.

The majority of rural grown produce will be distributed in the local towns to a variety of informal sector traders or retailers, they in turn will retail the produce in many different areas. This system provides evidence to suggest that in a small island economy, the processes of rural-urban interaction work to transfer goods and capital between regions. The presence of imported goods adds a further input into the local system, as imported vegetables appear in most rural settlements, brought in by local traders who buy from the Central Market. Therefore, in any rural or urban market in Trinidad, it is common to find traders selling a variety of local, national and imported fruit and vegetables, a factor highlighted in chapter 4 .

Ethnicity and Gender in the Informal Food Sector: An Historical Overview

The nature of both rural and urban poverty in Trinidad is such that many low-income households with access to land will attempt to grow food for their own consumption, and/or for retailing. This tradition extends from the 1700s, when slaves were allowed to cultivate their own subsistence plots, and women sold their produce in local markets (Mintz, 1964). Marginal production flourished with the arrival of East Indian indentured labourers who replaced the emancipated African slaves on the plantations, and in agriculture as a whole.

After emancipation land was more available in Trinidad than in other Caribbean islands, and many East Indian families continued to work in agriculture after their indentureships had finished. Many chose to exchange their passage back to India for free Crown land offered after 1869. According to Weller (1968), land ownership became an obsession with the East Indians, and between 1885 and 1912, 35,680 hectares of land were sold or given to East Indians by the government. In this way, East Indian communities came to dominate small farming in Trinidad in the growing of sugar cane, vegetables and cocoa.

Meanwhile, large groups of emancipated African slaves fled to urban areas in search of higher paid waged-work. Despite their rejection of agriculture as a way of life, many families continued to cultivate small plots in order to supplement their consumption and income. The growing of fruit, such as mangoes and grapefruit, flourishes in Port of Spain today, and is an additional source of household income. As Drakakis-Smith (1990) points out, subsistence food production is usually only associated with rural areas, but is also important in many developing cities. Although Caribbean examples are limited, urban production has been covered in other regions (Gefu, 1992).

From the 1950s onwards, agricultural production began to decline in Trinidad with the development of the industrial sector. The Peoples National Movement (PNM) did not give priority to agriculture, or rural development, as the country was seen as a producer of oil, and iron and steel. As a consequence, a large proportion of the Indian population felt neglected, and rural poverty increased throughout the boom period of the 1970s. In addition, there was a rise in imported high status foods which further undermined domestic production. In 1975, per capita food production was half of the amount in 1965. This coincided with a rise in food import bills, from TT$161 million in 1973 to TT$904 million in 1982 (Vertovec, 1990). Increasingly, young workers became attracted to higher paid public sector occupations, and the agricultural work force fell dramatically.

Domestic agricultural production is still suffering from a lack of diversification and investment. The natural and labour potential for food cultivation in Trinidad is vast, but it still remains largely untapped with the exception of a growing group of informal operators. Domestic food production is characterised by Government negligence, a lack of market organisation and a disregard by a large proportion of the work force for agricultural occupations. Agriculture in Trinidad is held in low esteem due to low wages, and the association with slavery and backwardness (Harry, 1993).

Despite this unfavourable situation, there are a growing number of small-scale farmers who have capitalised on the lack of government control. Trinidad has a more liberal land tenure system than other islands, whereby a large proportion of land is either owned or leased from the government. Despite this fact, an analysis of the distribution of agricultural holdings shows that a large number of farmers cultivate less than one acre of land (Vertovec, 1990). A larger component of the system consists of squatters on private or state land who engage in legitimate crop production for sale to the government on a small scale. This has not only resulted in an increase in informal domestic production, but in the national marketing and distribution of both domestic and imported produce. With the stagnation of agricultural investment, many farmers have also turned to supplement their farming incomes by distributing more profitable imported produce.

Historically, therefore, there is a visible dominance of agriculture by Indo-Trinidadians, but there is also a noticeable contribution by other groups which is less well documented. Harry (1993) has suggested that there is a distinct division of labour in the production and marketing of produce in Trinidad, a factor which has been influenced by history and cultural tradition. Although valuable, Harry's work concentrates on the Indo-Trinidadian role within agriculture and there has been little consideration of the activities undertaken by other ethnic and socio-economic groups. Together they contribute to one of the most visible manifestations of informal activity in Trinidad.

Informal agricultural retailing is also a suitable area to observe cross-cultural differences in gender roles. Boserup (1970) highlights the Caribbean as an area with a high participation of women in agriculture, and women are particularly responsible for the marketing of produce (Momsen, 1984). Despite this being the case in other islands, such as Jamaica, it is suggested that female participation may be more restricted in Trinidad due to cultural considerations, a factor which is also addressed within the survey.

A Nationwide Survey of the Informal Food Distribution and Retail System in Trinidad

It was partly to overcome the paucity of information that the field research began by examining the most basic characteristics of the informal sector, notably people, products and places. In line with the general call for an holistic approach to the food distribution system, this chapter will provide an overview of the informal food distribution system in Trinidad, a task made possible through the conduct of a series of reconnaissance surveys.

This preliminary stage of the research, referred to as the reconnaissance survey, incorporated a series of surveys of traders/retailers in four different areas of Trinidad. The objectives were to establish patterns of food retailing and production which highlighted the involvement of different social groups, identify the rural-urban flows of goods and people, and examine the influence of ethnicity and gender in agriculturally-related occupations. It was also designed to enable the preparation of the principal focus of the research, the detailed ethnographic work reported in chapters 7 and 8.

In order to be effective but quick to administer, the field surveys focussed on six selected characteristics. It was decided that the survey should concentrate on the method of retailing, the size of the operation, the type of products retailed, the number of workers employed in each activity, and finally, the ethnicity and gender of each worker. Further details regarding these characteristics are shown in Table 5.1.

Consideration of the method of retailing adopted by the operator was included in the survey for a number of reasons. Firstly, the method employed may be indicative of the type of produce traded by the operator, or the nature of their business. In many cases, the use of a permanent stall may suggest that the operator engages in trading on a permanent basis, as she/he has invested in a solid structure. By contrast, mobile trading restricts the number, and type of goods to be sold, and often suggests that the operator is engaging in selling on a survival or temporary basis. Stalls were also classified according to their size, measured in terms of width, which enabled further evaluation as to the availability of space or the prominence of the business.

Secondly, method of trading is also linked to government legislation and police control. As official comment on informal trading in Trinidad is not forthcoming, the method of trading adopted by operators in a given area may indicate the level of police tolerance. For example, fixed structures are only likely to be raised when the authorities are tolerant of informal trading. A trader will not risk erecting a visibly, permanent stall if he/she suspects that they will be subject to police harassment. The use of flexible stalls, which can easily by dismantled, is more likely in areas where the clearing of informal activities by police is frequent. Mobile trading is the most effective method of police evasion. Thirdly, as vehicles are expensive in Trinidad, their use by traders provides some indication of the level of wealth and success of their business. In addition, the use of a truck may link the operator to a shared family business due to its high capital outlay.

Classification of the types of products retailed by informal traders was an important consideration in the survey. There was no pre-specified list of product categories, but the survey showed that product specialisation was limited to the items listed in Table 5.1. Furthermore, most traders specialised in the sale of products of a particular type, but where this was not the case, classification was determined by the most dominant product type.

The quantity of workers present was recorded for each activity/operation. Workers were also asked to broadly classify their ethnicity and gender. During the analysis, activities were grouped according to whether

Table 5.1 The Characteristics Examined in the Reconnaissance Survey

Characteristics	Survey Criteria
1. Method of Retailing	Stall - fixed or flexible Mobile Trading Trading from vehicle
2. Size of Stall (if appropriate)	Small Medium Large
3. Type of Produce Retailed	Fruit Vegetables Single Products Fish/Poultry Confectionery/Nuts Grocery Cooked Food
4. Number of Operators per Activity	Number
5. Gender of Operators	Male/Female
6. Ethnicity of Operators	Indo-Trinidadian or East Indian descent Afro-Trinidadian or Afro-Caribbean descent European descent Other (Syrian, Chinese, Lebanese)

they were associated with the food distribution system or with non-food production and services. The survey aimed to provide a general overview of the geography of the informal sector rather than a definitive quantitative measurement of informal activities.

The Administration of the Reconnaissance Survey

When deciding upon a suitable methodological approach to the administration of the surveys, a random sample survey was deemed to be appropriate. However, a pilot study using a random sampling technique, consisting of one in four traders, revealed a number of problems. In locations with small numbers of traders, the study would provide little data. Since details concerning informal sector activity are scarce, omitting a large number of activities appeared to be unsatisfactory. As a wide-ranging, comprehensive survey was required, a decision was made to undertake a complete survey of all the informal activities operating in the locations surveyed. The small size of the island made a comprehensive survey of this nature possible in a number of regions. It was believed that this approach would provide sound coverage without jeopardising the validity of the results.

Due to limitations previously mentioned, the surveys were undertaken throughout the main and accessible regions of Trinidad. As observed in chapter 4, the prominence of informal activities along the main transport routes, their accessibility and general safety, highlighted their suitability. The survey was therefore administered along three main transport routes in Trinidad, a process which incorporated many towns and settlements. A fourth part of the survey selected three urban informal gatherings of traders, for the purpose of comparison.

Along each route, the survey included every individual operation/activity encountered along the side of the road. For ease of administration, each route was divided into manageable sections, which coincided with settlement locations. Surveys were conducted on Fridays, when informal activity is most visible in Trinidad. In many cases, a number of sections along a particular route could be covered in a single day but where this was not possible, the survey was continued on the following Friday.

The Survey Locations

The first transport route shown in Figure 5.1, subsequently referred to as the *West-East Highway* extends from the far west of the island, at the old US military base at Chagaramas, and extends along the dual-carriageway of the Western Main Road through Port of Spain until it joins the national west-east Churchill-Roosevelt Highway. This route was divided into three sections for operation:

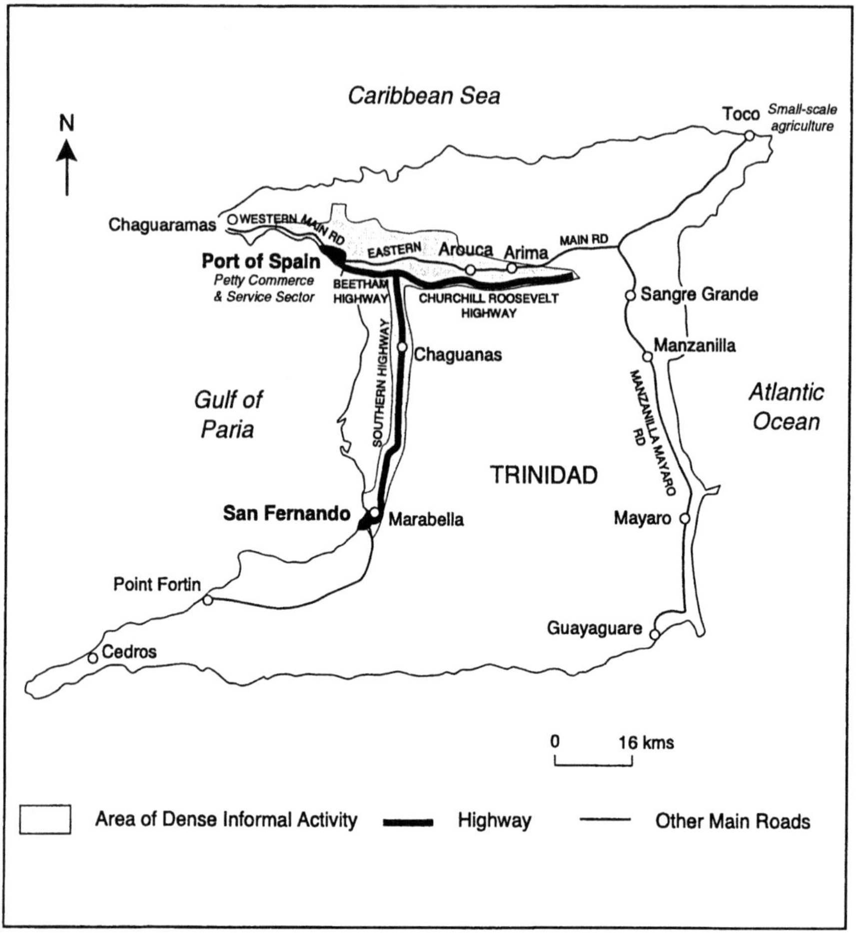

Figure 5.1 The Survey Locations

(i) the Western Main Road from Chagaramas, through Carenage to central Port of Spain;
(ii) from central Port of Spain, along the Beetham Highway to the Churchill Roosevelt Highway at St Augustine;
(iii) the Churchill Roosevelt Highway extending past Arima to its termination.

The second route follows the *Eastern Main Road* from its source in Port of Spain to Manzanilla in the East, where it becomes the Manzanilla Main Road to Mayaro. This long section of road, one of the oldest in Trinidad, needed to be divided into nine parts:

(i) Lady Young Road, Barrataria and San Juan in east Port of Spain;
(ii) St. Joseph/Curepe;
(iii) Tunapuna;
(iv) from Tunapuna via Arouca to the outskirts of Arima;
(v) Arima town to Valencia;
(vi) Valencia to Sangre Grande;
(vii) Sangre Grande Town;
(viii) Sangre Grande to Manzanilla;
(ix) Manzanilla to Mayaro.

The final transport route was the main north to south arterial, the Solomon Hochoy Highway locally referred to as the *Southern Highway*. It was only necessary to divide this route into four sections:

(i) the northern junction with Churchill Roosevelt;
(ii) the highway to San Fernando;
(iii) the San Fernando Junction;
(iv) San Fernando to Gulf City junction.

As already noted, in addition to the main routeways, surveys were also undertaken in three urban centres near to each of the main routes, referred to as *urban gatherings*. This additional sample was needed to provide information on informal urban groupings and serves to highlight patterns of activity which will be expanded upon in chapter 8 and 9, where the issues of occupational differentiation are examined in more detail. The three areas were chosen for their proximity to each of the three transport routes, and their diverse locations:

(i) the Savannah in Port of Spain (near to the West-East Highway);
(ii) Arouca centre (situated near the Eastern Main Road);
(iii) Marabella centre (near to the Southern Highway).

A total of 672 informal operations/activities, involved in food production and retailing, were sampled in the four main locations. Due to the concise nature of the survey, co-operation was given by all the operators approached. However, although there were no refusals as such, the survey recorded a number of empty stalls which were included in the total of 672. Their inclusion in the survey was important as it gave some indication of the number of part-time informal operators in a given location, and of the visible number of sites which are used for the purpose of informal retailing. The total number of empty stalls recorded was 169, although the proportion differed greatly between locations.

In the first location, the *West-East Highway*, a total of 229 activities were sampled along the route. Some 258 activities were sampled along the entire stretch of the *Eastern Main Road.* The *Southern Highway* provided a smaller sample of 139 activities, and in the additional *Urban Gatherings*, 46 activities were recorded. In order to examine the results in a contextual manner, the data have been analysed in two different ways. Firstly, the overall results for the survey are presented to enable the reader to gain a general picture of the informal food distribution system. Secondly, comparison will be made between the data collected along the three main routeways, omitting the urban locations which will be discussed in detail in chapter 7. This will allow the observance of any spatial patterns relating to gender and ethnic differentiation in occupations, and highlight the importance of the routeways in establishing rural-urban flows of people and goods.

General Characteristics of the Informal Food Sector in Trinidad

One of the first characteristics to be established was the method of retailing (Table 5.2). Within Trinidad, as a whole, it appears that retailing from a stall is the preferred choice by most traders, with some 80 per cent of all operators using a stall. Trading on foot, otherwise referred to in the survey as 'mobile trading', accounted for only 12 per cent of the total. This category also included the use of wheeled carts. These results immediately provide an indication of a general tolerance of informal trading and associated structures by the Trinidadian government. The abundance of fixed structures suggests that the operators do not fear repercussion from the authorities. A low level of mobile trading also relates to the inability of operators to carry large amounts of perishable produce around in the heat. There are also problems associated with making a decent living from selling small quantities of produce, as food, in general, does not have a large profit margin.

The use of vehicles for trading, accounting for only 7 per cent of the sample, is not widely practised in Trinidad. The large capital investment involved in purchasing a truck, is such that owners cannot afford to keep it in one location for long. The general exception to this rule is the highway fish sellers, who transport their catch from the south to retail from ice-filled trucks in the north. Alternatively, some traders may have a truck-load of eggs to sell, and they will move along the highway to find the best location. The remaining 1 per cent of the sample utilised both a stall and a

Table 5.2 Preferred Method of Retailing in the Informal Sector

Method of Retailing	Percentage of Operations (n=672)
Trading from Fixed or Flexible Stall	80
Mobile Trading	12
Trading from Vehicle	7
Trading from Stall and Vehicle	1

Table 5.3 Structure and Size of Stalls

Classification	Percentage of Stalls	
Structure of Stall	Fixed	72
	Flexible	28
		100
Size of Stall (width in metres)	Small (under 1.5m)	51
	Medium (1.5-3m)	39
	Large (3m and over)	10
		100

vehicle, indicating the profitable nature of the business concerned. Here, vehicles were only recorded at large fruit and vegetable stalls.

Those operations utilising stalls were also categorised according to the structure and size of the stall. Table 5.3 shows that 72 per cent of stalls were of a fixed and relatively permanent variety, whereas 28 per cent were flexible and temporary. Furthermore, an evaluation of size showed that small stalls, with a width of under 1.5 metres, were most commonly used. Approximately half of all stalls recorded were of a small size, a fact which reflects the high demand for space in popular locations and the desire not to attract attention by building large irregular structures. In this respect, large structures of over 3 metres in width accounted for only 10 per cent of the total.

Both fixed and flexible stalls take on many different forms in Trinidad. In most cases, fixed stalls are wooden, but they differ in their degree of consolidation. These range from stalls with no roof, to those with a temporary plastic roof, to an enclosed stall with corrugated roof and shutters. Flexible stalls are moveable structures which may be carried by the trader. Most frequently used are collapsible wooden and plastic tables, or empty oil drums.

A fixed stall with a secure roof often indicates a permanent place of trade, whether it is 'owned' by one trader, a family or shared amongst friends. These types of stall also highlight locations where business is permanently good. This is well exemplified by the many permanent structures located along the main highways, which sell fruit and vegetables. In many cases, extended family arrangements allow different members to use the stall on different days. As these structures are more visible, these operators are more likely to be fined for unlicensed trading, than traders who can move around more easily. However, there appears to be a widespread tolerance of fruit and vegetable trading due to the government's recognition of the nationwide importance of the activity. Over time, a fixed structure may be consolidated to form a more formalised retail unit; evidence of this can be widely seen in Port of Spain.

Notwithstanding the overall results, the nature of trading varies according to location, a factor which will be discussed in the next section. Not surprisingly, downtown Port of Spain and other commercial centres are mostly devoid of fixed structures due to stricter legislation and police control. The majority of traders in the city are mobile, and carry their goods around with them. Many move around frequently from street corner to office doorway according to the time of day. Older women will often sit in the street and lay a few goods on a blanket for sale to passers by.

Product specialisation appears to be very important in Trinidad. Two major informal categories of food can be identified in Trinidad. Firstly, there are imported fruit and vegetables and secondly, there are a number of local products, such as fish, local fruit and vegetables, confectionery and cooked food. It is important to note that grocery items, including packaged and processed foods, are rarely found in the informal sector. These goods are often high in price and are supposed to be subject to VAT. Likewise, poultry does not appear to be as widely sold in the informal sector, as first thought.

Table 5.4 illustrates the prominence of fruit and vegetable trading in Trinidad. A total of 11 per cent of all activities sold fruit, from both imported and local sources. The same percentage of activities sold only vegetables, but a further 15 per cent of the sample sold both fruit and vegetables. Overall, 37 per cent of the sample traded in fruit and/or vegetables. The next most important category is that referred to as 'single-product'. This category was established, as a large number of operators sold only small amounts of one type of produce, such as mangoes or coconuts. It was deemed important to identify these operations as different to the fruit and vegetable traders, who tend to deal in large amounts of imported and local produce. In addition, this category appears to include only local produce, unlike the other categories.

The types of businesses trading 'single-products' were identified in a separate category, for a number of reasons. Firstly, a trader who only sells locally grown produce may have direct links with the production process, for example, they may be subsistence producers. This type of retailing is more likely be undertaken by traders engaging in informal trading for survival or part-time purposes, as opposed to the mixed fruit traders who can afford to sell different products, many of which are imported. Single-products are often traded only in season for additional income, and many of the operators do not engage in trading as their main occupation. Products included in the single-product category were: coconuts (25 per cent), mangoes (22 per cent), corn (15 per cent), eggs (9 per cent), vegetables (11 per cent), other fruit (18 per cent).

When the data on operations selling 'single-products' are subject to cross tabulation with the method of retailing, the results indicate that single-product retailing is more likely to be associated with flexible, temporary stalls and mobile traders. Nearly 30 per cent of all the flexible stalls were recorded as selling local single-products. Of this total, nearly half sold only mangoes or coconut/coconut water. The widespread availability of mangoes in Trinidad, which grow in gardens and by roadsides, and their subsequent low price of TT$1.00/2.00 each, suggest that mango selling occupies the lowest place on the product hierarchy in Trinidad. This type of retailing is often undertaken for subsistence, and does not provide enough income to make it a full-time occupation, indicating that flexible trading may also be associated with poorer and lower status occupations.

Furthermore, nearly 75 per cent of all mobile traders sold single-products, with the remainder selling confectionery, such as nuts, or cooked food. On the highway junctions, it is common to find a group of traders selling only handfuls of mangoes, spring onions or berries for a few extra dollars. Once again, this is the subsistence end of the market. Product specialisation is operative in the informal sector, and it can provide a good

Table 5.4 Type of Food-Related Products Sold in the Informal Sector

Product Category	Percentage of Total Sample
Fruit	11
Vegetables	11
Fruit and Vegetables	15
Single-Products	32
Fish/Poultry	13
Grocery Items	2
Confectionery (sweets and nuts)	10
Cooked Food	6

Table 5.5 Informal Sector Workers by Ethnicity and Gender

Classification	Percentage of Total Workers (n=740)	
Gender	Male	66
	Female	34
		100
Ethnic Origin	Indo-Trinidadian	70
	Afro-Trinidadian	30
		100
Gender and Ethnicity	Indo-Trinidadian Male	48
	Indo-Trinidadian Female	22
	Afro-Trinidadian Male	18
	Afro-Trinidadian Female	12
		100

indication of a trader's potential income, and motive for working within the sector. In this respect, the category of single product can be associated with a more subsistence and temporary type of informal retailing.

Other categories of products such as fish and confectionery accounted for around 10 per cent of the sample (Table 5.4), although fish sellers were mainly found along the highways. A small presence of cooked food vendors, selling Doubles, Roti (filled chapati), Hot-roasted Corn and Snow-cone (ice-cream) was also noted in the survey.

In addition to providing information on the nature of informal sector trading, investigation was also centred upon the operators themselves, in particular their ethnicity, gender and involvement in certain types of retailing. It was anticipated that the results would assist in the investigation of the social and ethnographic stratification of informal sector occupations. A total of 740 informal workers were included in the survey. Taking into account that 169 operations were visibly empty, a total of 740 workers were found to work in 503 activities. The average number of traders per operation was 1.5, indicating that the majority of activities only employed 1 or 2 people. Furthermore, 66 per cent of the traders were male, and only 34 per cent female, a fact witnessed in Table 5.5. This contrasts with the general stereotype Caribbean pattern of female domination of informal food retailing (Ellis, 1986).

Although female participation in the sector is considerably lower than male, there are examples where women tend to dominate in a particular occupation or market position. Firstly, a greater percentage of women use flexible stalls than men. One-quarter of all female traders used a small, temporary structure for trading. Secondly, a similar proportion of women were selling single products, particularly mangoes, which appears to be a female occupation. Thirdly, women account for nearly 80 per cent of traders selling home-made confectionery, an occupation which is often taken on as a means to supplement household income. These patterns suggest that women working in Trinidad's informal food sector occupy the lower-paid and part-time occupations. In comparison, nearly 100 per cent of all the large fruit and vegetable outlets were occupied by men. Where women were present in these outlets, they occupied a subsidiary role.

When ethnicity is considered, a significant 70 per cent of the entire sample was of Indo-Trinidadian descent. The survey did not encounter any traders of European, Chinese or other ethnic group and the remaining 30 per cent were all Afro-Trinidadian. The absence of other ethnic groups provides evidence that informal sector occupations, particularly those associated with food, are considered to be of low-status by other more prosperous social and ethnic groups. Further analysis showed that nearly half of all traders/workers in this sector were Indo-Trinidadian males. Although Indo-Trinidadian females accounted for a further 22 per cent of the sample, it is important to note that over 80 per cent of these women worked with male family members and not alone. Indo-Trinidadian women were mainly found assisting husbands, or other family members, on the fruit and vegetable stalls. The only solo occupation which they dominated was the sale of hot corn from the roadside or highway. The participation of Afro-Trinidadian workers in this sector is generally much smaller, for reasons discussed in the next section. Afro-Trinidadian males accounted for 18 per cent of the sample, and females for only 12 per cent. When further comparisons are made with the data on gender, a number of interesting patterns come to light.

Having already discussed the prominence of women in the lower-status occupations of the sector, it is further possible to establish that it is mainly women of Afro-Trinidadian descent who take on this role. Nearly 40 per cent of all Afro-Caribbean women were recorded as selling small quantities of single-products, mainly a home-grown fruit or vegetable. Furthermore, this group of women also dominate the selling of confectionery, roti and other home-prepared products. The exception to this rule is the higglers who trade in large amounts of fruit and vegetables, but whom were not generally found in the sample areas, as they tend to occupy markets.

In a similar manner, the Afro-Trinidadian men recorded in the survey were more likely to engage in flexible or mobile trading, and the trading of single-products than the Indo-Trinidadian male. Although, fruit and vegetable trading is also undertaken by Afro-Trinidadian males, this is often done by using flexible stalls and selling much smaller quantities of products. By contrast, nearly 90 per cent of all the large highway fruit and vegetable stalls are operated by Indo-Trinidadian men. Other less profitable occupations undertaken by the same group include the retailing of cooked food, such as doubles, and coconut trading. The only single-product predominantly sold by Indo-Trinidadian males is corn, when it is in season.

In summary, the informal food sector has projected a number of interesting patterns. The basic image of this sector is one which relates to the dominance of fresh fruit and vegetables by operators of Indo-Trinidadian descent. Despite the overall domination of this sector by the male Indo-Trinidadian workforce, local products are also sold by men and women of Afro-Caribbean descent. Here, Afro-Trinidadian males tend to be employed in a middle-strata of smaller-scale, more temporary and less-profitable occupations. With the exception of higglers, women of Afro-Trinidadian descent are usually engaged in the sale of low-profit commodities, such as confectionery and nuts, associated with the use of informality as a survival strategy (Potter and Dann, 1990). Despite, these overall patterns of informality, results do vary greatly between the different survey locations.

The Nature of Food Production and Retailing in Trinidad: A Spatial Analysis

In order to provide a spatial approach, this section analyses the data recorded in three of the four main survey areas, namely the major transport routes of the West-East Highway, the Eastern Main Road and the Southern Highway. This comparison will facilitate a greater understanding of the nature of rural-urban interaction in the informal sector. Although valuable to the overall survey, the fourth location, incorporating urban informal markets, has been excluded from the analysis as it does not provide data which are subject to spatial comparison. By taking a geographical approach to the analysis, a greater understanding of the influence of space on informality in Trinidad will hopefully emerge.

The Spatial Pattern of Trading: Preferred Methods

Firstly, it is important to note that the predominant method of retailing in all three sites was the use of a stall, with the highest level found along the Eastern Main Road. Figure 5.2 also highlights the greater use of vehicles along the highways. The distribution of stalls, according to whether they were fixed or flexible, showed greater differences between the three sites. As shown in Table 5.6, the lowest level of fixed stalls was recorded along the West-East Highway, with the highest, amounting to 95 per cent, along the Southern Highway. Stall size does not differ greatly between any of the locations. The high level of flexible stalls used along the West-East Highway, is indicative of its status as the busiest, and most congested, routeway in Trinidad. Police control is high, and there have been a number of violent clashes between traders and the authorities. As it is a major commuter route, it is also the most profitable location for produce trading in Trinidad, and as such, it is a popular location. However, recent accidents involving vehicles pulling off the highway to buy fruit and vegetables, have heightened a governmental move to clear traders from this route.

The highest number of stalls, and indeed fixed stalls, were recorded along the Eastern Main Road. This road extends through many rural areas in the East, and there is much land available. The road around Arima and Sangre Grande is scattered with permanent stalls, which have been fixed outside a house or land-holding for the purpose of selling any spare fruit or vegetables. Here, it is not uncommon to see the sale of a dozen mangoes from the garden. This type of subsistence trading, commonly found along the Eastern Main Road, is more akin to popular views of the informal sector.

Furthermore, government regulation is not as stringent along the Eastern Main Road, as the traders provide a much needed service to the local residents. One of the greatest problems for the traders along the West-East Highway is its passage through areas of high-income housing,

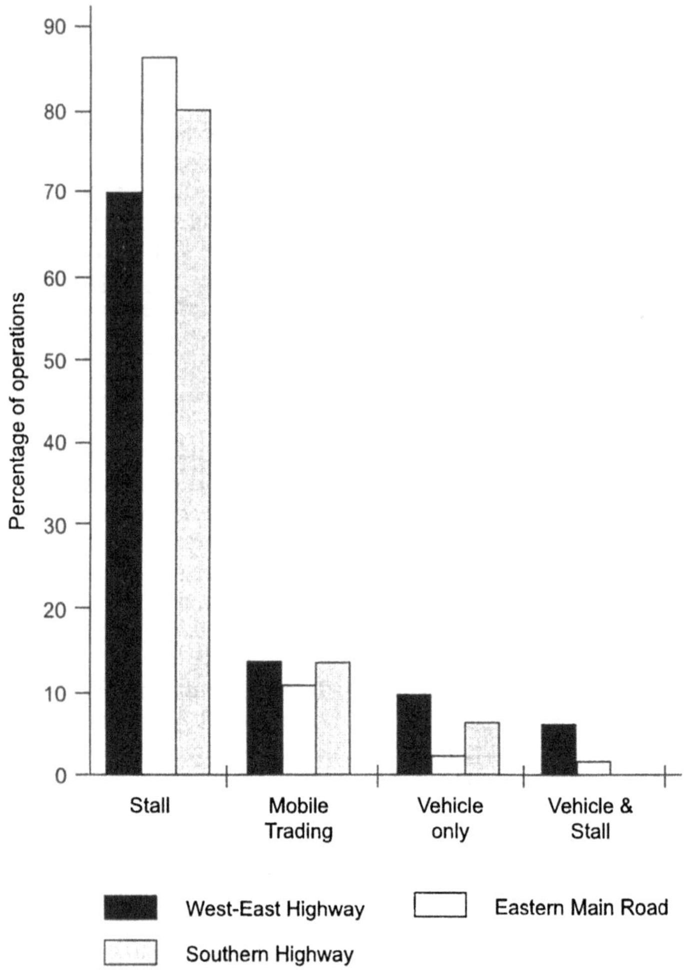

Figure 5.2 Method of Trading by Survey Location

Table 5.6 Spatial Distribution of Fixed and Flexible Trading

	Percentage of Operations		
Nature of Stall	West-East Highway	Eastern Main Road	Southern Highway
Structure of Stall			
Fixed	57	75	95
Flexible	43	25	5
	100	*100*	*100*
Size of Stall (width in metres)			
Small (under 1.5m)	52	46	52
Medium (1.5-3m)	33	46	38
Large (3m and over)	15	8	10
	100	*100*	*100*

where residents campaign to eradicate street vending. This is not a problem in the lower-middle income housing areas situated along the Eastern Main Road. Within Trinidad, levels of police regulation over the informal sector reflect popular and political opinion.

In contrast to the West-East Highway, 95 per cent of all stalls along the Southern Highway were fixed. This location is also a prime trading position, but its rural nature posses less problem to the authorities. Competition for space is much lower than the West-East arterial, and there are no residential areas along its boundaries. This also explains why less activities were recorded within this location. In general, the police appear to ignore trading along this route, which has resulted in the establishment of a number of very large structures. The rurality of the Southern Highway also means that it is too inaccessible for the small trader who has no transport. It is occupied by prominent and well-stocked stalls, operated by the entrepreneurial highway traders who appear to control this part of the market. Most of the stalls are of a high standard, and of a well-established nature, which partially indicates the higher status and income earning potential of the highway sellers.

Product Specialisation in the Informal Sector

Figure 5.3 provides a comparative analysis of the major types of produce sold in each location. In accordance with the overall figures, all three locations show a preference for fruit and vegetable trading, with a tendency towards selling one type of product only. The greatest occurrence of vegetable selling is along the Western Main Road where the largest quantities of imported vegetables are sold. Collectively, fruit and vegetable selling accounts for 41 per cent of trading along the West-East Highway, 40 per cent along the Southern Highway and 35 per cent along the Eastern Main Road. However, the sale of both fruit and vegetables together, which is synonymous with large operations, is of greatest importance along the Southern Highway. The sale of single-products is also prominent in all three areas, but is of equal importance to fruit and vegetable trading only in the Eastern Main Road. Of the total operations trading in single-products, 41 per cent were found in the Eastern Main Road. It may be surprising to note that the sale of single types of produce, notably corn and coconuts, is also prominent along the Southern Highway.

Table 5.7 provides a breakdown of the products found in the single-product category. Cross-tabulation of the data in the earlier part of the chapter revealed an association between the trading of single products, particularly mangoes and female sellers. Table 5.7 shows that the retailing of mangoes is only important along the Eastern Main Road, suggesting that this location is utilised by subsistence and part-time traders, many of whom are women. The availability of corn, eggs and coconuts along the highways highlights the traders' connections with East-Indian agriculture, as these products are derived from farms in the south and east of the

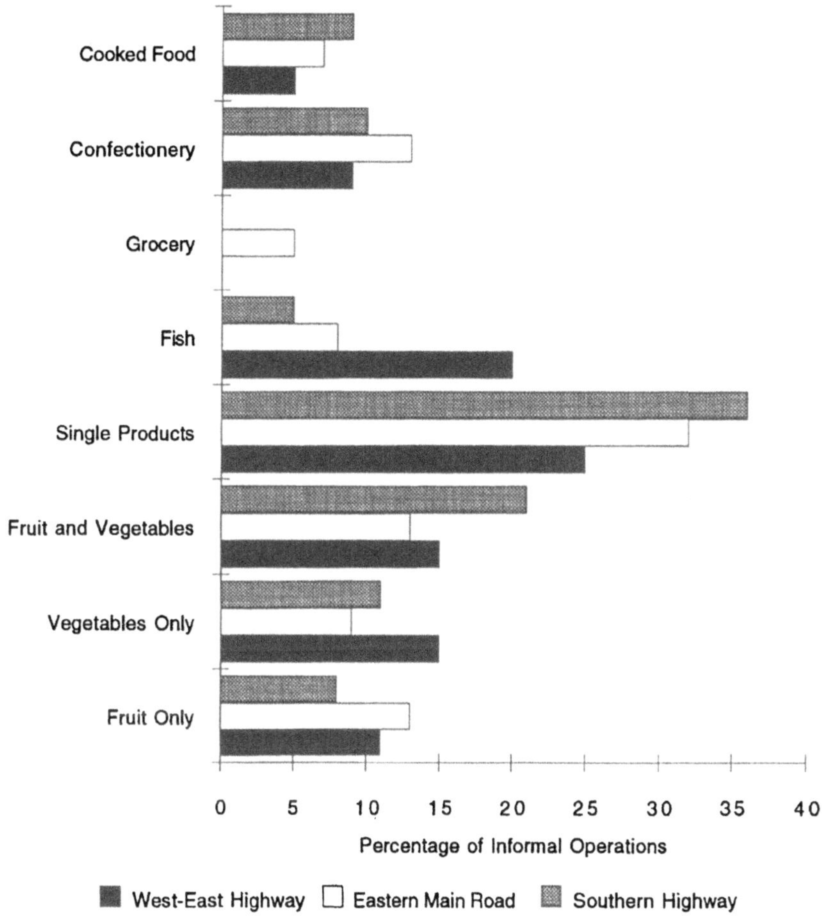

Figure 5.3 Product Specialisation by Location

Table 5.7 'Single-Product' Categories by Location

Category	Percentage of Operations West-East Highway	Eastern Main Road	Southern Highway
Mangoes	6	47	12
Coconuts	18	12	30
Corn	15	9	36
Seasonal Fruit (greengages, melons)	21	20	10
Eggs	25	3	0
Seasonal Vegetable (root vegetables)	15	9	12
	100	*100*	*100*

country.

The retailing of fresh fish is another popular informal occupation in this sector. The selling of fresh fish is another successful component of highway. The fish are brought up from the fishing areas in the south, near Cedros, to be retailed on certain days of the week, especially Friday. Fish sellers have trucks and set up in the same location every week, thereby attracting regular customers. The most popular location is along the West-East highway, where Port of Spain commuters stop to visit regular traders. As always, there is a contrasting and less successful side to fish retailing in Trinidad. This sector incorporates the small boys in Carenage selling crabs to supplement incomes and the odd trader who has managed to catch half a dozen fish every once in a while for extra money.

The sale of confectionery, such as nuts and Pepper-Mango are to be found in all three locations. However, all the confectionery traders along the Southern Highway were located at the junction with the Churchill Roosevelt Highway, where they trade among the cars at the traffic-lights. A similar situation is also found at the major junctions of the West-East Highway. Once again, only along the Eastern Main Road is there a more widespread distribution of sweet and nut sellers. The availability of informal cooked-food establishments was found to be limited to Doubles, Roti, Hot-roasted Corn and Snow-cone, as shown in Table 5.8. Notably, the highest proportion of hot-corn sellers was found along the Southern Highway, as corn appears to be a product associated with Indo-Trinidadian farmers. As expected, snow-cone vendors were only seen in the Eastern Main Road.

In summary, the Eastern Main Road offers a more diverse range of products, with higher levels of confectionery, cooked food and mangoes. Although, the sale of fruit and vegetables is also important, analysis of the specific sections of the road show that fruit and vegetable traders were mainly located to the east of Arima. The section of the road which passes through the urban continuum was subject to a wide range of vending. This is in contrast to the two highways, where fruit and vegetables are the most frequently marketed goods.

Gender and Ethnicity: The Importance of Product and Place

The data included in Table 5.9 highlight the marked gender and ethnic differences found between informal workers in the three areas. Despite the overall dominance of male traders, female workers still account for 30 to 40 per cent of the workforce in each location, with the highest proportion found in the Eastern Main Road. Furthermore, all but six of the women present along the Southern Highway were accompanied by male family members. In this respect, women were generally present to assist male workers, but were not left alone to trade. The six remaining females were hot-corn sellers, which is strictly a female-occupation in Trinidad. The differences in the occurrence of women between areas may be related to

Table 5.8 The Distribution of Cooked Food Operations

Category	Percentage of Operations		
	West-East Highway	Eastern Main Road	Southern Highway
Doubles	70	38	25
Roti	10	24	0
Hot-roasted Corn	20	0	75
Snow-cone	0	38	0
	100	*100*	*100*

Table 5.9 Gender and Ethnicity Differentiation between Locations

Labour Category	Percentage of Operations		
	West-East Highway (n=321)	Eastern Main Road (n=233)	Southern Highway (n=142)
Gender of Workers			
Male	71	60	66
Female	29	40	34
	100	*100*	*100*
Ethnicity of Workers			
Indo-Trinidadian	81	44	93
Afro-Trinidadian	19	56	7
	100	*100*	*100*

three factors. The first is again associated with the nature of trading in different locations. The prominence of traders selling small amounts of local products, such as mangoes, and the subsistence-oriented trading of the Eastern Main Road is more accessible to women, who can enter the business on a flexible basis. The larger businesses of the highways require credit for large purchases plus transport, both of which are more difficult for women to obtain.

Secondly, there is the question of safety on the highways. Highway locations are isolated, and are regularly subjected to robberies by armed gangs. Here women are seen as a more vulnerable target. Finally, and most importantly, there is a question of ethnicity which influences the presence of women along the highways. Of the women interviewed along the East-West Highway, 91 per cent were of Indo-Trinidadian descent. This figure was as high as 99.5 per cent for the Southern Highway. Interestingly, Afro-Trinidadian women were only prominent along the Eastern Main Road, where they accounted for 70 per cent of female workers. Figure 5.9 shows this differentiation.

Traditional Indo-Trinidadian views which influence some families often confine women to the household rather than allowing them to engage in visible economic activity such as trading. It is often more acceptable amongst low-income Indo-Trinidadian families for women to work in 'private' rather than 'public' spaces. Where they are found, it is usually as part of a group or family unit. Table 5.9 attests to the dominance of Indo-Trinidadian traders within the sector as a whole, and of the more profitable businesses along the highways. Between 81 and 93 per cent of the traders operating along the West-East and Southern Highways, are of East Indian descent. Whilst the ethnic distribution of traders along the Eastern Main Road is more equitable between dominant ethnic groups, there is a noticeable dominance of traders of Afro-Trinidadian descent.

Further analysis of the data shown in Figure 5.4, clearly highlights the Eastern Main Road as the only important area for the participation of Afro-Trinidadian women. This provides evidence to suggest the type of occupations taken by this group of women. Firstly, the high number of flexible stalls along the Eastern Main Road, suggest that it is connected with a level of trading associated with lower-incomes and lower status. The high level of single products being sold from temporary stalls, particularly the sale of mangoes which is primarily a female occupation, supports the notion that this is an area dominated by part-time workers, and those with less-established businesses. This evidence lends support to the idea that it is women who are forced to occupy the lower-income and lower status occupations within the informal sector, thereby mirroring Trinidadian society as a whole.

Part-time trading is frequently associated with women, who often take to the street selling fruit and vegetables in order to support their family, either as a result of poverty or the unemployment of the husband. Alternatively, the increase in female-headed households in the Caribbean

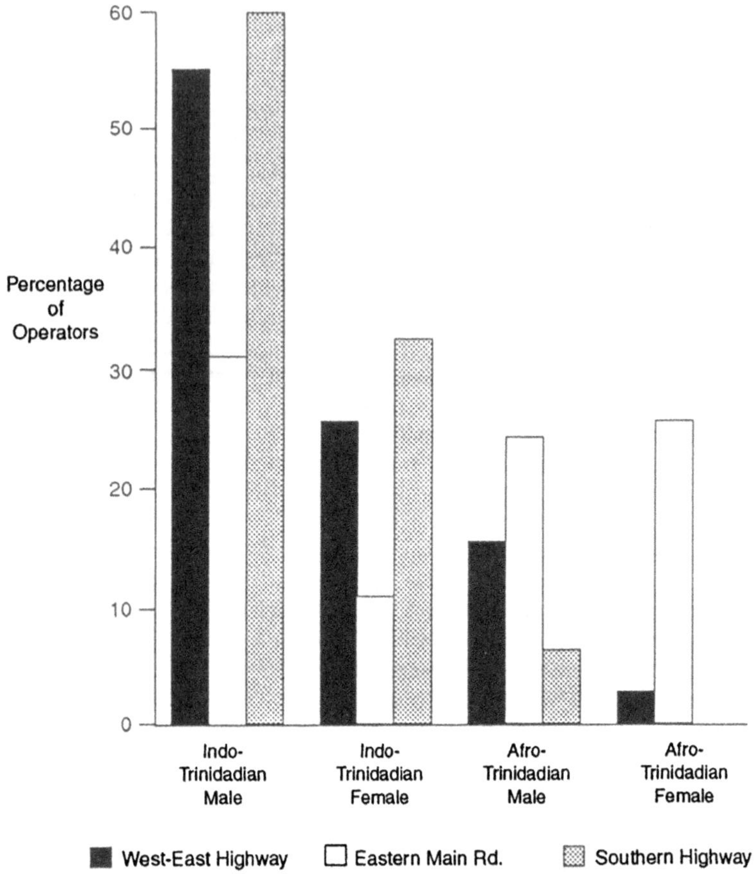

Figure 5.4 Gender and Ethnicity of Workers by Location

(Ellis, 1986) has lead to an increase in female trading as supplementary to other income-earning activities. This type of activity is often adopted on a part-time basis at weekends, or between other jobs, purely as a means of survival. Female traders are frequently seen wandering along the streets of Port of Spain and other urban areas carrying their goods in a bag. Many will only be selling a single product, often mangoes, berries or limes which have been picked from their own trees or local ones. Traders will frequently need to spend an entire day on the street in order to sell two-dozen mangoes.

The fact that some traders, particularly women, only sell a small amount of one locally grown product, indicates that they may be using the informal sector as a last opportunity to make money. As one female trader indicated, nobody would spend a whole day in the sun trying to sell a dozen mangoes for TT$2.00 each unless they had to for survival. Once better times arrive, it is these traders who will disappear to engage in more favourable activities. Unfortunately, evidence from the fieldwork suggests that this type of survival trading is on the increase in Trinidad, particularly in the sale of local products. This type of trading highlights the dynamic movement of people and goods as a major characteristic of the informal sector. It is also similar in nature to the retailing of confectionery, nuts and processed goods by small children in urban areas. In this respect, it is also important to note the prominence of grocery and confectionery sales along the Eastern Main Road, as compared to the highways.

In general, the smaller proportions of Afro-Trinidadian males working in the food sector (18 per cent), in comparison to their Indo-Trinidadian counterparts, could be connected with the undesirable stigma attached to agriculture. In Trinidad, agriculture is associated with backwardness and slavery, a view which is widely held. Where Afro-Trinidadian males are operating along the highways, they occupy flexible stalls, trade by foot and are more likely to sell local products. Poor perceptions of informal employment lead many workers of Afro-Trinidadian descent to adopt it only on a temporary basis, or as a last resort. This is in direct contrast to the Indo-Trinidadian family who has entered the food sector as entrepreneurs, determined to expand and to succeed. This highlights the importance of perceived prestige and status in occupational choice in Trinidad. The contribution of popular perceptions to the stratification of occupations is an area where greater research in needed.

The dominance of the Indo-Trinidadian traders along the highways is a factor which is indicative of their prominence in the food sector. A random sample of small-scale farmers undertaken in Trinidad in 1979, showed that only 18.5 per cent of small-scale farms were owned by farmers of Afro-Trinidadian descent (Harry, 1993), as opposed to 73 per cent of Indo-Trinidadian descent. An extended family network also provides labour and financial support which is not so readily available amongst Afro-Trinidadian communities. Reasons for the dominance of this sector by the Indo-Trinidadians also relate to their desire for social mobility through entrepreneurial activity.

In the main, Indo-Trinidadian traders with a higher income potential own their own permanent stall in a good location on a busy main road, such as the Western or Eastern Highways, or a regular market spot from where they operate on a fairly regular time-table. Many highway traders will only retail for 3 or 4 days a week, according to supplies and market days. They know the market place well and what the customer will buy. These are the traders who often sell imported produce in addition to local goods. They usually have a decent range of produce and due to their ability to buy in bulk are able to make higher profits. They are often not from the locality where they trade, as they own a truck or have access to transport, and will travel across the country in order to trade in the best locations. Although the majority of this group will have fixed stalls on the highways, it is more likely that a family will own more than one between them. This sector also includes a number of more flexible traders who locate a temporary structure according to the day of the week or select a favoured location, near a social gathering or a marketplace.

Another important dimension to food retailing is the popular occupation of selling cooked snacks in the street. This is slightly less informal than fresh produce retailing in that hot-food retailers are supposed to carry a licence of hygiene which they purchase annually from the Department of Health and Safety. The licences are relatively inexpensive (TT$35.00 in 1991), but failure to carry one can result in a hefty fine. This is the only type of formal control over snack sellers, as they are still free to trade where they please and are not subject to VAT. There is a popular feeling that the endorsement of taxes will be the next step taken by the government. If they become subject to tax, many traders have expressed their intention to leave the occupation, arguing that their profit margins will become too small, particularly in the light of increased competition not only from the numerous other traders but by the American-style burger outlets.

The occupation of cooked food selling is often entered into on a longer term basis than other types of selling, mainly because the success of a business relies on the ability of the trader to develop a regular custom. Many roti and doubles sellers have been selling for over ten years, and have adopted a regular routine, so that a customer knows that a particular trader can be found at a certain time. These activities are found in abundance anywhere where there are people. It is most frequently practised at lunch time, evenings and weekends. On a typical Friday night, a trader may start at the bus station, then move outside the cinema, and finally finish outside a bar or night-club in Port of Spain. They work long hours and often need to return home several times in a day to re-stock.

The selling of hot-snacks often requires a family or kinship network which provides help to buy and prepare the food, and to take over the selling if necessary. This type of family network, which is well associated with Indo-Trinidadian families, explains why Indo-Trinidadians are prominent in many types of informal sector trading. The very nature of informality requires a labour network which will help with different types of duties, from child care to cooking food. This does, however, emphasis the number of people who are being supported by a single activity, thereby stretching the income earnt.

In summary, therefore, the operators who engage in the informal sale and distribution of food are not homogeneous in character. The sector is a haven for irregular, low-paid and part-time traders, located along the Eastern Main Road, as well as those larger operators who utilise the sector for a long-term occupation. As there are many part-time fruit and vegetable traders, there are also a great number who have turned to it as an occupation, either as a small-scale producer, market trader or highway trader. These are the 'entrepreneurs', many of whom are to be found on the highways, who have realised the potential involved in undertaking the role of food distributor to the majority of the population.

Conclusions: Space, Ethnicity and Gender

So far, this chapter has provided evidence to suggest that ethnicity, gender and space are all important in explaining the marked stratification of occupations in three locations of Trinidad. The importance of spatial preference in influencing employment decisions is demonstrated in the subsequent examination of the spatial variation in the gender and ethnicity of workers in the survey locations. This detailed analysis also brings to light a series of more complex patterns of informal sector activity, which relate strongly to urban-rural interaction.

Specific locational data on the ethnicity and gender of operators in each section of the survey also show that levels of urban or rural development appear to influence workers' choice of occupation. Firstly, Table 5.10 analyses the nature of workers along the three sections of the West-East Highway. The first section of the route, which is in the west of the country shows a higher participation rate of Afro-Trinidadian workers. This area is closer to Port of Spain, which is traditionally associated with Afro-Caribbean culture. In general, the West-East Highway is the most densely populated area of informal food traders. Although the Indo-Trinidadian traders appear to control the market, they are often in competition with a number of Afro-Trinidadian vendors who live in this area, and who turn to fruit vending on a sporadic basis. The majority of the Indo-Trinidadian traders commute every-day from rural settlements, far from Port of Spain, and see this occupation as a full-time career.

The Southern Highway, detailed in Table 5.11, shows a complete domination of the entire highway by Indo-Trinidadian traders. The only participation of Afro-Trinidadian workers is, once again, near urban settlements at the junction with the Churchill Roosevelt Highway in the north. Here, a number of traders sell confectionery to cars stopping at the

Table 5.10 Ethnicity and Gender Differentiation along the West-East Highway

Section	Percentage of Workers in Each Section			
	Indo-Trinidadian		Afro-Trinidadian	
	Male	Female	Male	Female
West Main Road to Port of Spain	26	16	47	11
Port of Spain, to Churchill Roosevelt at St Augustine	64	23	6	5
Churchill Roosevelt to Arima	53	29	17	1

Table 5.11 Ethnicity and Gender Differentiation along the Southern Highway

Section	Percentage of Workers in Each Section			
	Indo-Trinidadian		Afro-Trinidadian	
	Male	Female	Male	Female
Junction at Churchill Roosevelt	39	17	39	5
Highway to San Fernando	61	37	2	0
San Fernando Junction	82	18	0	0
San Fernando to Gulf City	61	39	0	0

junction. It is a convenient location for many traders to make a little extra money, without having to travel far. As the south of the country is traditionally perceived as 'Indo-Trinidadian', as discussed in chapter 3, it is not surprising that this group controls informal trade in this area. Thus, spatial division within the informal sector appears to mirror the spatial polarity in the nation as a whole.

The vast area covered by the Eastern Main Road necessitated its division into nine sections. The extension of this road, from the centre of Port of Spain through many settlements, to the sparsely populated eastern coast, provides a more varied set of results. Table 5.12 highlights the marked differences between the participation of different ethnic and gender groups along the Eastern Main Road. Firstly, the presence of Afro-Trinidadian workers is greater in areas which are perceived to be local or regional centres. Afro-Trinidadian workers are more prominent than Indo-Trinidadians in central Port of Spain, Tunapuna, Arima to Valencia, Sangre Grande and Manzanilla. By contrast, Indo-Trinidadians occupy a greater proportion of the workforce in the more rural, and less commercial locations along the road. These include, the more residential area of St Joseph/Curepe, the edge of the urban corridor between Tunapuna and Arima, the road between Valencia and Sangre Grande, and the road between Sangre Grande and Manzanilla in the east. Figure 5.5 clearly shows this sequential spatial pattern of ethnicity. In conclusion, informal traders are influenced by perceptions of whether a location is more rural in character, or a more urbanised central place. This judgement is partly influenced by a worker's ethnicity, where a liking is held for a particular life-style or environment, based on cultural values and tradition.

Within Trinidad, a large proportion of the Afro-Trinidadian population lives and works in town, which they associate with modernisation and entertainment. Their association with slavery has culminated in a rejection of both agriculture and rural life-styles. By contrast, a large proportion of the Indo-Trinidadian population have chosen to remain in their rural settlements, and adopt agriculture as a way of life. Many entrepreneurs will travel long distances to trade in busy locations, but prefer to stay away from the urban centres. Furthermore, the Eastern Main Road runs through sparsely populated areas between Arima and Manzanilla, where many Indo-Trinidadians farm and trade from stalls outside their homes.

A second interesting pattern which emerges concerns the working of Indo-Trinidadian men in the same locations as Afro-Trinidadian women. Significant numbers of both groups were recorded in Tunapuna, Valencia to Sangre Grande, Sangre Grande, and Sangre Grande to Manzanilla. This points to the fact that women also gravitate to areas away from Port of Spain, towards what they perceive to be quieter, safer environments. Afro-Trinidadian women appear to target a different market, and as such, do not provide competition for the Indo-Trinidadian traders of imported produce. In areas where Afro-Trinidadian male traders dominate the market, there tends to be very few male traders of Indo-Trinidadian origin. This is

Table 5.12 Ethnicity and Gender Differentiation along the Eastern Main Road

Section	Percentage of Workers in Each Section			
	Indo-Trinidadian		Afro-Trinidadian	
	Male	Female	Male	Female
Central Port of Spain/ Barrataria/San Juan	0	0	70	30
St Joseph/Curepe	71	0	11	18
Tunapuna	42	4	4	50
Outer Tunapuna to outer Arima	36	36	16	12
Central Arima to Valencia	0	18	55	27
Valencia to Sangre Grande	36	18	1	45
Central Sangre Grande	35	5	30	30
Sangre Grande to Manzanilla	29	29	13	29
Manzanilla/Mayaro	21	7	31	41

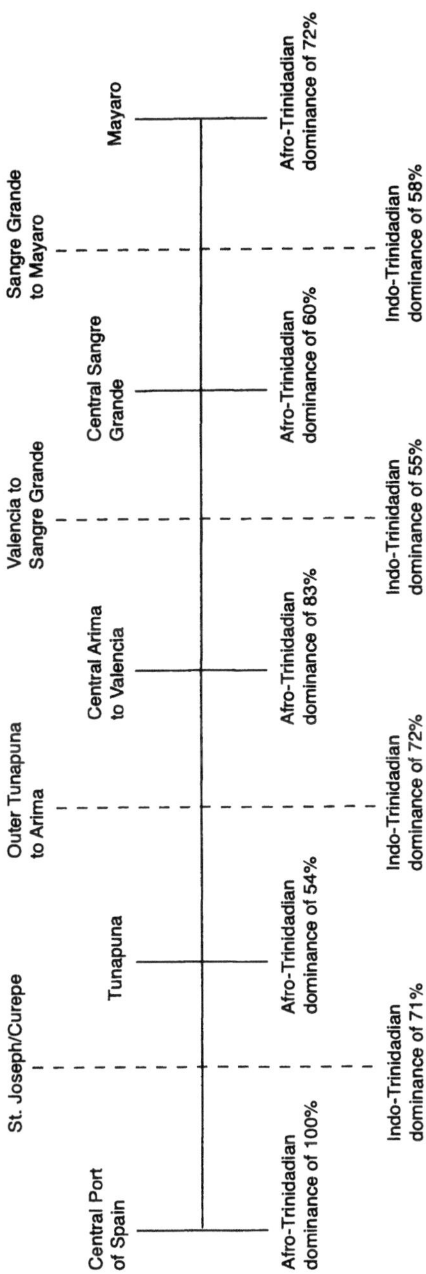

Figure 5.5 Rural and Urban Preferences in the Informal Food Sector

particularly apparent in Barrataria/San Juan, and Arima to Valencia. By contrast, Indo-Trinidadian male domination is seen in St Joseph/Curepe and Sangre Grande. Tunapuna, the road between Valencia and Sangre Grande, and Mayaro, by contrast, were areas of great Afro-Trinidadian female participation. The presence of the female higgler of fruit and vegetables is also strong in these locations. Although higglers were not greatly featured within this survey, as they tend to confine themselves to markets, their appearance may attract other women to work in the area.

A number of interesting explanations for the prominence of Indo-Trinidadian workers in informal food-related occupations in Trinidad can be identified. The first is concerned with the extended family support network, which is common amongst Indo-Trinidadian families. This provides a network of child-care, the sharing of resources and duties, and also the ability to borrow capital from the family to improve the business. Although informal networks amongst Afro-Trinidadian families do exist, these are not as strong or as extended. They are more likely to be female networks, where women of one family help one another in times of hardship. This evidence reinforces the concept of the importance and strength of Afro-Trinidadian women in the household. Issues relating to social capital will be discussed further in chapters 7 and 8.

The second factor relates to the perceived ideology that Indo-Trinidadians have a powerful work ethic, and a desire to succeed by working long hours in order to achieve higher social status through small business development. Research undertaken at the Institute of Social and Economic Research, University of the West Indies, in Trinidad has explored the issues behind the Indo-Trinidadian dominance of the private sector in Trinidad. Preliminary conclusions, based on work undertaken by Brereton (1979), indicate that as the poorest and lowest section of the population in the plantation era, Indo-Trinidadians were scrupulous in their savings and worked hard to build for their future (Ryan, 1991a). As they saw that prominence in the public sector was closed to them, they identified the private sector as their only way to status in society. It is argued that this desire to succeed, combined with their hard work and ability to save, has paid off in both the formal and informal sectors.

A third trend concerns the control over domestic-agriculture by Indo-Trinidadian families which has lead to their participation in the informal distribution of food. Further, job location is also influenced by a settlement pattern which is subject to ethnic polarity, with the predominant Afro-Trinidadian occupation of urban centres. Fourthly, and more importantly it appears, is the fact that polarity is also influenced by people's perceptions of a location, whether it is urban or rural, safe or unsafe, female or male, 'Indo-Trinidadian' or 'Afro-Trinidadian' in character. This factor, combined with the hierarchical structure of market participation and product specialisation, forces some social groups into a narrow margin of occupations. A prime example is provided by women, many of whom are only able to engage in trading on a part-time basis, due to their limited supplies of home-grown produce, in a limited number of locations. Chapters 7 and 8 focus in detail on women's perceptions of work in the informal sector, in order to pursue this issue further.

Food production and retailing are important functions in providing incomes in the informal economy in Trinidad and elsewhere in the Caribbean. The absence of large-scale public or private sector control opens up the market to small-scale entrepreneurs and individuals who are quick to seize the opportunity to supplement their incomes. The nature of food retailing and distribution, its relative ease of entry and minimal capital required, makes it a favourable activity for part-time or temporary workers who are suffering the effects of structural adjustment policies. These advantageous aspects are contrasted with a range of negative factors, which include difficulty in earning a decent income, high competition and general social attitudes which see food retailing as low on the scale of desired occupations.

Despite these drawbacks, the sector allows a large number of people to earn some kind of a living. A more formalised and regulated system of food distribution would render the street hawker unemployed, and placed once again in an overcrowded economy in search of work. Food retailing is also a part of the informal sector which is not seen to be greatly unfavourable to the authorities or to the public who benefit from the convenience of the street-located stalls. Problems which do occur often involve the trader causing a 'nuisance' in a public place, but often this is solved by asking them to move around the corner. The more serious disturbances which have resulted in traders being fined and jailed nearly always involve the highway traders, as they cause serious congestion on the highways, an issue which is discussed in detail in chapter 8.

Data from the survey also suggest that the type of produce sold in the informal sector differs according to traders' ethnicity, gender and location. Indo-Trinidadian workers tend to dominate the sale of both imported and local fresh vegetables and fruit. The Afro-Trinidadian female is more likely to sell ground provisions, nuts and local goods, although the female market higgler will also sell imported vegetables. It is also a fact that it is the Afro-Trinidadian traders who sell only small amounts of one product, often local and from their own garden, such as mangoes and limes, berries and home-made confectionery. This small-scale retailing, and the absence of bulk supplies of produce suggests that to these traders, street selling is a last resort at earning a little extra money.

Apart from its benefits in terms of distributional capacity, the informal food sector in Trinidad has many problems. It includes the most demanding occupations, in terms of labour and hours worked, and often pays low wages. It is also considered by many to be one of the least desirable and most demeaning occupations, both within society as a whole, and as compared to other informal sector jobs, a topic which will be addressed subsequently. This is partly due to its association with agriculture and also the fact that due to its unfavourability, it is a visual sign of poverty and desperation: 'the last option'. Therefore, it is not only the perceptions of the workers which are hindering the system, but the perceptions of wider society. Evidence suggests that a greater emphasis should be placed on understanding the role of the informal food distribution network in developing countries and the people who work within its confines. Only with a greater knowledge can assistance be targeted at the sectors and groups of workers which are most in need.

6 Informal Sector Petty Commodity Production, Service Provision and Retailing

Introduction

Predominantly urban based, Trinidad's petty commodity production and service sectors are becoming increasingly important to the national economy, as the country is unable to sustain a successful formal manufacturing base. In a pattern which is similar to domestic food production, formal commodity manufacturing in Trinidad is dominated by the petroleum sector and related industries, with little potential for the development of a successful secondary sector. As a consequence, Trinidad is forced to import a wide-range of raw materials and goods for its markets. These include, amongst other items, a large proportion of raw materials for industry, electrical components, motor vehicles, textiles and luxury goods. Domestic production is essentially confined to small-scale and petty commodity production, the majority of which is home-based and constitutes a growing part of the informal sector.

During the boom period in Trinidad in the 1960s, large investments were directed into petroleum and oil-related production. Today, the manufacturing sector is heavily nationalised, severely restricted and inefficient. As a result, the formal economy is devoid of a large productive sector which is capable of producing the modern consumer goods demanded by the population. Trinidad is under pressure to import large quantities of products, from machinery to household items, due to its lack of resources, expertise, and until 1992, restrictions on imports of raw materials. As a consequence, the informal sector is also limited in its scope and capacity for expansion. In a format which bears resemblance to the non-petroleum formal economy, the informal sector in Trinidad is mainly concerned with service provision, textiles, household items and the production of indigenous crafts. At present, the sector exists to provide employment, and produce a limited amount of goods for the domestic market, with the only growth potential being in the clothing industry, most of which is still informal.

In addition to the informal sector's reproduction of consumer goods, there is a growing informal service industry which has followed the demand of a population which cannot afford official prices. Here, the informal sector provides a wide range of employment opportunities which capitalise on providing a range of personal, household and business services throughout Trinidad. The development of the informal business sector has been rapid in the last ten years due to a combination of social and economic factors. Firstly, there is the lack of a successful and diversified manufacturing base, which has left a considerable gap in the market for the small-scale entrepreneur, an opportunity which has been grasped by increasing numbers of unemployed workers. Secondly, with increasing poverty and hardship, there has been greater demand for lower cost goods and services which can be provided by many small-scale informal businesses. Furthermore, the informal entrepreneur has the ability to adapt to changing consumer tastes and price changes as a result of demand.

Thirdly, there is an increasing number of people seeking employment in the informal sector as a result of unemployment and recession. Increasingly, new entrepreneurs are looking to establish their businesses in the informal sector due to the advantages of tax evasion and the absence of planning laws and bureaucratic procedures, a change documented by De Soto (1989) in his research conducted in Peru. Finally, many workers prefer to engage in informal sector production and employment as it is more flexible, independent and is often based either at home or in the local neighbourhood, where kinship networks can assist in its development. Other less fortunate workers, such as women with young children, have no choice but to engage in home-based activities as they are unable to work away from home.

As the previous chapter dealt specifically with the internal food distribution system of Trinidad, so this chapter focuses upon the production and retailing of non-food items and the rapid growth of service industries. Over the years, these sectors have expanded to cater for every demand of Trinidadian society.

The majority of goods and services available in the formal economy have similar informal versions which serve the lower-income sectors of the community. However, many cultural activities can only be found in the informal sector, and as such, are utilised by all sectors of society. Notable examples are those based on the provision of entertainment such as Carnival, the organising of large fetes (parties) and informal music gatherings, all of which attract large incomes and customer demand. Within this chapter, an analysis of a number of informal operations, including Carnival, will illustrate the wider cultural importance of the informal sector in Trinidadian society. As detailed in chapter 4, the informal secondary and tertiary sectors of the economy are extremely diverse in nature. Activities range from the production of clothes, crafts and leather goods, to the provision of domestic services and recycling.

In direct contrast to food retailing, petty commodity production and the service sector are, by nature, more urban based and in this respect, provide an interesting addition to this research by incorporating an exploration of the Greater Port of Spain capital region and associated urban periphery. Similar to many retail traders, the location of many small workshops are located on the main routeways of the country. Once again, the Eastern Main Road is a central location for many informal sector businesses.

Petty commodity production and service provision incorporate a diverse range of operations which are in accordance with the overall heterogeneous character of the entire informal sector. Consequently, a broad overview of the sector will be followed by an analysis of the occupations offered within it. In continuation, the chapter provides a detailed analysis of the data collected by means of the reconnaissance surveys detailed in chapter 5, which relate to petty commodity production and associated activities. Finally, attention will focus upon an evaluation of the importance of perceptions of space, ethnicity and gender in ascribing occupational roles to different socio-demographic groups within the informal sector.

Petty Commodity Production, Service Provision and Non-Food Retailing in Trinidad

Within the informal sector there are a number of small-scale producers, retailers and service providers, many of whom operate beyond the reach of government agencies and registration. Their degree of informality differs greatly according to a number of salient characteristics. These include the type of commodities produced, the production process, the type of ownership, market strategy, the number of additional people employed and the location of the business. Informality is becoming increasingly widespread throughout Caribbean society and therefore, participants in this division of the informal sector come from a wide range of different social and income groups. In addition, there is less social stigma attached to informal petty commodity production than there is in street occupations, such as hawking or vending. Greater status is awarded to production and service-oriented occupations due to their perceived association with modernisation and skill. The annual Carnival provides the best example in illustrating the wealth generated by, and widespread respectability given to, some informal activities.

An Overview of Informal Sector Replication: Indigenous Production, Retailing and Service Provision in Trinidad

Unlike other, larger-developing nations, specifically those of Latin America, Trinidad does not posses a large manufacturing sector either of a formal or informal nature. As discussed in chapter 3, Trinidad has channelled investment into the development of an industrial sector based on petroleum, at the expense of the domestic economy. Efforts to construct a successful manufacturing sector in the 1970s have largely failed, with the exception of a limited number of local construction industries, textiles, food processing, rum and beer production plants and a consortium of Transnational Corporations such as Coca-Cola, Nestlé and Unilever. The domestic manufacturing sector is restricted to producing a number of clothing, food and household items for local consumption. Even here, a large amount of raw materials and machinery needs to be imported, a process which conforms to a pattern of continued dependency on the international economy.

With the informal sector often duplicating the activities of the formal economy, it is not surprising that the informal manufacturing base is also limited in size and diversity. The ability of the informal sector to fulfil its potential is often dependent on the technology and expertise found in the formal sector. Without a dynamic sector from which to learn and which to imitate, informal operations are restricted by a lack of knowledge, technology and innovation. Many informal sector operators are experts in replicating cheap versions of goods produced in the formal economy, but they have difficulty in developing new products. Without goods and ideas to emulate, the informal sector struggles to provide low-cost versions of expensive imported goods.

Despite the incorporation of a large amount of ingenuity and enthusiasm, the informal sector remains limited and is not as diverse as the tertiary sector. This so called 'petty commodity sector' is dominated by clothing and textiles, local crafts and leather items, furniture, limited electrical items, household goods, construction and food processing. Within this broad classification the present research has identified a number of different types of outlets, all of which may be regarded as 'informal' in one respect or another. Although this classification stems from research undertaken in Trinidad, it may also be adapted to the realities of the informal sector in other developing countries.

The heterogeneous nature of the informal sector denotes the existence of a vast array of different types of production units which display differing levels of informality. Firstly, there are many small-scale independent producers, many of whom could be termed 'artisans', operating in traditional industries such as footwear, clothing, leather goods, crafts and jewellery. The majority of these artisans own their means of production, such as tools, and they purchase their own materials from indigenous sources. These entrepreneurs conform to a typical categorisation of informal operators which highlights a small-scale, labour intensive mode of production with limited growth potential (Davies, 1979). Production is usually customer-oriented and therefore responds to current popular demand. Producers have autonomy over the quantity and quality of their work, which is often undertaken at home. Retailing of the crafts is also undertaken by the entrepreneur on the streets and markets, or increasingly, in formal outlets.

A second category refers to a number of enterprising entrepreneurs in distribution, or manufacturing, who employ a small number of people. In some cases the business is family owned, or run by friends and associates, in return for a share of the profits. Essentially, this category incorporates a number of small businesses which operate for the mutual benefit of the workers involved. In addition to units being run by kinship networks, there are also those entrepreneurs who employ workers on an hourly or piece-rate basis in a manner similar to that in the formal sector. This third categorisation is particularly applicable to many businesses which manufacture clothing, and employ women on a part-time basis in haphazardly constructed additions to the entrepreneur's home. This group of businesses may also be aligned to the 'profit operators', discussed in chapter 4.

Many of these producers also engage in outwork operations, most commonly associated with the footwear and clothing industries. Workers, often women, work for small clothes shops, and large department stores, for a meagre piece-rate. In this way they are specialising in a single part of the production process that has connections throughout the economy, but the skills which are needed prevent recruitment for many of the unemployed. They are often subject to low wages and stringent quality tests. This type of putting-out system leads to a large sub-contracting chain. For example, a small tailor employs people on a basis of outwork contracts from large chains. In many cases, Trinidad's successful businessmen started out by following this path of development (Ramsaran, 1993). Good examples of this type of business are found in the production of furniture, tools, clothes, pottery, electronic components and the production of glassware from recycled materials.

The informal service sector in Trinidad is of a greater size than its productive counterpart due to its replication of the formal sector. Tertiary activities are important in Trinidad, particularly as the country acts as a service centre for the smaller Caribbean islands, a fact which has led to the expansion of informal service suppliers. Due to the highly-skewed distribution of income in the country, which results in the high demand for low-cost services, there are numerous informal service providers for every legalised counterpart. In addition to those replicated activities, there is also a category of cultural services which are not provided by the formal sector, leaving the informal sector to undertake a monopolistic role. It is also important to note that customers from all social groups often engage the services of informal operators, rather than the high priced legal alternatives. For example, it is not uncommon to find informal caterers providing food for a nationally important function. In Trinidad, informality is part of a cultural tradition of an informal life-style, where most customers will take advantage of a low-cost, flexible arrangements where possible. In the Caribbean, documentation and legal connections are viewed with caution, and often deemed an unnecessary waste of time.

The retailing of petty commodities represents the visible side of the informal production process. Here, the street trading of clothes, crafts, imported goods and household items provides visible evidence that the production sector is continuing to employ workers. Trading in these items is mainly undertaken in urban areas, with Port of Spain and the Greater Capital Region proving the favoured locations.

A Nationwide Survey of the Petty Commodity Sector, Service Industry and Retailing in Trinidad

Whilst chapter 5 presented a series of insights on those activities related to the food production and distribution system, this chapter examines the remaining categories of activity which were recorded by the reconnaissance survey. These activities include petty commodity production, service provision and the retailing of non-agricultural products. Although a full evaluation of the methodology has previously been provided in chapter 5, it is worth stressing that the main aim of the survey was the establishment of the size and nature of the informal economy in Trinidad with a focus on the gender and ethnic background of its participants. Six important characteristics, listed in Table 6.1, were recorded for each operation sampled.

The investigation into the non-food sector, was undertaken in June-August, in conjunction with the previously documented survey of the internal food distribution system. The survey was administered throughout the locations outlined in chapter 5, with the exception of a slight adaptation to include areas in what are referred to as the *Informal Street Gatherings* category, which were important to the non-food sector, and to exclude those which were not. Here, the survey was extended to include Frederick Street in central Port of Spain, and excluded the Savannah, Arouca and Marabella. The reconnaissance survey recorded a total of 818 individual operations, out of which 672 were activities related to food, with the remaining 146 operations forming part of the informal service, production and retail industry of non-food sectors.

Unlike the vast dispersion of the food distribution system, visible non-food operations were only recorded in a handful of locations. As indicated by Table 6.2, no activities of this nature were recorded along the *West-East Highway* or the *Southern Highway*. Along the *Eastern Main Road*, activities were only recorded in four of the nine sections; San Juan to Curepe, Tunapuna, Arima and Sangre Grande. With the addition of Frederick Street in Port of Spain, this suggests that the sector is restricted to urban areas.

The data collected in the reconnaissance survey highlight the marked difference in the prominence of activities in the food and non-food retailing sectors. A total of 82 per cent of the sampled operations were related to the food distribution system. These findings suggest that the informal petty commodity production sector in Trinidad is visibly small in scale compared to the informal food distribution system. This fact is also supported by governmental documentation, based on individual studies

(Central Statistical Office, 1991) that informal petty commodity production in Trinidad provides a far smaller contribution to the informal economy than the tertiary sector.

With the aim of this research being a general investigation of visible informal activities, it is fair to note that although few visible signs of production, such as workshops, were identified by the reconnaissance survey, the work recognised that many production outlets are not visible from the street. The lack of visible signs of production in Trinidad clearly shows the dominance of home-based production in residential areas, locations which were never intended to be a focal point of this research. Furthermore, greater attention was paid to the importance of the main transport routes in their role as components of rural-urban interaction. As the reconnaissance survey was designed to be brief and easily facilitated, time did not allow the incorporation of a detailed house to house survey. It was not the intention of the survey to provide a complete synopsis of the informal sector in Trinidad, but rather to highlight important sectors which could be focused upon in the more detailed research (see chapters 7 and 8).

As petty commodity production is of less importance to the Trinidadian informal sector at present, this omission was not deemed to invalidate the work undertaken. Instead, it was hoped that a survey of services and retailing on the streets, and the main trading areas, would reveal important linkages with the production process. The presence of such linkages had been confirmed during a number of interviews, with formal store owners and a selection of street traders, who were also the producers of their own goods. This chapter uses a different format to chapter 5, in that it focuses specifically upon the spatial, gender and ethnic dimensions of the sector. As chapter 5 highlighted the importance of the regional highways in the location of informal activity, this chapter, by contrast, serves to stress the salience of urban areas, specifically the Eastern Main Road, in promoting employment opportunities.

An examination of 146 sampled activities, in the five locations where they were recorded, highlighted the spatial concentration of visible commodity-related activities in Trinidad. Table 6.3, clearly shows an association between the type of activity and the level of urban settlement. Frederick Street is the main retailing core of Port of Spain, while San Juan is a residential borough in East Port of Spain and part of the urban continuum which extends through St Joseph to Curepe. The Eastern Main Road arrives at Tunapuna, and extends to the eastern towns of Arima and Sangre Grande. Not surprisingly, commodity retailing was not located on any of the country's main highways, or along rural routeways. Petty commodity production, retailing and associated services perform a mainly urban function and appear to be concentrated in areas of high customer potential.

In direct contrast to informal food retailing, the majority of activities sampled were either of a mobile or flexible nature. Table 6.3 indicates that only 57.5 per cent of operations used stalls to display their goods, whilst

Table 6.1 Characteristics of Informal Activities Examined in the Reconnaissance Survey

Characteristics	Operational Criteria
Nature of Activity	Stall: Fixed or Flexible Mobile Trading Vehicle
Size of Operation (if appropriate)	Small Medium Large
Type of Product Retailed/Service Offered	Repairs - shoes, pots, tools Clothing Shoes, Leather Goods Jewellery, Trinkets Cosmetics Household Goods Newspapers and Magazines National Lottery Tickets Crafts - pottery, souvenirs Auto/Mechanical Products Plants and Flowers Furniture
Number of Traders per Operation	Number
Gender of Traders	Male Female
Ethnicity of Traders	Indo-Trinidadian or East Indian descent Afro-Trinidadian or Afro-Caribbean descent European descent Other (Syrian, Chinese, Lebanese)

Table 6.2 Number of Activities Present in the Survey Locations

Location/Section	Number of Activities Recorded
West-East Highway	0
Eastern Main Road	
San Juan-Curepe	14
Tunapuna	25
Arima	48
Sangre Grande	17
Southern Highway	0
Informal Street Gatherings	
Frederick Street, Port of Spain	42
Total Sample	146

42.5 per cent of operators were mobile. It was also noted that 66 per cent of stalls were flexible structures. This relative increase in mobility and flexibility is indicative of the urban nature of commodity retailing which necessitates movement around the city. The remaining 34 per cent of stalls which were fixed, were located in the country's easterly urban centres. Figures relating to mobility support an argument which identifies urban informal occupations as legally hazardous and spatially limited. High levels of flexibility also provide evidence of substantial home-based production where the producer/trader does not sell on a regular basis, but rather when products are available. Due to the high mobility factor, the size of the stalls was not deemed to be an important factor in determining wealth or status of business.

More significantly, the type of product retailed, and the nature of the service provided, was established in order to construct a functional typology. The results of this procedure, as displayed in Figure 6.1, highlight the repair business as the only notably visible informal service, one which accounted for 7 per cent of the sample. The remaining activities involved the retailing of a number of different products (Figure 6.1). Here, the prominence of clothing sales, accounting for a 39 per cent share of the market, was most noticeable. Following this, the sale of crafts (12 per cent), leather items and shoes (10 per cent) and jewellery (12 per cent), constituted important parts of the sector. A number of other less frequently recorded activities included the sale of cosmetics, household items, music, auto-related products and national lottery tickets. This breakdown by function suggests that the informal sector is mainly restricted to the production and sale of personal items such as clothing, specialised crafts and everyday goods.

A total of 170 workers were recorded as being employed within these activities. The ethnicity and gender of workers are summarised in Table 6.4. An evaluation of the labour figures from a gender perspective highlighted a preponderance of female operators. A total of 56 per cent of the sampled operators were female, as opposed to 44 per cent male, a fact which displays a marked contrast to the male-dominated food sector. Further evaluation also raised an issue of ethnic differentiation, as operators of Afro-Trinidadian descent accounted for 85 per cent of the sample, whilst Indo-Trinidadian workers only constituted 11 per cent of the labour force. Interestingly, this survey brought to light the inclusion of another ethnic group, the Syrians, who tend to dominate formal clothes retailing in Trinidad. Again, the participation in this sector by Afro-Trinidadian workers is in contrast to the Indo-Trinidadian dominated food distribution system.

Once data relating to gender and ethnicity were subjected to cross-tabulation, an interesting pattern emerged. As shown by Figure 6.2, as many as 52 per cent of the operators were Afro-Trinidadian women, whilst Indo-Trinidadian women accounted for a negligible 3.5 per cent. Afro-Trinidadian males constituted 33 per cent of the sample whilst Indo-

Table 6.3 The Characteristics of Informal Activities by Location

Variable	Frederick Street	San Juan/ Curepe	Tunapuna	Arima	Sangre Grande
Percentage of total sample	29	9.5	17	33	11.5
Percentage who are stall users	5	57	72	87.5	82
Percentage who are mobile traders	95	43	28	12.5	18
Total	*100*	*100*	*100*	*100*	*100*
Percentage employing fixed stalls	0	37.5	0	36	79
Percentage employing flexible stalls	100	62.5	100	64	21
Total	*100*	*100*	*100*	*100*	*100*
Size of Stalls:					
Small	100	100	61	38	36
Medium	0	0	39	52	64
Large	0	0	0	10	0
Total	*100*	*100*	*100*	*100*	*100*

Trinidadian males were also sparsely represented. This distribution clearly displays two important factors relating to occupational stratification in Trinidad. Firstly, it is clear that there is marked ethnic differentiation of the types of occupations undertaken. Secondly, there is a dominance of women of Afro-Trinidadian descent in the urban retailing of petty commodities, a situation which suggests that they may also be involved in the production process. It is evident that Indo-Trinidadian workers rarely seek occupations which involve the retailing of petty commodities, or the provision of personal services. Issues relating to the relative importance of choice, constraints, and location in occupational decision-making need to be considered in this context.

It has already been established that location, and the perception of space, is an important component in evaluating occupational stratification in Trinidad. Although the total figures from the survey highlighted a number of interesting divisions in the labour market, it is equally important to re-evaluate the individual data gained from each sample location. As in chapter 5, the importance of location and place may show further differences in the results. Table 6.5 shows the types of goods most frequently sold at each of the five locations. It displays the fact that although the most prominent activity is the sale of clothing, the degree of dominance varies according to distance from Port of Spain. Clothing accounts for 12 per cent of products sold in Frederick Street in central Port of Spain, and only 7 per cent along the San Juan stretch of the Eastern Main Road, until the borough of Tunapuna is reached. The higher share of the sample, undertaken by operators in the clothing trade in the easterly settlements of Tunapuna, Arima and Sangre Grande, is indicative of a number of factors relating directly to employment opportunities and constraints, which will be examined in the next section.

The only significant areas of visible repair work are along the Eastern Main Road between San Juan and Curepe, and in the remote settlement of Sangre Grande in the east. Repair services are attracted to semi-industrial locations, such as San Juan, where their services are in high demand and where stalls and small workshops can easily be erected. Repair work is also important in Sangre Grande, which is the only service centre for the eastern coast. The production and sale of crafts, leather goods and jewellery were also important in all areas, a fact displayed in Table 6.5. These types of goods are commonly associated with the traditional image of the local 'artisan' or craftsman. The sale of crafts constitutes between 12 to 17 per cent of recorded activities in all five areas. In a similar manner, the production of shoes and leather products is also widespread, but is most important in Frederick Street (19 per cent) where there is the greatest customer potential and little tourist trade. The higher level of craft related activities, which were most prominent in Port of Spain, conforms to the traditional image of African, West Indian and Rastafari culture.

The retailing of hand-crafted and imported jewellery is linked to perceived customer demand. Traders will concentrate in areas of high

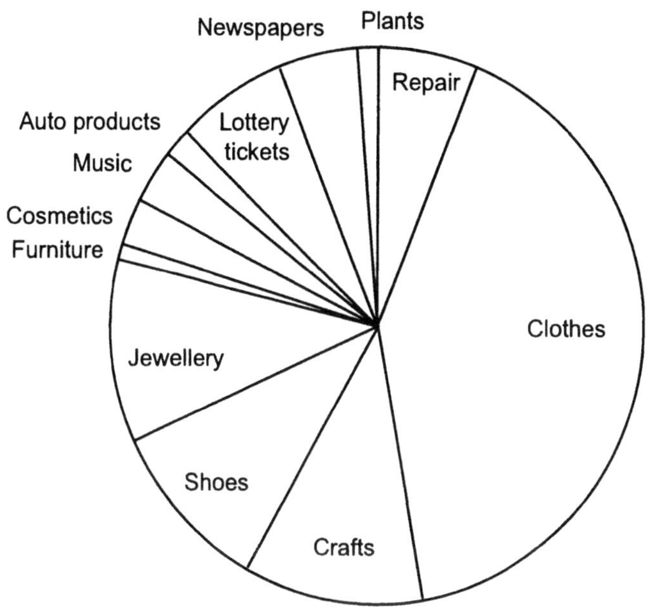

Figure 6.1 The Distribution of Activities by Function

Table 6.4 The Gender and Ethnicity of Informal Operators

Characteristic	Percentage of Operators
Gender:	
Male	44
Female	56
Total	100
Ethnicity:	
Indo-Trinidadian	11
Afro-Trinidadian	85
Syrian descent	4
Total	100

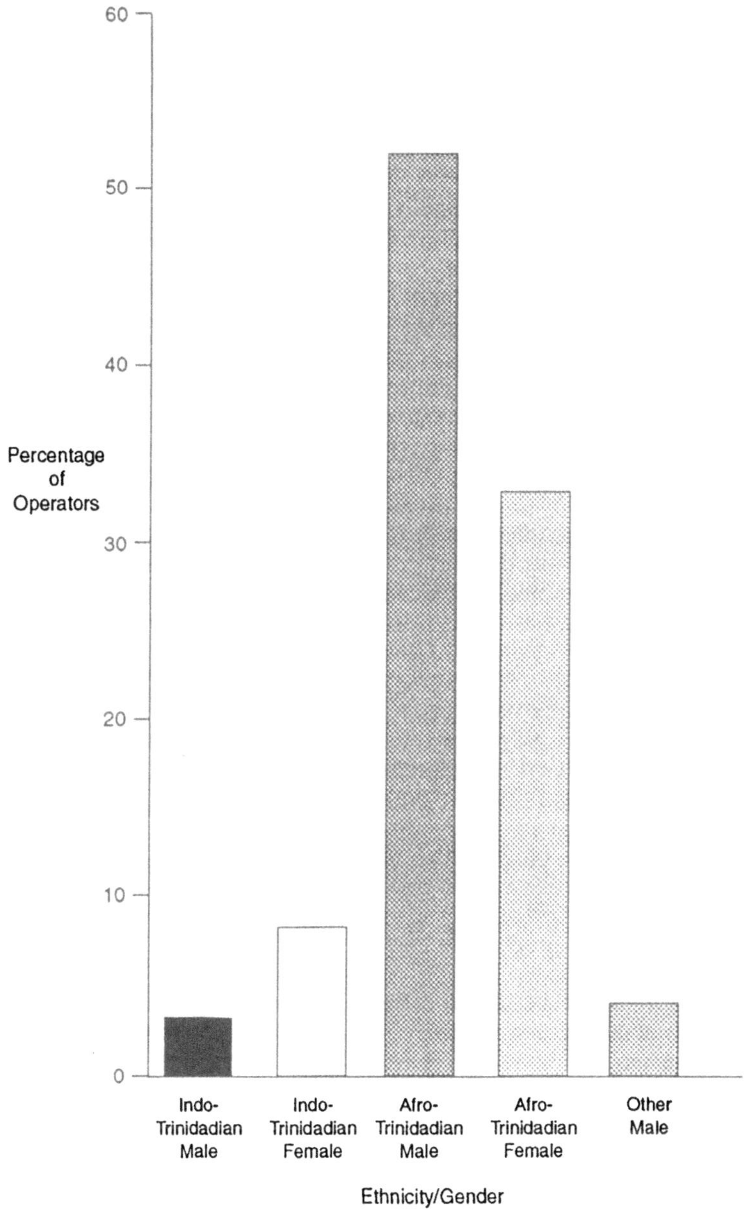

Figure 6.2 Representation of Operators by Gender and Ethnicity

population flows such as San Juan/Curepe and Frederick Street, residential areas and near-by office blocks. Nearly one third of activities sampled along the San Juan/Curepe stretch of the Eastern Main Road were connected with jewellery and trinkets. A wide selection of other goods was occasionally found in a number of sample areas, with the only significant occupation being the sale of National Lottery Tickets, by individuals to raise money for government projects, and the sale of newspapers in Port of Spain and San Juan. As shown in Table 6.5, other products such as furniture, household goods, music, auto products and plants were sparsely distributed.

An analysis of the labour force figures gained as part of the survey also indicates spatial variations in the division of labour. From the overall results displayed in Table 6.4, it can be seen that the frequent occurrence of women in this sector is a prominent feature. Following on from this, however, is the need to investigate differences in female participation rates according to spatial location and type of occupation undertaken. Table 6.6. illustrates the noticeable differences in female participation rates between areas. An analysis of the locational distribution of operators according to their ethnicity and gender also shows evidence of a divided labour market. Table 6.6 clearly shows that within the commodity retailing sector, regions are strongly dominated by workers of a single gender, with little interaction occurring between the sexes. The locations of Frederick Street, San Juan/Curepe, and Sangre Grande exhibit male participation rates of around 70 per cent. In contrast, Tunapuna and Arima show female participation rates of over 80 per cent. The male dominance of trading appears to be greater in prime urban spaces, namely Frederick Street and San Juan, which have a close proximity to Port of Spain. Male operators appear to control activities in the urban core and the surrounding area, whilst females are seen to dominate the marketing centres of Tunapuna and Arima. Sangre Grande also conforms to the male-dominated model despite its rural environment, an issue which requires further analysis. Also noticeable is the fact that despite overall figures indicating a female domination of petty production and retailing, men are still more prominent in three of the five areas.

Further evidence of social differentiation emerges from comparisons made as to ethnicity and gender. Figure 6.3 illustrates the fact that Indo-Trinidadian women were barely represented in the survey. Furthermore, out of the 11 per cent of male workers of Indo-Trinidadian descent who were recorded, only their presence in San Juan/Curepe and Tunapuna is prominent enough for recognition. At the other end of the scale, Afro-Trinidadian men were prominent in Frederick Street, the Eastern Main Road and Tunapuna with participation rates of over 50 per cent. An even more prominent feature is the presence of Afro-Trinidadian women throughout the survey, particularly in Tunapuna and Arima, where they exceeded 75 per cent. Further analyses, presented in the following sector, will show that within this broad division of labour there exists a complex

Table 6.5 Type of Products Most Frequently Sold in the Survey Areas

	Percentage of Sample Activities				
Type of Goods	Frederick Street	San Juan/ Curepe	Tunapuna	Arima	Sangre Grande
Repair	0	21.5	0	4	29
Clothes	12	7	80	50	41
Crafts	12	14	0	17	12
Shoes and Leather	19	0	4	10.5	6
Jewellery	17	29	0	8.5	12
Cosmetics	7	0	0	2	0
Furniture	0	0	0	2	0
Music	9.5	0	0	2	0
Auto/Mechanical	0	7	0	0	0
Lottery Tickets	19	0	8	2	0
Newspapers	4.5	21.5	4	2	0
Plants and Flowers	0	0	4	0	0
Total	*100*	*100*	*100*	*100*	*100*

network of social and political factors which may help explain the reasons behind this rigid spatial division of informal sector labour.

Spatial Boundaries: Occupational Stratification along the West to East, Urban-Rural Corridor

Although the importance of the contribution of space, gender and ethnicity in Trinidad has already been established in this work, the results presented in this chapter provide evidence to suggest that societal divisions are even stronger than previously suspected. Thus, this section examines the reasons behind occupational stratification in the petty commodity sector, and looks at space as a possible explanation. In addition, the gender division of labour is re-examined, looking in greater detail at the results from the survey. Ethnic divisions within occupations are also explored from a similar standpoint. In order to achieve this aim, this section re-appraises the data from each main sample area, providing a spatial appraisal of the prominent types of occupations within each location, and the nature of operators who work within them. Particular attention is paid to the reasons why workers from different social groups gravitate towards certain occupations and locations.

Product Specialisation: Occupational Preference and Constraint in Trinidad

The results clearly identify the clothing industry, both retail and production, as a popular source of employment and one which is primarily female dominated. Table 6.7 clearly shows the prominence of women in a restricted number of occupations, which include the clothing industry, and the sale of newspapers and lottery tickets. There are two possible reasons for this.

Firstly, when location is considered, it is notable that the two areas which have a high female participation rate, Tunapuna and Arima, also identify clothing as the highest recorded activity. Table 6.7, and Figure 6.4, both highlight this spatial pattern of activity. Secondly, further cross-tabulation of the variables 'product type' and 'gender' shows that 92 per cent of clothes retailers were women. The sale of clothing appears to increase with distance from Port of Spain, suggesting that such highly recognised female occupations are not successful in the more hostile environment of Port of Spain. As noted before, women are often excluded from trading in Port of Spain due to perceived fears about safety and vulnerability, and the inability of women to successfully compete for a sound pitch due to restrictions in incomes, contacts, and competition from formal stores.

Successful male-dominated trading groups like the People's Mall on Frederick Street, present great competition for the small-scale female

Table 6.6 Gender and Ethnicity of Workers by Location

Factor	Percentage of Sample Activities				
	Frederick Street	San Juan/ Curepe	Tunapuna	Arima	Sangre Grande
Gender of Workers					
Male	76	64	19	18	74
Female	24	36	81	82	26
Ethnicity of Workers					
Afro-Trinidadian	79	86	87	88	87
Indo-Trinidadian	7	14	13	12	13
Other	14	0	0	0	0
Gender and Ethnicity					
Indo-Trinidadian Male	7	14	10	5	9
Indo-Trinidadian Female	0	0	3	7	4
Afro-Trinidadian Male	55	50	10	13	65
Afro-Trinidadian Female	24	36	77	75	22
Other Male	14	0	0	0	0

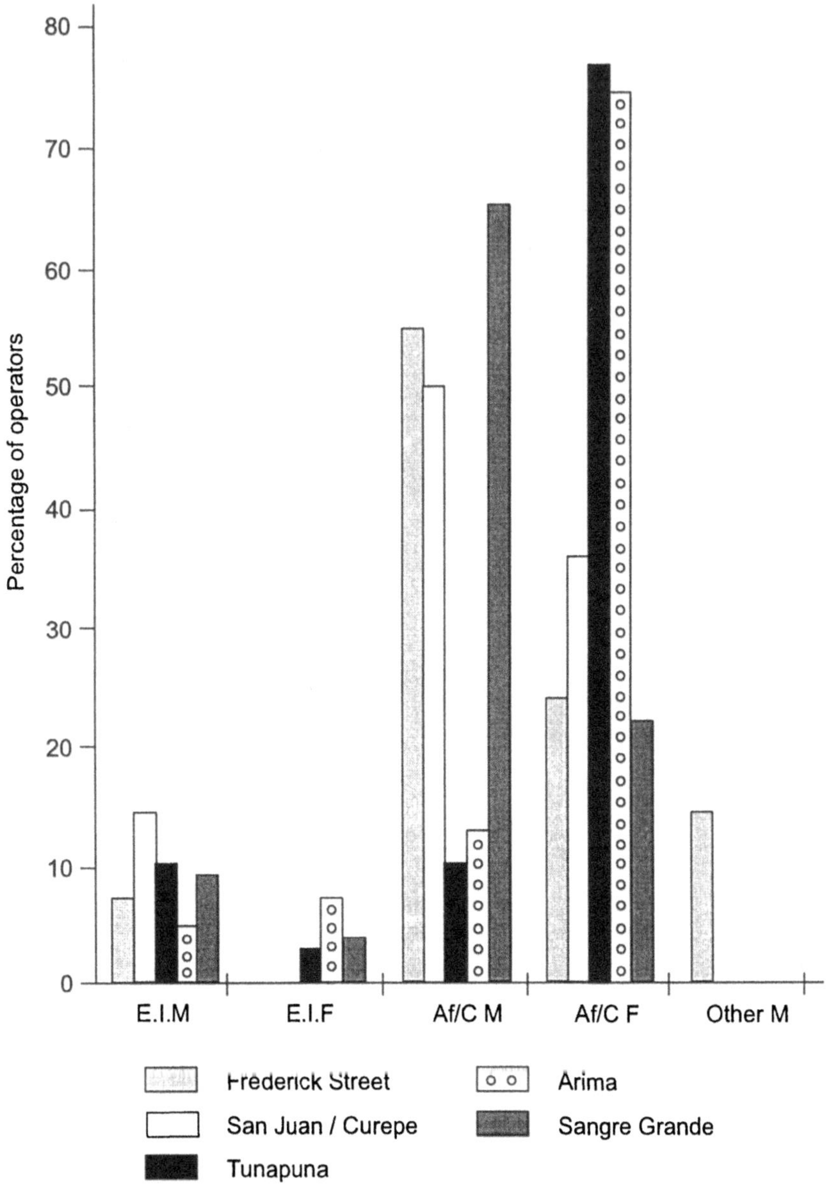

Figure 6.3 The Spatial Distribution of Workers by Gender and Ethnicity

entrepreneur. Instead of facing a daily battle in Port of Spain, many female traders gravitate to areas which are synonymous with female presence, such as the traditional market centres of Tunapuna and Arima. These areas are also important locations for the rural higglers examined in chapter 7, thereby contributing to a 'female environment', where concerns relating to safety, unfair competition and sexual harassment are reduced. The female domination of clothing sales is also a sign of the participation by women in garment production. This occupation, one which is traditionally seen as adhering to the stereotypical female role of house maker and carer, is also low paid and involves long hours. Many of the women in the survey produced a proportion of their goods individually, and supplemented their range by purchasing a number of imported items from suitcase traders.

A further interesting point relates to the ages of the clothing vendors, who were often between their late 20s and mid 40s, a much younger age than the fruit and vegetable traders. Many younger vendors highlight the selling of clothes as a better occupation than the higglering of fruit and vegetables, although they work under similar conditions and in the same areas. Contrasting levels of perceived status are attached to different goods, with the majority of goods sold by females occupying the lowest ranks. Although the production of clothes is the largest informal productive sector in Trinidad, there exists a network of clothing producers who operate under differing conditions of informality. Most social groups within Trinidad, regardless of income and class, will have outfits made by a local dressmaker. Within this broad category of production, a number of different types of production unit can be identified. Firstly, there are individual repairers of clothes, and seamstresses, mainly female, who undertake small repairs and alterations from home for a small fee. Advertisement is through word of mouth and contacts, and everyone knows an 'Aunt May' or 'Mrs M' who will fix it for a few dollars. The majority of work is undertaken by hand, and may only be one of a series of income earning activities undertaken by the worker.

Following on from this are the individual dress-makers, or partnerships, incorporating a couple of women, often in the family, who make and design outfits for customers and friends. This operation may involve limited machinery such as a sewing machine and cutting tools. Although the skills of these women are high, they are often underpaid for their services. Most locals know a dressmaker who will copy any outfit required, as long as the material is provided. The average Port of Spain price for a dress is $35.00 (£4.00-£5.00). This process of unequal exchange presents one of the fundamental problems with informal sector activity.

Further up the hierarchy of the clothing industry are the small workshops which employ four or five people, and which are less 'informal' than the previous operations as they have a number of direct links with the formal sector. It is operations such as these which prove

Table 6.7 The Gender Division of Labour in Petty Commodity Trades

Type of Goods	Percentage of Total Workers	
	Male	Female
Repair	100	0
Clothes	8	92
Local Crafts	84	16
Leather Shoes	94	6
Jewellery	62	38
Cosmetics	40	60
Furniture	100	0
Music	100	0
Auto/Mechanical	100	0
Household	0	0
Lottery Tickets	36	64
Newspapers	29	71
Plants and Flowers	0	100

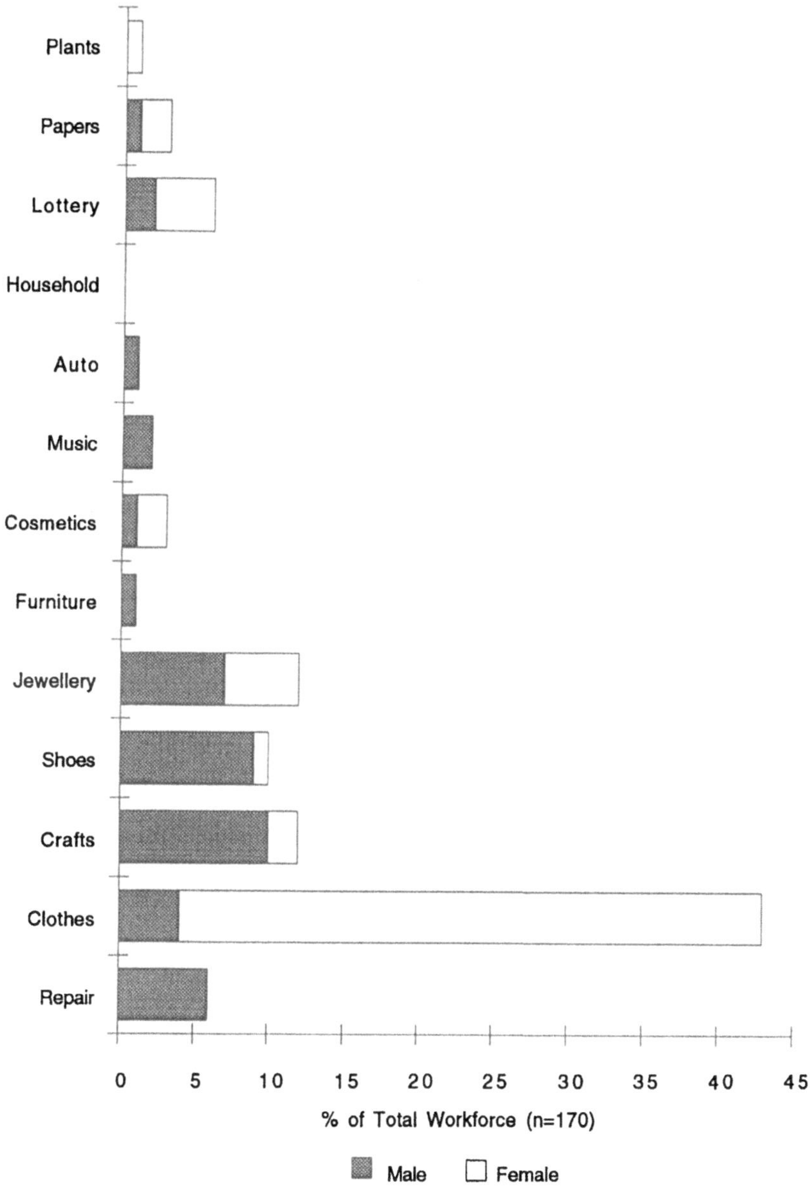

Figure 6.4 The Distribution of the Total Workforce by Product/ Specialisation and Gender

problematic to any definition of the informal sector. The business owner may employ four or five people on an hourly, or piece-rate, to work in an extension of their house. Although the owner may act as designer, their role is also one of attracting customers, and undertaking contracts for formal stores and designers. This is where the division between the informal and formal sector becomes unclear.

Although workshop employees do not pay tax and hold no contracts or terms of employment, they are essentially working for the formal economy. The owner will sell a number of outfits to a store for an agreed value. The problem of identification and definition also arises when one considers that there are also a number of small scale enterprises in the so called formal sector which operate similar operations, with the only exception that they are subject to registration and tax. Both types of workshop are likely to employ women on low-wages.

Other female dominated occupations were the retailing of lottery tickets, cosmetics and newspapers. Within the survey, 64 per cent of lottery ticket sellers and 71 per cent of newspaper vendors were women. Lottery ticket vending accounted for most of the 24 per cent of women recorded in central Port of Spain. It is one of the most insecure and lowest paid occupations in Trinidad. Retailers buy the tickets from the government and then aim to sell them for a small fixed profit. As tickets only cost a few dollars, the potential profit margin is narrow, with sellers having to work all day just to make a few dollars. The undesirable nature of this type of retailing makes it one of the least sought-after jobs in Trinidad. It has been adopted by women, particularly the elderly, who cannot find an alternative occupation. The retailing of newspapers and cosmetics also conform to a similar pattern. Both products need to be bought from large companies and sold for a small mark-up.

In contrast, occupations which hold a connection with crafts and indigenous skills or imports, are undertaken by male entrepreneurs. As shown in Table 6.7, the production and sale of crafts, shoes, leather goods and jewellery is mostly undertaken by men. Leather work and copper jewellery production is particularly favoured by followers of Rastafari. In general, production which is seen as skilled and crafted is regarded as being part of the male domain, whereas, the production of basic items, such as clothing, is lower paid, deemed to incorporate less skill and is therefore seen as 'women's work'. Here the perception of the skills required for different occupations is fundamental is ascribing status, income and gender roles.

The use of indigenous materials and local skills is held in high regard in the West Indies as it is seen as adhering to a 'back to roots' lifestyle, currently popular amongst lower-income groups. This view is supported by locational evidence which showed that male craft workers who produce metal work, shoes, and leather craft, were more likely to be granted assistance with cheap rent and equipment, than women. The reality of this fact was evident in Arima where the women sold their clothes in the sun, surrounding a number of production units occupied by male craft producers. Indeed, it further supports an argument which suggests that in addition to a product-based division of labour, there is also a strong locational influence which shapes occupational selection. A number of in-depth case studies, undertaken as part of the research, have thrown light on the daily lives of many women employed in the clothing industry. A brief insight into the experiences of women who make their living in the clothing industry can explain some of the reasons why women dominate this occupation, and why they work in certain locations. These constraints are well exemplified by a middle-aged seamstress, Vena, whom I met through a friend in Port of Spain.

"Making Do": The Daily Work of a Seamstress

Vena is 30, and lives in Laventille, East Port of Spain, in a house which she has rented from a local landlord. She has three children, and a husband who visits her on an irregular basis. Vena cannot rely on her husband's income as it is sporadic. As she explains, this is due to his part-time employment, liking for 'feteing' and the keeping of another family. This situation is typical of many lower-income families in Port of Spain. This means that it is essentially her responsibility to provide for her three young children. Her occupation as a seamstress is her main source of income.

Vena started making clothes as a child when she used to help her mother. She never thought that this would be her chosen occupation, but it is one of the only skills that she has. Educated only to primary school level, and with little work experience, Vena is limited in her access to many occupations. Furthermore, her household and child-care responsibilities restrict her to a flexible occupation which she can do at home. Fortunately, she also has the help of her mother and sister who live nearby.

Vena started making clothes as a favour to friends in order to, as she says, "make do". At that time she was working in a fast-food restaurant in Port of Spain. Friends would bring her an item of clothing, with the material, and she would reproduce it to the best of her abilities. Her obvious talent for copying shop-bought items soon heightened the demand for her business, and she gained many new customers through an informal network of friends and neighbours. After the birth of her second child, she had to quit her waitressing job as her son was ill. At this point, with the assistance of her family, she started making clothes on a full-time basis. Money was tight to start with, particularly as she had to borrow money from her sister to buy a better sewing-machine, but she is now in a position where she manages.

As Vena explains, things were alright for a while but she could not rely solely on 'word of mouth' recommendations, particularly in a recession. Her neighbour suggested that she should make clothes to sell on the streets as an addition to her customised work. She thought hard about a possible product and decided to make children's clothes, as mothers like to see their offspring "looking real nice". Having decided on her product, she then had to find some money to buy the material, another difficult task. Her next problem was where to trade, which to Vena was a major consideration.

Living in East Port of Spain, Vena's nearest potential source of customers was central Port of Spain. However, she felt unsure about trading here due to the 'bad talk' and 'wickedness' that her friends had told her about. On a number of visits to Frederick Street she had felt unsafe as "all de rastas wid de drugs is all over de place, dey look real mean". Local hearsay had told her that all the good spots downtown were already spoken for, and she expanded upon the story of a friend who had been violently threatened when trying to vend mangoes.

After much deliberation, she decided to trade on Tunapuna High Street every Friday, which involves a 20-30 minute bus journey. When asked about her reasons for this choice, she explained that Tunapuna is a friendly place, where people "don't get vexed" and there are other women trading nearby. Although, there were certain area which had been 'taken' by other traders, she soon found a good position near a fast-food outlet. Four years later, she has many friends in Tunapuna, and enjoys the social life as much as the work. Her mother cares for the children when she trades, and she has started taking her eldest daughter with her sometimes to "feel the atmosphere".

Despite Vena's initial enthusiasm about Tunapuna, she later admited that she has trouble making ends meet. Recently, people have stopped buying clothes and there are days when she sells nothing, only to return the next day. As she comments, "times are real hard and people don't hav de money for dressing-up n'feteing no more". Even her orders for tailor-made clothes have reduced as her customers are "makin do". Her current monthly income is well under TT$1000 a month (£140) which places her in the lowest income earning group. In order to supplement her income, Vena has tried offering a child-minding service on the days when she is at home, but within her neighbourhood, mothers can only afford to pay her small amounts or 'in kind'.

Vena makes a vast amount of clothes for very little return. Unfortunately, her charge of $40.00 for a dress, is an average price for a seamstress, as prices are low due to high competition. An additional consideration is that few of her customers earn a decent wage. Despite the quality of her goods, Vena's market potential is limited by her low-income environment and customers. This prohibits the growth of her business and ability to raise her prices. Vena's story is a prime example of the restrictive and exploitative nature of some informal sector work, which in many instances also happen to be women's work. Although, Vena will work solidly for three days, she may only receive TT$80 (£10.00) from her customer. With the current price of basic goods soaring to meet Western prices, due to the IMF's adjustment policies, this income means little buying power. Vena's situation is typical of the many women in Trinidad who strive to support their children by irregular means. It also highlights the importance of women's perceptions of place in determining their working environment.

The Gendering of Informal Places in Trinidad

When following the Eastern Main Road from Port of Spain through to Arima and Sangre Grande, the trading environment visibly alters according to occupation, gender and ethnicity as shown in this chapter. The results, summarised in Tables 6.1 to 6.7, clearly indicate that there are marked differences in the occurrence and distribution of production and service activities, and between those persons who operate them. The hectic capital, Port of Spain, displays the greatest visible evidence of informal petty commodity production, a factor supported by two main types of evidence.

Firstly, there are the numerous hand painted signs which advertise goods and services, which are attached to telephone posts and buildings. Not surprisingly, little detail is given about the location of the business, due to fear of police awareness. Instead, they are mostly referred to by name and a broad location. Signs such as "Mufflers repaired, ask for Eddie in Barrataria", "Hair by May, off Williams Trace, Laventille" or "Retreads, ask at Al's rum shack", are commonplace. In other cases, telephone numbers are left but these numbers are usually friends or relatives so the chain can be broken when desired.

A second source of evidence in Port of Spain is the retailer, mainly male street traders or vendors, who operate in the Central Business District. Many of the traders observed during the survey were either the producers of the retailed goods, or a member of a partnership where they undertake different stages of the production process in turn. Many of the younger traders were in an informal apprenticeship where they worked at a set wage for an older, more experienced entrepreneur. Due to the highly visible nature of trading along Frederick Street, and the governmental concern over invasion of the street and pavements, traders are mobile and rarely construct stalls. Instead, they may mark their space with a cloth or basket and move away when suspicion is aroused.

As clearly indicated by Table 6.6, the majority of traders in central Port of Spain are male, of Afro-Caribbean descent, and appear to be under 40. Traders often work together in a territorial manner, and are unwilling to allow unfamiliar vendors to obstruct their business. As Port of Spain still retains a strong Afro-Caribbean identity in both population and culture, there are few Indo-Trinidadian traders to be found located here. Furthermore, the sale of the types of products found there is dominated by males of Afro-Caribbean descent. The most familiar products are jewellery, leather crafts, imported clothing, smuggled items such as electronics, pirate music and crafts. These traders represent the hard-core entrepreneurial class who know their markets and obtain the highest incomes.

Suitcase trading, which is essentially smuggling, is a highly desired and high status occupation amongst urban informal sector participants in Port of Spain. It is an occupation which is prolific within the Caribbean islands due to their close proximity to the USA and South America. Policies of protectionism, operative at the time of the research but now weakened by IMF directives, encouraged traders to bring negative listed goods into their own markets in exchange for higher profits. Although highly-illegal items such as drugs, liquor and currency are often brought into the country, many of the traders are content with importing clothing such as US jeans, foreign music, household items and cosmetics and jewellery. A percentage of these imports can be found in formal stores but the largest proportion is still sold by the vendor. One of the main locations for suitcase vendors is the People's Mall, also known as the Drag Mall, located on Frederick Street, a government scheme which is examined in chapter 9.

Although there are female suitcase vendors, fears for their safety in travelling alone to Caracas, and perceived connections with drug smuggling in downtown Port of Spain makes such work unattractive to many. Furthermore, women's commitments in the household makes it difficult for married women to travel abroad twice a month to obtain new stock. It is also more difficult for women to obtain the capital and networks needed to illegally obtain foreign currency. It would appear that the streets of downtown Port of Spain fundamentally represent a male dominated environment, where female traders are often barred from entry.

Visible trading of non-food items and petty commodities decreases with distance from central Port of Spain. Following the Eastern Main Road out from Port of Spain towards the east, there is a dramatic drop in visible trading as lower class residential areas are passed. There is a notable amount of small advertisements for a range of services in the districts of Laventille and St John, where a large proportion of home-production units is located. Auto repair services, electrical and mechanical operations all operate from lower-income residential areas in haphazardly constructed additional rooms.

Home-based production units are generally found in the lower class urban suburbs of Laventille, East Dry River and further east in Tunapuna. It is important to note that a large proportion of production takes place at home in order to escape detection and to reduce costs. The Eastern Main Road from Port of Spain, through San Juan and Curepe to Tunapuna, displays evidence of repair booths which are operated by male Afro-Trinidadian workers. However, this area contained the highest proportion of traders of Indo-Trinidadian traders (14 per cent), of which none were female. Indo-Trinidadian traders appeared to be restricted to selling newspapers and repairing household items on the streets. The sale of jewellery, auto products, crafts and a majority of the repair booths were operated by Afro-Trinidadian males. The 36 per cent of female workers in San Juan/Curepe accounted for a small amount of clothing, newspaper sales and the limited sale of imported jewellery. In general terms this area acts as a service centre for lower income Afro-Trinidadian households. As it is a part of the urban conurbation, it also has a tendency to attract more occupations perceived as being male, such as repair work.

The male dominated environment begins to disappear towards the settlement of Tunapuna which acts as a market centre for both sides of the Eastern Main Road. Its peripheral location is a favourite location for female traders, many of whom live in Port of Spain, but who prefer this location to the downtown area. The high street of Tunapuna is congested by female clothes traders who set up along the paths and outside shops. The 81 per cent female occupation rate dovetails with the fact that 80 per cent of the activities recorded in this location were clothes-related. Although there were a number of Indo-Trinidadian traders selling lottery tickets, newspapers and plants (13 per cent), commodity trade in this region is still dominated by traders of Afro-Trinidadian descent.

As the Eastern Main Road stretches to Arima it finally leaves the urban continuum behind. Arima, the most easterly located centre in Trinidad, is a hive of commercial and social activity, as it is the main commercial, retail and service centre for the entire north-east and east of Trinidad. It is not dissimilar in appearance to San Fernando in the south, in that it lacks the modernity and size of Port of Spain, but still provides everything that is needed. First impressions characterise Arima as a busy market town with a small commercial centre, dominated by a covered market. More important, is the informal market which covers a large area to the back of the market where many of the female higglers operate.

The images of tranquillity and peace which are ascribed to Arima, make it an attractive place to work. These images of security may influence the large number of female traders who come to trade. Here, a reasonable living can be made without the insecurity, congestion and violence of Port of Spain. The combination of the rural higglers and women selling clothes and trinkets, make it an attractive female-dominated environment in which to work. As it is widely perceived in this manner, Arima continues to attract Afro-Trinidadian female workers. Although occupations relating to clothing make up 50 per cent of the activities, there are also a number of craft units, occupied by males, which surround the market. It is interesting to note that despite the female-dominated trading environment, the majority of repair, crafts and jewellery outlets were still operated by men.

The last remaining location of importance is the small settlement of Sangre Grande which acts as a supply centre to the eastern coast. Trading in this settlement does not conform to either a perceived female/male environment, a fact that may be explained by the isolated location of this settlement, providing a lack of interaction with other regions. Sangre Grande conforms to a pattern which identifies Afro-Trinidadian male traders as the prominent group (65 per cent). Traders within Sangre Grande only operate a restricted number of types of operation, repair services, clothing, crafts, jewellery and shoes. Despite the reasonably high proportion of clothing vendors (41 per cent), the remaining occupations are all typically male dominated. This fact may be associated with the isolation and traditional status of Sangre Grande, a town which has not changed for decades. Thus, the male dominated trading environment may have more to do with traditionally prescribed gender roles than any environmentally-related perceptions of traders elsewhere.

Conclusions: Perceptions of Place, Gender and Status

The predominant historical division of Trinidadian society, based on race and class, has left its mark on the population. Trinidad still continues to display settlement patterns which conform to a divided society based on ethnicity. It is not surprising that these divisions have been replicated within the sphere of work. What is surprising, however, is the extent to which cultural divisions based on gender and ethnicity have also influenced patterns of work in the informal sector. Evidence has shown that within Trinidad there are a number of distinct areas which, by choice or constraint, are dominated by different social groups. Furthermore, for each group, there appears to be a traditionally perceived list of appropriate occupations, a convention which tends to be adhered to. Within Trinidad, there are unwritten laws and ideas on occupational roles which have developed from a mixture of traditional behaviour, ethic tension and legitimate constraints.

Within the informal sector in Trinidad, a person's occupation is strongly influenced by their gender, ethnicity and place of work. Evidence suggests that female workers are restricted to the traditional occupations which are seen to cater for the female skills of caring and home-based production. Societal pressure is often so great that many young women are socialised into thinking that these are the only jobs they can do. In contrast, men have a wider range of jobs that are considered suitable, many of which are also seen to involve high levels of skill. It is ironic that the making of leather belts is seen to be a more highly skilled occupation that the production of garments. The important factor here is not the actual level of skill, but the fact that male jobs must appear to be of a higher status than their female equivalents.

In a society which is strongly regulated by the desire to do what is expected, there will be a tendency for many people to conform. After undertaking traditional occupational roles, workers choice of location may also be restricted by their own perceptions on the nature of a potential workplace. It may be difficult, or impossible, to work in areas which are already dominated by a specific cultural group to which the operator does not belong. For this reason, urban occupations such as petty production are dominated by Afro-Trinidadian workers, as they have always lived and worked in the towns. Port of Spain is unfamiliar territory for many rural based Indo-Trinidadian families.

Evidence from the surveys suggest that female workers tend to gravitate towards smaller, more friendly locations with less threat from male dominance, and fears for their safety. Men are equally affected by this pressure, as Port of Spain is considered the prime location for 'real business'. Workers on the urban periphery are often accused of not being able to 'take the heat'.

Table 6.8 characterises the five sample locations according to common perceptions of their identities, and other factors, taken from the survey. Here, the Port of Spain locations show signs of a male dominated environment where skilled occupations are highly visible. These assertions conform to a traditional image of an unsafe, corrupt and congested city. By contrast, the market centres of Tunapuna and Arima, appear to be more popular with women traders, who together evoke an image of a less-congested, safer environment, perhaps a more 'female-environment'.

The interaction of traditional codes of behaviour, and perceptions relating to occupational choice, have resulted in a strict division of labour within the informal sector. Boundaries and divisions may be crossed or broken down, however, only when it is deemed to be appropriate. The prime example of 'occasion' is Trinidad's annual Carnival, which is one of the most substantial informal industries in operation. It provides an example of how informality has always occupied an important place in society. The annual Carnival is one of the most important events in the calender, some argue that Trinidad's whole existence is built around the Carnival mentality. The celebration is also important to the country's economy, as the amounts of money spent on preparation, and in the three days of festivities, contribute large amounts of money. It is also a time when people from all sectors of society try to capitalise on the event and make some extra money. Most importantly, Carnival is informal in spirit and in design.

The nature of Carnival itself is so 'informal' that there are few rules or regulations governing economic activities or behaviour. It represents an extravaganza of music, art, culture and fashion which reflects the true nature of a society that often hides behind a masquerade. For the organisers and artists there are large amounts of money to be made, either by organising the bands or by capitalising on refreshments for the thousands of participants. Many entrepreneurs, from all sectors of society, try to supplement their incomes by providing a service during the holiday. Stalls selling refreshments and food are located in all possible free spaces with the most profitable location being Queen's Park Savannah, where the bands congregate. With a general lapse in policing, Port of Spain becomes a free enterprise zone.

More importantly, it is the one time when many barriers, incorporating cultural and ethnic traditions, are broken down as the society attempts to mix as one. It is also a time when men dominate the otherwise female occupations of dressmaking-production and design. Carnival bands are

Table 6.8 Perceptions of Place and Associated Factors

Characteristic	Frederick Street	San Juan/Curepe
Gender	Male	Male
Ethnicity	Afro-Trinidadian	Afro-Trinidadian
Main Occupations	Crafts, jewellery, leather, music	Repairs, crafts, jewellery
Nature and Form	CBD, prime retail locations, crime	Semi-industrial, urban, low-income residential
Perceived Image	Congested, unsafe, dirty, unfair competition	High crime, industrial, busy
Characteristic	Tunapuna	Arima
Gender	Female	Female
Ethnicity	Afro-Trinidadian	Afro-Trinidadian
Main Occupations	Clothing, personal goods	Clothing, crafts, basic goods
Nature and Form	Semi-urban, market centre, residential	Regional centre, marketplace, residential
Perceived Image	Friendly, safe, good trade	Prime marketplace, safe, semi-rural
Characteristic	Sangre Grande	
Gender	Male	
Ethnicity	Afro-Trinidadian	
Main Occupations	Clothing, repairs, jewellery, personal goods	
Nature and Form	Semi-rural, small town, isolated	
Perceived Image	Traditional, rural, backward	

organised by men, because here clothes production is seen as a skill and an artform. The largest task in Carnival is the preparation of costumes, which take nine months to be designed and constructed. Although the outfits will be stitched by workshops of women, it is mainly male entrepreneurs who organise the production. In addition, it is the one time when participants of all races can be seen working alongside each other in many locations. Carnival is a prime example of how societal barriers can be broken down when people's perceptions of work deem it to be advantageous.

Carnival is a prime example of the potential scope for the economic and social development of the sector. Problems in the promotion of small businesses, particularly with regards to policy formation, will continue to exist if there are still marked divisions in the labour force. This chapter has highlighted the importance of societal and individual perceptions of work in constraining the advancement of certain social groups. The example of Carnival has shown how occupational barriers can be broken down when it is deemed appropriate. If this is the case, further attention must be paid to gradually reforming traditional images of people and place. Having established that perceptions of place, as well as gender and ethnicity, are important in ascribing occupational roles in the informal sector, the present work aims to further support this assertion. By providing a series of in-depth studies, chapters 7 and 8 provide a detailed examination of the complex issues raised by the reconnaissance surveys.

7 Gendered and Racialised Spaces: Petty Commodity Trading in Trinidad

> These are people whose societies are reserve societies, drawn into the system when the profits of single crops boom, and expelled when the single crop booms burst. In this world, a job becomes not a matter of course, a right, but a magical possession. The identity of labour is not the norm. It is rather a privileged status... (C.L.R. James, 1993: 5).

Introduction

While much has been learnt about the nature of informal sector participants, and their multiple roles in recent years, there is still tremendous ignorance of the social, economic and political factors governing the survival, behaviour and aspirations of such workers. Despite heightened awareness of the role of informal participants in society, improvement of their general status remains an important goal for development in many regions of the globe. As occupation is a major determinant of societal status, the equality of opportunity, and the treatment of men and women in employment, has been a longstanding concern.

It is widely understood that women and men participate in the paid and unpaid-labour market, on a different basis (Brydon and Chant, 1989). As shown clearly in chapters 5 and 6, womens' work in Trinidad is segregated horizontally to a limited range of occupations, of jobs within occupations, and vertically at the bottom of the occupational ladder. Within the informal sector, women are most frequently found in small retail and productive operations involving clothing, trinkets and food. They are often forced to combine income-earning activities with household responsibilities, and in many cases, they are the sole providers of income. Often operating outside commercial centres, women are more likely to be found in quiet rural areas.

The importance of womens' work is often obscured by a view of reproductive labour that dismisses it as a natural part of a womens' biology, instead of a socially determined gender role (Mosse, 1993). Problems also arise when the ideology of work is synonymous with formal labour in a full-time, paid occupation (Pahl, 1984). The line between reproductive and productive work is a fine one, and the failure to recognise women's work is a hindrance to development (Young, 1989). Existing studies of gender and labour market segregation in the Third World have tended to focus upon three types of variable; material conditions, institutional determinants and "unobservable factors" such as tradition (Afshar, 1985; Redclift and Sinclair, 1991). Greater weight is often given to the first two, as the latter is extremely difficult to measure. Likewise, feminist geographers have looked to women's reproductive and household roles as an explanation for their societal position (Beneria and Sen, 1981).

Female segregation in the workplace appears to be as a result of a combination of factors, and there is a need to analyse the inter-relationships between them. Such factors include, not only material variables, such as wages and the availability of credit, but ideological determinants, among which gender and ethnicity appear to be two of the most influential. Although research has focused on general views and ideologies of women, it has often neglected the other gender group - men. Men's ideology on work, societal status and women's position within it, is equally important in shaping the labour market, both in the informal sector and elsewhere. As Sinclair (1990: 3) argues, "the labour market is not a gender neutral context to which women simply bring a set of pre-conditioned attitudes, but it is permeated by an implicit gender ideology activated through government, management, male and female workers".

In this respect, there have been a number of problems associated with the popular theories on gender and work. Firstly, it is not solely women who have provided the labour power for capital accumulation. The nature of the plantation economy, and the pattern of transnational development, is such that male labour is also exploited. Secondly, if we are to talk of "women" as an all embracing group, consideration must be given to the many successful women in the Caribbean. In this respect, the gender variable on its own is not enough to explain the positions of many women in the Caribbean region and elsewhere.

As previous chapters have attempted to show, Trinidad is a nation which is shaped by ethnicity and it provides a good example of how racial difference can be expressed through the use of space (Clarke, 1993; Yelvington, 1993). In Trinidad, as elsewhere, the process of identity formation has involved the attachment of meanings and values to different ethnic groups in what has been referred to as the commodification of ethnicity (Appadurai, 1986, 1990). Yelvington (1993) and others (Clarke, 1993) have argued that this commodification of ethnicity is most obvious in the allocation of places in the labour market. In the Trinidadian labour market, different groups of job seekers are weighted by essentialised notions of cultural norms, appropriate behaviour and skill. In particular, the racialisation of difference has resulted in the marginalisation of different ethnic groups into certain informal sector occupations. Although some research has focused on occupational stratification in the formal sector (Ryan, 1988, 1991), little work has considered the role of ethnicity in defining the informal sector (but see Ryan and Stewart, 1994).

As we mentioned earlier, gender relations are clearly significant to the social processes of the labour market, and they provide another axis of segmentation which shapes men and women's search for work. The maintenance of specific gendered roles is of particular importance in the workplace as women's behaviour is often crucial to maintaining the distinctiveness of a group's cultural and religious practices (Anthias and Yuval-Davis, 1992). In Caribbean culture, women are assumed to, and usually do, play a particular significant role in the socialisation of children and the maintenance of the household. The feminisation of domestic and 'inside' spaces, and their identification as suitable working environments for women, are produced by processes which are also subject to racialisation. The ways in which Indo-Trinidadian and Afro-Trinidadian women define 'work', for example, are often based on spatial notions of the workplace. Spatial metaphors of the labour market, such as private/public or inside/outside are particularly important in ascribing gendered roles in the informal sector. Hence, Indo-Trinididadian women may define informal labour as 'helping out' rather than 'work' because it is more likely to be undertaken in the household, a reality which stems from a negative view of female waged labour in the public sphere. In relation to the informal sector, there is a need to understand how the dynamics of gender, ethnicity and class operate in the real life experiences of Trinidadian men and women.

For most informal sector workers, racialised and gendered identities are performed and re-formed through activities which are part of their working lives. How do men and women see the informal labour market and their relative positions within it? As mentioned in chapter 1, the concept of racialised gendering can provide a useful connection between economic, cultural and broader socio-political processes which shape Trinidad's informal labour market. It is well established that people's success in the labour market depends on availability of work, skills and qualifications. However, evaluation of skills depends on the social processes and power relationships through which particular stereotypes of people are created and coupled to notions of their capacities as good, bad, skilled or unskilled (Lloyd-Evans and Bowlby, 2000).

Ideas about appropriate work and behaviour can also be expressed in spatial terms in what Peake and Trotz (1999) identify as an intertwining and mutual construction of place and identity. Contemporary ideas about the different jobs deemed suitable for Afro-Trinidadian and Indo-Trinidadians are geographically grounded (Peake and Trotz, 1999), and reproduced in real as well as imaginary terms. For example, women's negative images of certain parts of Port of Spain may be largely produced and maintained by societal ideas about appropriate spaces for women, but these images serve economically to exclude women from profitable business opportunities. Boundaries of ethnic groups are not only marked by occupation but also by the identities of different places (Massey, 1994). The importance of considering space in a study of the informal sector is eloquently expressed by Peake and Trotz (1999: 7) who argue that "Space is not just the backdrop against which social interaction takes place; space constitutes difference and is deeply implicated in the production of identities and inequalities". As the next two chapters will show, these processes help shape the daily practices of working in the 'lived spaces' (Lefebvre, 1991) of Trinidad's streets and informal markets.

Social capital is of particular importance to informal sector operators who are often dependent on trust, assistance and community loyalty for their livelihoods. Interestingly, the informal sector also illustrates the paradoxical relationship between economic crisis and social capital. On the one hand, whilst informal activity often increases under economic austerity and some activities thrive (Le Franc, 1994), it also stands to suffer most from increased competition, as community networks become strained and vulnerable to breakdown. As Moser (1996) poignantly argues, economic crisis and structural adjustment can exert positive and negative forces on social capital, both by strengthening it in times of hardship through reciprocity networks, but also reducing household coping strategies and ability to 'help out'. Vulnerability is associated with decreasing interhousehold reciprocity and the erosion of community level organisations, of which small informal enterprises are an integral part.

Furthermore, as these processes are often place specific, there is also a need for greater understanding of locally embedded social networks (Hanson and Pratt, 1995). As this chapter illustrates, informal petty-commodity traders are heavily dependent on their stocks of social capital in order to maintain productive livelihoods. In relation to the informal labour market, traders often rely on well-established social networks, trust and reciprocity in order to operate successfully. Traders will often give preferential treatment to their associates seeking work, assistance or credit. The structure and basis of relationships within a group may also ensure that favours are reciprocated and promises honoured. For example, members who do not behave appropriately can be ostracized or excluded from further economic relationships between the group. Common values, often based on shared ethnic ties, which promote a willingness to work on behalf of others in the group are of particular importance in the informal sector. For example, the ability to work together to improve the overall position of the group because of a feeling of solidarity is important for grassroots mobilisation, home based enterprises and community businesses. Given the highly gendered and ethnically segmented nature of petty commodity trading in Trinidad, groups with a lower stock of social capital remain unassisted. In order to illustrate these points in greater depth, it is important to look at the ways in which the various groups construct and maintain social capital.

We now turn to look at the backgrounds and daily experiences of Trinidadian men and women working in the informal petty commodity sector. Throughout chapters 7 and 8, we ask how gendered and racialised ideas about informal work and images of Trinidad's trading places have been significant to the practices of petty commodity trading. What are the dominant representations of ethnicity and gender in different places and how do men and women negotiate these invisible boundaries? We examine the spatial processes by which groups deal with these notions of difference, and explain how they are spatially expressed on the streets of Port of Spain, along the nation's highways and inside urban markets.

Whilst the previous chapters examined the general operation of two major components of the informal sector, chapters 7 and 8 examine in detail the nature of four distinct informal trading occupations, and their participants: female higglers in Arima; female higglers/traders in Central Market in Port of Spain; male suitcase traders in Port of Spain; and male highway traders. This cross-section of occupations was chosen to allow detailed information to be gathered on gender, ethnicity and work.

The four occupations were selected for their inherent roles in providing employment which is characterised by its gendered and racialised nature. Rural higglering is inherently a female Afro-Caribbean occupation, but within Trinidad it also incorporates a number of Indo-Trinidadian participants, who work for family businesses. Trading in Port of Spain's Central Market was included in the research to provide a comparison between the different types of higglering jobs available to women, and to provide further information on the importance of location in job preference. By contrast, two male dominated occupations were chosen for their contrasting uses of the city and the countryside, and their representation of distinct working identities. Highway trading is essentially an Indo-Trinidadian occupation, whilst suitcase trading in Port of Spain's People's Mall, has been associated with an Afro-Trinidadian ideology.

Following the results of chapters 5 and 6, this chapter aims to investigate the influence of gender, ethnicity and space in the development of the occupations and more specifically, on the lives on the traders themselves. Following on from this, chapter 8 will focus specifically on the results of ethnographic work undertaken to evaluate the participants' perceptions of work. The chapter is divided into three main sections. Firstly, there is an introduction to some of the historical and theoretical concepts behind the specific occupation of informal trading in the Caribbean. Secondly, a detailed appraisal of each of the four occupations is presented, with particular reference made to the gendering of different occupations. A third section presents the results of a series of in-depth ethnographic interviews, conducted with a sample of 15 participants from each of the chosen occupations. Through these in-depth ethnographic interviews and case studies, this chapter aims to explore the differences and similarities between men and women's experiences as informal traders, and examines whether such 'difference' is not only translated into unequal access to power and resources, but is spatially expressed.

Informal Trading in the Caribbean: Different Lives

Within the Caribbean region as a whole, there is still a lack of published literature on informal sector participants, and more specifically on the occupation of informal trading (but see Lloyd-Evans and Potter, 1992; Witter and Kirton, 1990; Witter and Anderson, 1994). The one exception to this, has been the research undertaken on women in the Caribbean. The last fifteen years has seen the growth of an extensive literature on Caribbean women, with a large proportion coming from within the region (Barrow, 1986; Ellis, 1986; Reddock, 1988, 1994; Antrobus, 1990; Massiah, 1989, 1993; Senior, 1991; Mohammed, 1994). Literature from a number of western academics has been equally valuable in understanding the complexities of women's lives in the region (Momsen, 1984, 1993; Stubbs, 1993; Peake and Trotz, 1999). A smaller literature has concentrated on gender relationships between men and women in the workplace (Beechey, 1987; Momsen 1987; Hart, 1989; Yelvington, 1993).

Historically, Caribbean women have always played a more dominant role in their societies than other Third World women. Women have been engaged in a variety of economic activities, particularly trading, since the mid 1800s (Brereton, 1979; Momsen, 1993). Furthermore, the image of the strong, dominant Caribbean mother, has always been a powerful image in the region (Clarke, 1954). In-built in Caribbean society is a tradition of female economic autonomy, the female-headed household, and a family structure which does not rely on male involvement. Although there is a multiplicity of household forms in the Caribbean, female-headed and extended women only households are both common (Barrow, 1988; Chant, 1997). Colonial influence and male migratory patterns of work, discussed in chapter 3, have resulted in a high proportion of female-headed households in the Caribbean, currently estimated at 30 per cent (Momsen, 1993). Even, with the presence of a male partner, Caribbean mothers are usually responsible for household decisions and for supporting their children.

According to Momsen (1993), women's high degree of autonomy can be explained by three factors. Firstly, female slaves worked alongside men in the plantations (Brereton, 1979). Male migration after slavery served to reinforce women's sole responsibility for their children and led to their marginalisation from production. Secondly, women in the Commonwealth Caribbean have enjoyed legal equality in their access to land, a right not recognised in many other regions (Safa, 1986). As Besson (1987) argues, land is an important consideration in ascribing societal status in the Caribbean. Finally, Caribbean women are one of the most highly educated groups in the developing world and as such, they value education for their children. Many women take on a number of jobs to finance their children's education, many of whom will aspire to migration when they are adults (Dagenais, 1993).

Despite women's long history of economic activity and strong reproductive roles, lower-income women still occupy a disadvantaged position in the wider society. Momsen (1993: 1) argues that Caribbean gender relations exhibit a 'double paradox', as domestic ideology co-exists with the economic independence of women. The roots of this situation lie in colonialism. The Caribbean is still subject to patriarchal forces, remaining from the colonial era, where social and economic processes are still controlled by men. This factor is particularly evident in the workforce, where women still receive lower wages than their male counterparts, and have few good opportunities for job enhancement. As discussed in chapters 5 and 6, women are confined to a limited number of occupations in the informal sector in Trinidad, many of which are deemed to be of lower status that male dominated jobs.

As discussed at length in chapter 3, the utilisation of labour is an important process in Caribbean society. Women comprise over 40 per cent of the official labour force in the Caribbean (Ellis, 1986), of which the government is a major employer. As many traditional occupations are not included in the above calculations, such as their role in more informal occupations, it is clear that female contribution to the economy is substantial. Caribbean countries are among those having high female economic activity rates. Over 20 per cent of the female population in the Caribbean is officially economically active, which compares favourably with the world average of 28 per cent (Reddock, 1993). This figure is almost twice as high as Latin America, the region with which the Caribbean is often categorised. In the age range 25-44, the female activity rate for the Caribbean is higher than the average world figure of 48 per cent. However, these high female participation rates conceal facts which demonstrate the unequal status of women. Antrobus (1990), notes that within the female labour force, 70 per cent of women workers are low paid and occupy insecure jobs, despite the fact that female education standards are as high as those of their male counterparts. The majority of women are found in traditional occupations, which are seen by many as backward and not worthy of financial support.

Although the lives of many low-income Caribbean women in the region may not differ greatly, they are not a homogeneous group. Divisions of ethnicity, colour, class, society and economic status, affect their lives and are responsible for significant differences in their perceptions of themselves, and their role and contribution to the development of their countries. Within Trinidad, gendered identities are also subject to varying degrees of racialisation which are economically, socially and politically expressed. As discussed in chapter 5, the mixed racial structure of Trinidad, with a ratio of 45 per cent East Indians to 50 per cent of black African descent in 1990, adds another dimension to the scenario.

Chapters 5 and 6 highlighted a rigid gender division of labour in Trinidad's informal sector. However, contrary to some of the research on Caribbean women (Le Franc, 1989, 1994), the inclusion of women in the Trinidadian informal sector appears to be highly compartmentalised, and not as widespread through informal occupations as the literature suggests. One explanation for this may be the presence of a mainly patriarchal Indo-Trinidadian small business community, which has grasped many of the opportunities offered by the informal sector. Valuable research has been undertaken on women's informal activities in Jamaica (Durant-Gonzales 1985; Le Franc, 1989; Harrison, 1988, 1991; Anderson and Witter, 1994), Guyana and the Eastern Caribbean (Massiah, 1993), which identifies women as the main actors in both the internal food distribution system and petty commodity trading. A large proportion of these trading occupations are referred to collectively as 'higglering', 'huckstering' or 'hawking', and are said to be dominated by women. Research presented in chapters 5 and 6 showed that this is not the case in Trinidad, although it may appear to be so in other Caribbean islands.

Informal trading in Trinidad takes on many varied forms and guises, and as with other occupations, is highly differentiated. Despite a heightened gender perspective, little research has been undertaken on male informal workers in the Caribbean. As highlighted in chapters 5 and 6, men also undertaken a large role in many informal occupations, including those in the higgler/huckster category. Traditionally 'higglering' was the term given to Caribbean traders of fresh produce, but the term had been expanded by many to include imported goods and petty commodities, a large proportion of which are not controlled by female traders. This is particularly the case in Trinidad, where the inclusion of Indo-Trinidadian workers in the informal sector has led to a more complex occupational strata which is explained in the following section.

Female Higglering/Informal Trading in Trinidad

The role of the higgler, or huckster, is relatively well-documented in the Caribbean (Lloyd-Evans and Potter, 1992; Potter and Dann, 1990), and is one which is seen to be a female occupation. It has been argued that higglers are the true entrepreneurs of the informal sector. Historically, higglering dates back to the days of slavery, when female slaves sold surplus from their household plots in local markets. The importance of higglering in most countries of the Caribbean cannot be underestimated, as they play an essential role in the food distribution system in many countries (Jordan, 1984).

In Jamaica in 1975, a government minister concluded that 80 per cent of the fruits and vegetables consumed were sold by higglers (Senior, 1991). This fact has been further supported by a growing body of literature which considers the economic role, and contribution of higglers to their society (Katzin, 1960; Durant-Gonzalez, 1985; Phillips, 1985; Mason, 1988; Le Franc, 1989; Harrison, 1991). Although writers such as Harrison (1991), and Le Franc (1989, 1994), have undertaken in-depth research into the lifestyles and social roles of higglers, particularly in Jamaica, there is still a lack of information on the motives behind the occupation.

Higglering is an extension of the Caribbean ideology, and need for, economic independence. It is an occupation which does not require large amounts of start-up capital, and allows flexibility and control. Although higglering represents economic improvement, it is still a small-scale business. Much research has questioned the reasons why higglering has not evolved into a small formal business (Jordan, 1984; Cuales, 1989). In Caribbean society, higglering is an occupation which is open to many women from a range of ethnic backgrounds.

Much of the work on higglering has involved studies of women in Jamaica and the eastern Caribbean. Few studies have observed the Trinidadian higgler who, it is argued in this chapter, undertakes a different role (but see Phillips, 1985). Le Franc (1989) in her study of Kingston, argued that higglering is a heterogeneous occupation which covers all aspects of petty trading. She identified five different groups of higgler, from the traditional fruit and vegetable trader to informal commercial importers (ICIs). In Kingston, the increased urbanisation of women has led to a 10 per cent decline in traditional food higglers, and a corresponding increase in the trading of trinkets, clothing and imported items.

Higglering has become almost synonymous with informal trading in the Caribbean, highlighting the belief that it is also a female dominated occupation across the region. As documented in chapter 5, it could be argued that higglering is not the single most important informal trading occupation in Trinidad. To suggest that the majority of informal Caribbean trade is undertaken by a single homogeneous group of women traders is simplistic. Rather, many of the occupations classified under the umbrella of 'higglering' should be regarded as distinct, and very different activities. In addition, little research has observed the other types of trading occupations which are also prolific and equally important in the Caribbean.

In Trinidad, the informal food distribution system is highly influenced by an informal network of East Indian family businesses. Chapter 5 highlighted the fact that female traders, or higglers, undertake an important but secondary role in many areas of Trinidad. Furthermore, they are restricted to trading in small amounts of goods, particularly along the main transport routes. Chapter 6 identified a greater proportion of female traders selling petty commodities, but only in a limited number of occupations, and not across the board as suggested in other islands. Within Trinidad, informal trading is an equally important occupation for males.

Within this chapter, higglering is a specific term given to female traders of fruit and vegetables. This conforms to the traditional image of food higgerling in the Caribbean, and serves to identify the group from traders of other petty commodities such as clothing, jewellery and imported consumer goods. As in many other islands, it is an occupation associated with vendors of an Afro-Caribbean identity, although a small number of

East Indian women have adopted a similar market role. The majority of Trinidadian higglers trade within well-established markets, such as Arima and the Central Market. These served as the locations for two in-depth studies which explored the different lives of female traders in Trinidad. These are reported in the account which follows.

Highway Trading in Trinidad

On arrival in Trinidad, an outsider becomes aware of the presence of a large number of roughly constructed stalls selling fruit and vegetables along the main routeways of the island. The observer may well expect to come across the traditional female higgler, rather than a vast selection of traders selling from purpose-built stalls.

One of the most highly visible, and economically important, occupations in the informal sector in Trinidad is the production and vending of fruit and vegetables along the major highways. The highway trader undertakes one of the most lucrative and distinctive informal occupations in the country. Although some of the largest permanent stalls are licensed to trade, the majority are not. With the internal food system placing a heavy reliance on informal methods of distribution, the highway fruit and vegetable trader occupies an important role in the country's economy.

Highway trading not only represents the highly entrepreneurial capabilities of the informal sector, but highlights an occupation which is mainly undertaken by an ethnic and gender specific social group. As discussed in chapter 5, the majority of highway traders are males of East Indian descent, with women generally assisting in a secondary role. As the term 'highway trader' suggests, this occupation is also location specific. The term refers to those groups of vendors which are abundantly located along the country's central highways, and deal in large amounts of fresh fruit and vegetables. The only potential competition comes from the female higglers, who adopt a more localised and spatially limited role in the market. The differences in locations of the two groups lead to different customer thresholds, and result in the fulfilment of two important services.

This distinct pattern is very different from other islands, with the exception of Guyana, and has been influenced to an extent by history. The continued settlement of East Indian families in rural areas, has necessitated the utilisation of agriculture as a source of income, particularly in the production and retailing of agricultural produce. This domination has recently extended from locally grown produce to imported foodstuffs. Having found an important growth area, many families have ceased the opportunity of social advancement through small business development. There are many successful informal highway businesses, which represent one of the best income earning opportunities of the informal sector. Despite the great potential in agriculture, and associated activities, other social and ethnic sectors of the population still refrain from these occupations due to traditional stigmas.

Unlike other islands, the substantial Indo-Trinidadian population has continued to dominate agriculture since their arrival as indentured labourers. One of the greatest points of the social history of Trinidad was the arrival of indentured labour from India in 1844. From 1845 to 1917, the growth of the Indian population in Trinidad rapidly changed the social geography of the country. It is estimated by Roberts and Byrne (1966), that 143,000 migrants arrived in Trinidad between these years. The central location of the major sugar estates in Trinidad, in the flatlands in the centre and along Caroni's western sugar belt, influenced the concentration of the Indian population in these areas. Following the end of their indentureship, usually 10 years, only one in five Indians returned home to the mother country (Roberts and Byrne 1966). The majority decided to remain in Trinidad as employment was guaranteed, and there were greater opportunities for obtaining land. Trinidad also offered an easier progression along the social ladder for those of a lower caste.

It has been documented by Vertovec (1990), that by 1894, a large number of East Indian villages had been set up all around the plantations. As indentureships ended it appeared that families would move to one of these new settlements. A 1914 Colonial report stated that the majority of Indian families cultivated 5 to 20 acres of private or leased land, which were manned by large families of household labour.

Following the decline in the sugar estates in the early 1900s, Indo-Trinidadians were allowed to grow sugar cane on their own land, and it is estimated by Beachey (1957) that these farmers produced half the country's sugar cane. They were also active in rice, vegetables, cocoa and fishing along south coast. During this time, many families were able to establish themselves as small-scale producers, and provided competition with the traditional female higgler in the market place.

Isolation from language, and education opportunities, led to the development of strong kinship networks, on which highway trading survives. Systems of shared and un-waged labour, and informal loan schemes, have enabled enterprises to accumulate large profits. Highway trading is becoming a popular occupation amongst Indo-Trinidadians, particularly due to the high unemployment in other employment sectors.

Suitcase Trading and Smuggling in Port of Spain

The demand for foreign clothing, music, and other consumer goods, has led to an increase in the prominence of the suitcase trader in the Caribbean. As discussed previously, suitcase trading is seen to be a modern female higglering activity in many islands. Le Franc (1989, 1994) identifies these higglers as 'informal commercial importers'. Although women in Trinidad are involved in suitcase trading, it is not a mutually exclusive female activity. Rather, it is an occupation which is becoming increasingly male dominated due to the high competition for jobs. As Phillips (1985) documents, many inter-island traders of fruit and vegetables are female, but this chapter argues that the importation of non-food items is becoming the domain of male suitcase traders. Female traders from Trinidad appear to travel to other islands to sell these products, but male suitcase traders are more prominent in Port of Spain. This is supported by evidence from chapter 6, which highlighted the prominence of male street vendors selling jewellery, leather goods and electrical items.

Suitcase trading is also an occupation mainly undertaken by traders of Afro-Caribbean, Surinamese, Chinese and mixed descent, and is an area not popular with East Indian traders. Despite the Indo-Trinidadian ambivalence to suitcase trading, it is a well known fact that they operate a more clandestine smuggling operation through the Port of Cedras, in the south-west of the country. An informant advised of the smuggling of large quantities of alcohol, industrial machinery, and electrical items via boats from Margarita, Venezuela. One suspects, that more illegal goods such as drugs and arms may also be imported, and a number of murders have been carried out in Cedras in recent years. In 1990, two young men were shot after supposedly recovering a number of whisky bottles hidden in the sand. For this purpose, research concentrated on the more visible aspect of petty-smuggling which conforms to a highly urban, Afro-Trinidadian image and appears to be associated with risk, illegality and entrepreneurship.

Street trading of clothing, and other goods, is illegal in Trinidad, although a blind eye is turned in many areas. The police are instructed under the Highways Act to arrest unlicensed traders on streets, footpaths or those causing an obstruction. Since the mid 1980s, the Mayor of Port of Spain has launched several campaigns to periodically clear traders from the street. In 1990, an attempt was made to remove traders from around the Savannah, but this was met with public support for the traders.

Suitcase trading incorporates the illegal importation of small quantities of consumer goods to be sold in the domestic market. Popular destinations include the USA, particularly Miami, where many traders have family, Puerto Rico and other Caribbean islands, and the South American mainland. Venezuela is a popular location for Trinidadian suitcase traders, due to the country's proximity, and a more favourable exchange rate than the US dollar. Typical items brought in are designer jeans, T-shirts, clothes, music, cosmetics and electronics. All these items are brought in by air, or sea, and are illegal. If caught at customs, traders should be faced with import taxes and fines, although the reality is somewhat different.

All kinds of 'tricks' are used to get through customs, including bribes, the use of contacts and mere avoidance. One of us once observed the arrival of a late-night flight from Miami inside the customs hall, which was packed with traders carrying a vast assortment of goods in boxes, bags attached by string and various cases. Electrical goods such as radios and televisions were freely carried under the arms, and large amounts of clothing was carried in bags. Not one of these traders attempted to go through the green channel, which in Trinidad only ever seems to be reserved for tourists. Instead, each one rushed to a familiar customs clerk, who they knew by name, where following a brief search, and sometimes the exchange of a few dollars, they merely proceeded out of the airport.

Although there appear to be a number of ways to avoid detention by the police, one group of vendors has managed to secure government permission to import goods without paying duty. The suitcase traders of the Vendors Association at a location termed the 'People's Mall', or 'Drag Mall', are part of a government scheme designed to support the informal sector, and are the subject of the fourth detailed case study, presented at the end of the chapter.

Methodological Issues in the 'Field'

Before engaging with the substantive issues around gender, ethnicity and informal employment that arose out of this research, it is important to explore not only the methodological framework that informed the ethnographic fieldwork in Trinidad, but to address issues of reflexivity which research of this nature raises. In recent decades, there has been heightened interest in post-colonial theory, non-western feminism and reflexivity which encouraged researchers to think more carefully about issues of difference, ethnicity and gender in the research process (Bhabba, 1983; Mohanty, 1991; Crocker, 1991; Radcliffe, 1994; Madge, 1993, 1997). In particular, there was call from third world feminists to deconstruct the ways in which western or 'first world' feminists conduct research with 'others', and to explore ethnical issues which surround the relationship between the researcher and the 'researched' in greater depth (Sidaway, 1992). In an attempt to break away from neo-colonial modes of enquiry on 'developing nations', there was a much needed move away from research which homogenised 'third world women' as passive, marginalized victims in need of sympathy and a voice (Mohanty, 1991). Since then, a substantive body of work has deconstructed the research process in an attempt to evoke a greater understanding of the power dynamics involved in different methodological approaches (Silverman, 1997).

The prime motivation for this research was to raise awareness of the important contribution made by informal workers to local and international economies and to throw some light on the ways in which gender and ethnicity help shape the informal labour market. From the start, Sally's own positionality as a white female researcher from the UK led to much deliberation over the ethnical issues involved in undertaking research in a post-colonial society like Trinidad, where race and ethnicity are intertwined with a historical legacy built on inequality. Furthermore, the project focused on the conduct of in-depth interviews with men and women from different ethnic, religious and class backgrounds. The notion of 'First World' researchers undertaking research in 'Third World' nations is conceptually problematic as it raises issues of unequal power structures, research dynamics of 'insider' and 'outsider', as well as issues of ethnicity and difference (Anthias and Uyval-Davis, 1992; Frankenberg, 1993; Robson and Willis, 1997; Haraway, 1991). Questions relating to whether it is appropriate for white British researchers to 'do research' in the post-colonial societies of the Caribbean must be considered, and in particular whether an 'outsider' can understand the daily experiences of people from very different ethnic and class backgrounds. Ultimately, researchers must come to terms with their own positionality in relation to the academic research process and the wider production of knowledge. Academics can use their positions to challenge discrimination and inequalities in the patriarchal global system. The present authors believe that there is a role to be played by 'First World' researchers in the 'Third World' as long as they are aware of the power dynamics at play and are sensitive to issues of representation and subjectivity. As Madge (1997: 114) poignantly notes in a discussion on the ethics of undertaking research in the Third World, "ethnical research should not only 'do no harm', but also have potential 'to do good'".

Ethnographic Field Research in Trinidad: Logistics and Limitations

The field research for this project started on a summer visit in May 1990 when Sally was based as Visiting Research Fellow at the Institute of Social and Economic Research (ISER), University of the West Indies. At this time, there was little published research on the informal sector in Trinidad on which to base a research project, although the government had started to take interest in the growing incidence of informal economic activity. Unfortunately, an attempted political coup in July 1990 (Ryan, 1991b), and the subsequent implementation of a state of emergency in Trinidad for several months, meant that Sally's field research had to be postponed. Although in insurrection only lasted for a few days, there followed a public uprising in Port of Spain, which took the form of rioting, arson and theft. The Foreign and Commonwealth Office, and the Economic and Social Research Council, would not give permission for the research to be started until January 1991. Due to this disturbance, it was agreed that fieldwork had to be restricted to investigating those informal activities that were deemed 'safe', and were less likely to provoke hostility. The existence of criminal activities in informal economies, involving prostitution, drug smuggling, extortion and protection, highlighted the need for caution. Sally was unable to undertake research in isolated rural areas and parts of the city. Instead, she developed a framework of networks in communities near to where she lived in order to engage in her research.

As chapters 5 and 6 outlined, a simple, but necessary starting point was the observation of the location and frequency of prominent informal activities throughout Trinidad, which were recorded in field diaries. With the exception of this basic quantitative exercise, the field research enlisted participant observation and other ethnographic techniques in order to develop a more in-depth and reflective methodology. The field of ethnography appeared to offer a suitable approach to studying the sensitive issue of informality, and use of ethnographic techniques has been widely discussed elsewhere (Ely, 1990; Hammersley, 1990, 1992; Silverman, 1997). Ethnographic data can be gathered from a large range of sources, where participant observation and in-depth interviewing play a major role. Participatory observation techniques were employed throughout the fieldwork, and they ranged from working with local community groups, attending festivals and social gatherings, to assisting informal workers with their trading activities. With help and guidance from researchers at ISER, networks were developed with local community organisations and national institutions. In order to facilitate a relationship of trust with informal traders, Sally's early fieldwork was spent talking with and sharing the everyday life experiences of local communities. Days spent talking with higglers and assisting them with small errands, or fetching food and drink, provided an invaluable insight into their daily lives. Through these interactions it was possible to conduct a series of in-depth informal interviews, a flexible technique which is more sensitive to the needs of the 'researched'. Ethnographic techniques are particularly suited to the informal sector due to the 'illegality' and insecurity often faced by traders and their reluctance to be involved in more invasive structured questionnaire surveys. Trinidadians are generally friendly and talkative people, who are happy to pass comment and chat with strangers. Many informal workers were happy to talk about their work on an informal basis, and once mutual trust had been established it was easier to undertake interviews on more specific topics. In particular, the use of narratives and life histories provided a rich source of material, which began to unravel some of the issues which are prominent in the experiences of traders. The development of networks in local communities helped enlist the participation of vendors in in-depth interviews. For example, interviews with the suitcase traders in Frederick Street, Port of Spain, was facilitated by Sally's involvement with an ex-social worker who introduced her to the head of the 'Vendors' Association'. Endorsement by this particular vendor allowed her to move freely around the Mall and to talk to the vendors.

A total of 60 in-depth interviews were held with participants from four groups of informal operators: rural female higglers in Arima, female higglers in Port of Spain's Central Market, highway fruit and vegetable traders, and urban suitcase traders in the Frederick Street People's Mall. Participants were encouraged to relate experiences and attitudes relevant to the research with a particular emphasis on talking about ideas about work and typical informal jobs in Trinidad and reasons for seeking work in the informal sector. Throughout the interviews, respondents were invited to express their views on the ways in which gender and ethnicity shaped opportunities in the informal labour market, and to comment on their own working identities. The majority of participants refused to be taped, for reasons relating to their insecure legal status, so written accounts of the interviews were used instead. Interviews were then coded under main themes, and analysed to identify different sub-themes and interrelations between themes. These were then examined in relation to the respondent's ethnic background, gender, age, education and family circumstances. In addition to the in-depth interviews, field-notes and narratives were also used to develop an interpretative insight into Trinidad's informal sector.

As an addition to the main field research, a period of time was spent working with a number of governmental institutions and informal sector projects. Here, a series of interviews, and case studies, were undertaken with government officials on issues relating to the informal sector. Interviews were used to build up a picture of the differing remits, practices and ideological approaches of different institutions, and to develop a better understanding of the common views held by agencies on issues relating to gender and ethnicity in the Trinidadian labour market. An exploration into the success of a number of informal sector programmes operating in the early 1990s is undertaken in chapter 9.

Profiles and Experiences of Traders in the Informal Sector in Trinidad

Trading Spaces: Higglering in Arima and Central Market, Port of Spain

As an introduction to this section on higglering, recognition must be given to the numerous skills held by the higglers, along with their sense of independence and pride. Independence is a valuable and important goal of many Caribbean women, and partially explains their involvement in trading. Many of the higglers interviewed were experienced in a number of different occupations, but the majority had chosen higglering for its flexibility and independence. Higglering represents a means of economic survival and social interaction for many Caribbean women.

Higglering in Arima: a feminised space? Arima market is located near the Central Business District of the town. As established in the previous chapters, it is a popular market town, situated off the Eastern Main Road, which serves a large rural periphery. It is also popular with female traders due to its 'friendly' environment, a factor which will be addressed in the following chapter. The formal market is a covered concrete structure, located near to the main shopping area and bus terminal. Inside the building are located approximately 50 stalls selling fruit, vegetables and fish. The majority of these stalls are operated by men. Outside the market building is a large open piece of ground, without shade, which is almost totally occupied by traditional female higglers. Female traders of clothing and other items have adopted a smaller location further along the road.

Outside the formal confines of the market, there is a group of approximately 70 women trading, for long hours in the intense heat, from roughly constructed wooden stalls. They will only take a break whilst another watches their patch. Each higgler is equipped with a old pair of imperial scales, used for rough calculations. Some have small blackboards, where they chalk up the days prices, and will shout for customers. Others, just sit back and wait for regulars, or an interested passer-by. Money is kept in a purpose-made bag, tied around the waist of their familiar aprons and patterned dresses. Older women tie scarves around their heads to protect them from the sun while others attempt to erect a plastic canopy to shade themselves, and their vegetables. The open market is a hive of entrepreneurial activity, which is at its greatest in the mid-day rush.

Whilst the men tend to 'lime' in groups inside the building, it is the higglers who appear to get the most customers, as they catch the passers by. The dark, 'masculine' atmosphere of the formal market appeared to be a hostile environment for many higglers, and their customers. One higgler talked of how her husband, who was trading inside the market, liked to "lime and drink with friends", but it was her who made more money. Peake and Trotz (1999) have documented the fact that the 'lime' is an important space for Afro-Caribbean men and signifies, amongst other things, a resistance to certain forms of labour.

Higglering in Central Market In contrast to Arima, Port of Spain's Central Market is the most important trading environment in Trinidad. It incorporates a large site comprising warehouses, an open market space and a wholesale and retail division. As previously noted, a government backed supply of necessary foods is imported into the country via Central Market. Recently, this pattern of supply has been altered by the ability of private companies to import any goods they wish, at the cost of a government import tax. In 1992, the influx of food items was still abundant. Imported goods are sold wholesale to a number of the prosperous traders, who have access to storage and transport. The base price for these vegetables and fruits is set by the government according to the international market, and it varies daily. Wholesale prices are also based on quantity sold, with discounts for buying in bulk, and the prices are displayed on a board.

The Central Market trader is aware of the fluctuations of the international prices of goods, and also of any fall in the value of the TT dollar, as their profit margins depend upon it. The produce is then distributed in a number of ways. It is normal practice for the wholesaler to sell to a number of middlemen who will then travel to other markets in the country and sell to traders. This is particularly the case with the rural traders who seldom travel to Central Market as it is seen as a competitive environment with a number of urban and more 'street-wise' traders controlling the dealing. The wholesaler will also sell to individual traders, who either sell the produce in the retail section of the market, and/or to rural higglers.

Wholesalers and traders have to pay a nominal rent for their stall or space. This money is collected by representatives, and goes to government revenue. Little of the money is invested in the market facilities, which are poor. As fresh produce is VAT free there is no tax, and after the initial wholesale price, it is left to the trader to establish a retail price.

Phillip's (1985) survey on inter-island traders, conducted in Trinidad, highlights the domination of female trading of agricultural produce in Central Market's CARICOM Wharf, a free port area. Of the trade conducted in Trinidad and Tobago, CARICOM trade accounts for 10 per cent, and is associated with small trade. The CARICOM wharf allows inter-island trading to be conducted free of duties. Agricultural traders, from the nearby islands of the Eastern Caribbean, are allowed to work for three days per week (mainly Wednesdays to Fridays) at the market, where many of them also sleep. After sales, the traders can apply to the Central Bank to get their currency converted. Inter-island traders come to the market to sell their produce, and buy goods from other islands. The majority of traders come from Guyana, St. Vincent, the Grenadines and Barbados. As Phillips (1985) argues, Trinidad is a popular focal point for inter-island traders, as the country provides a western range of goods, popular in smaller islands.

Despite their dominance in agriculture, few Indo-Trinidadians appear to be involved in the inter-island trade, except in Tobago. Instead, this activity is left to the female traders, particularly as they dominate agricultural trade in other Eastern Caribbean countries. For the purpose of this research, interviews were undertaken with 15 higglers/traders in a variety of locations in Central Market, including the wholesale and CARICOM areas. The regional profile of female traders sampled included three traders from Tobago, one from Guyana, one from St. Vincent, and ten from a variety of locations in Trinidad. The traders from outside Trinidad were trading in the CARICOM area, whilst the ten Trinidadians were in the wholesale market buying and selling goods for the domestic market only. Whilst inter-island trading in agricultural products is dominated by women, the wholesale market exudes an atmosphere of male domination.

Higglers' Backgrounds: Contrasts between Arima and Central Market

According to Phillips (1985), there are two areas affecting women's roles; the relations of production and the relations of gender. She further argues that traditional family structures, and child bearing responsibilities, limit the sphere of women's economic activity. Although this is undoubtedly true, this section of the research explores whether relations of gender and production have different effects on women, depending on the specific nature of their occupations and how these jobs are racialised. Higglering in Arima involves working with a different set of processes than those required by higglers in the Central Market. But are the groups also different in terms of their personal backgrounds, or everyday experiences?

The 15 Arima higglers who kindly agreed to be interviewed were aged between 16 and 65 years of age. Table 7.1 clearly shows that the majority of the higglers in Arima were aged between 35 and 59, indicating the popularity of the activity amongst middle-aged women. Younger women were generally from Indo-Trinidadian families, and were working as part-time higglers for a family business. Arima appears to attract middle-aged Afro-Trinidadian higglers, with a few younger women assisting a mother, or a friend. One respondent was a 16 year old Indo-Trinidadian girl, who was running the stall during her school holidays, whilst her mother was making 'Doubles' for sale later that day.

In general, higglers trading in Central Market appear to be of a much younger age than those interviewed in Arima. As shown in Table 7.1, seven of the traders were aged between 25 and 35, with two between 15 and 19, and the eldest between 45 and 50. The Tobagonian traders were aged between 25 and 40, whilst the Guyanese trader was between 35 and 40, and the Vincentian was slightly older. The teenage traders were from Maracas in the north, and Mayaro in the far east of Trinidad. The remaining Central Market Trinidadians lived in a variety of areas, most of which were a long distance from Port of Spain, thus displaying the fact that most traders will travel to Port of Spain to buy their produce once a week.

Higglers do not necessarily trade in areas where they live, a factor established in chapter 5. In the Arima sample, older higglers tended to live and trade in Arima, although this is a practice which they have adopted in their later years. For Mrs M, a 60 year old higgler who lives with her husband in Greater Arima, the physical demands of moving around Trinidad carrying produce is now too much for her. With the exception of a weekly visit to Central Market, accompanied by two of her middle-aged children, she remains in Arima. This does not pose too much of a problem, as Arima is a thriving centre where customers from 'out country' come to buy from her. A well-known figure in the market, Mrs M displays an image of the traditional Caribbean higgler, well-respected and proud of her occupation, an image which appears to be changing. Of the 15 Arima respondents, six higglers lived in Arima, five lived in St. George near to the Eastern Main Road, one higgler travels from Eastern Port of Spain to trade in Arima, and three lived in Toco in the far north-east of the country.

As Indo-Trinidadian women were barely visible in the previous surveys, it was surprising to find that five of the Arima higglers interviewed were of East Indian descent. Although the occupation is generally dominated by Afro-Trinidadian women, Arima market appears to be a more favoured place for Indo-Trinidadian traders who work for family concerns. This research generally found that Indo-Trinidadian women's employment opportunities in the informal sector were largely controlled by male family members, and their presence in public spaces was more restricted. Specific reasons for this pattern will be explored in

Table 7.1 Comparative Ages of Higglers in Arima and the Central Market

Age	Number of Respondents	
	Arima	Central Market
15-19	1	2
20-24	-	-
25-29	1	3
30-34	-	4
35-39	3	3
40-44	3	1
45-49	2	2
50-54	2	-
55-59	1	-
60-64	2	-
Total	15	15

chapter 8.

The ethnic variation among Central Market traders was slightly more limited than found in Arima, with only three Indo-Trinidadinan higglers interviewed. Once again, two of these traders did not run their own business, but worked for their husband's family on an infrequent basis.

Households, Trading and Social Networks

Family forms and household structures in the Caribbean are diverse (Momsen, 1993; Barrow, 1996). The role of the Afro-Caribbean woman, often seen as a matriarch, has had great influence in household structure in the region. In the historical context, Afro-Caribbean women have been a vital source of cheap semi-skilled and skilled labour, first during slavery, and then in the plantations and industry (Reddock, 1994). In slavery, Afro-Caribbean women worked alongside men in the fields, with little sexual division of labour. As slaves, and descendents of slaves, the majority of women were accustomed to working outside the home, and became responsible for the economic and domestic welfare of their children. A long history of work has given women access to money and independence, and has broadened their social relationships beyond the home (Momsen, 1993). Motherhood is very important, and has resulted in a high proportion of female headed households in Trinidad. Chant (1987) identifies the African matrifochal family, where women are responsible for their children, as a predominant household structure amongst low-income groups.

After the abolition of slavery, Western European forms of household organisation began to be adopted. The ideology of western Anglican marriage encouarged a greater sexual division of labour in the household, which it is argued (Reddock, 1988) led to greater subordination of women in the region. Although, western forms of marriage and household structure were adopted by the middle and upper income groups in Trinidad, union status and visiting relationships are still popular amongst low-income groups. Single parent families and female headed households are common forms of organisation in Trinidad. Even when a partner is present, women still tend to maintain their responsibility for the household.

The household structure of Indo-Trinidadian families has often evolved around an extended patriarchal network or joint family. With the complex caste system in India, the domestic unit became the focus for social advancement and status amongst families. On arrival in Trinidad, as indentured labourers, East Indian families were housed according to the cultural norms of the family and forced to abandon their traditional household structures. Estate owners housed one nuclear family in each dwelling, and as a rule, no married couple was allowed to reside in the parental home. In this way, the plantation owners rearranged the domestic relations of Indo-Trinidadian families in accordance with European patterns.

Once in Trinidad, however, the roles of East Indian women were enhanced in the form of greater personal freedom around the estates (Vertovec, 1992). This was partially due to the fact that few female indentured workers were brought to Trinidad and as a result, they were sought after for marriage. When their indentureships were finished, those East Indian families who remained in Trinidad tended to re-establish themselves in extended family households, for a number of reasons. Firstly, extended households facilitate the organisation of labour and allow the development of small businesses, particularly for those Indians who remained in agriculture (Brereton, 1993). Secondly, kinship networks provide security and a network of assistance to low-income families. The extended family is still a popular form of household structure amongst low income Indo-Trinidadians today. Although there is great diversity between families, many low-income Indo-Trinidadian women are still subject to a patrilineal system of control which often confines their economic activity to the household. This is a major reason why working-class Indo-Trinidadian women are greatly underrepresented in the waged workforce. It is important to note that household structures differ between socio-economic groups in Trinidad, whereby middle-income groups tend to adopt a more European nuclear family structure.

The marital status of both the Indo- and Afro-Trinidadian higglers interviewed, was mixed, with over half the Arima women being married. This figure does not follow the popular Caribbean tradition of union status, but reflects the East Indian preference for marriage which has influenced Trinidadian behaviour, particularly amongst older women. Five of the married women were Indo-Trinidadians, and with the exception of one, they all worked for their husband's family. Only three of the women were in a union type arrangement, whilst the young girl was single, and four were either separated/divorced or widowed. In their research in Guyana, Peake and Trotz (1999) also found that Indo-Guyanese women who were household heads undertook headship as a result of divorce or separation. As elsewhere, Indo-Trinidadian women are more likely to be married than Afro-Trinidadian women who prefer common-law and visiting relationships. Amongst Afro-Trinidadian traders, female-headed households appear to be the norm, with the higgler often providing the main source of income. In contrast, only four of the Central Market sample were married, a factor shown in Tables 7.2 and 7.3. This relates directly to age, as the younger members of the group were either single or in union status, and to the different codes of behaviour between rural and urban areas.

Table 7.4 shows the differences in living arrangements between the samples. In Arima, a number of women owned their own house, which they often shared with children and other family members. It was not unusual to find a female adult household, where the higgler supported two or three daughters with children of their own. Four higglers, all East Indian, lived in an extended family arrangement, and three resided in rented accommodation. Household sizes varied greatly, and conformed to few patterns. In addition to the respondent, over half the women's households consisted of between 5 and 7 members. One elderly higgler only lived with her sister and husband, whilst two of the Indo-Trinidadian traders lived in a household with 14 other members.

Household arrangements of the higglers working in Central Arima were different from their rural counterparts, in that seven traders lived in their mother's home, or another family member's house. Many younger, Central Market traders lived with their mothers, as this allowed the sharing of child-care responsibilities. All the women had between 3 and 7 children, often from more than one relationship. Whilst Arima higglers supported their families, many of the Central Market traders were assisted by their mothers. This allowed the Central Market higgler more independence, freedom, and may account for their 'street-wise' attitude. An additional five of the sample owned their own house, and the remainder rented.

In the main, most households incorporate a number of the respondents' children, sometimes a male partner, and often another close relative. This arrangement assists higglers in combining childcare with a full-time occupation. The number of additional wage-earning household members was low in the majority of cases, with an average of two, highlighting the importance of the higglers' income. This evidence conforms to other research highlighting the importance of female economic activity in the Caribbean (Ellis, 1986; Gibson, 1986). A combined total of 77 per cent of the higglers in both areas, owned their business. The remaining Indo-Trinidadian higglers were working for a family business, with the exception of one woman in Central Market who was covering for her sister on a part-time basis. In a pattern which conforms to Le Franc's (1989) observation in Jamaica, higglering is not a family run occupation amongst Afro-Trinidadian women. More commonly, assistance is given by daughters, sisters, and other female family members, only when it is needed. The failure of higglers to engage in social networks for economic activites, as opposed to reproductive activites, is discussed in the following section.

As noted by Momsen (1993) and Phillips (1985), women in the Caribbean attain a reasonable level of eduction. The majority of the Arima higglers over 40 years old had only received primary education, but the remaining 55 per cent had attended secondary school. Out of this figure, five had not passed any examinations, but three had four 'O' levels or equivalent. Central Market higglers were more highly educated, which was probably a reflection of their younger years. Two-thirds of the women had attended secondary school, with four attaining qualifications. In Central Market, the better qualified women saw higglering as a means to an end, until a better opportunity came their way. Unfortunately, there is little evidence to show that a good education leads to upward social and economic mobility in Trinidad, particularly for low-income women.

Table 7.2 Marital Status of Arima Higglers

Marital Status	Ethnicity of Traders	
	Indo-Trinidadian	Afro-Trinidadian
Single/No Partner	1	-
Union status	-	3
Married	4	3
Separated/Divorced	-	3
Widowed	-	1

Table 7.3 Marital Status of Central Market Higglers

Marital Status	Ethnicity of Traders	
	Indo-Trinidadian	Afro-Trinidadian
Single/No Partner	1	3
Union status	-	4
Married	2	2
Separated/Divorced	-	2
Widowed	-	1

A young Indo-Trinidadian trader, Renuka, was studying for her 'A' levels, but would run a stall for her mother in the holidays. Although she was aspiring to read law at the University of the West Indies, helping her family was considered to be part of her socialisation. Amongst the Indo-Trinidadian community, involvement in agricultural trade does not have the same stigma as it does for many Afro-Trinidadians. Also in Central Market, was a Afro-Trinidadian trader of similar age, but with fewer qualifications. Angie detested working in Central Market, which she did for her mother on an occasional basis, as it was considered 'poor work' by her friends. Like many young women, she aspired to work in an office where she could lime with young people, and enjoy a more 'modern' lifestyle. Differences in trader's perceptions of occupations is discussed in detail in the following chapter.

For working women in Trinidad, the introduction of an IMF structural adjustment package has had adverse impacts on their purchasing power. Few women are fortunate enough to have income earning opportunities which support their families, and as a result, engage in a range of extra activities. When asked if this was their only occupation, 66 per cent of higglers in Arima, and 73 per cent in Central Market, stated that they undertook additional tasks, as shown in Table 7.5.

In Arima, this work had to be of a flexible nature, which the higgler could either do at home, such as sewing, processing fruits into jars, and preparing doubles for sale, or an activity associated with higglering such as farming. Mrs H, from St George, had worked during the Carnival period, for the last ten years, selling food and drinks for large profits. She would save this money, often in a credit union scheme, for her two youngest children's schooling, and for expensive items such as medicine. Separated from her husband, she has the total responsibility for six children, with only her eldest daughter bringing in a small income from working in a supermarket. Two other respondents said they would 'do any odd jobs' when they needed additional income, or during weeks when sales were down. The activities undertaken by the Central Market higglers were less associated with traditional activities. As previously mentioned, their assistance with child-care and household duties leaves them freer to take on work outside the home. Hairdressing was a popular job amongst the under thirties, whilst craft making and hotel work was undertaken by other higglers.

Multiple economic activities appear to be engaged in more by single or separated women, than by those who are married, if only by a small margin. Age and ethnicity also appear to be other factors. Older Afro-Trinidadian women (over 55 years), for whom higglering was their only job, could no longer sustain an additional workload. Interestingly, all but two of the Indo-Trinidadian higglers, in both locations, stated that they did not undertake other work, but later talked about their tasks on their in-law's farm. As mentioned in the introduction, Indo-Triniadian women are more likely to describe household labour as 'helping out' due in part to the

Table 7.4 Household Arrangements of the Higglers

Household Arrangements	Number of Respondents	
	Arima	Central Market
Living in own house	7	5
Living with parents	1	4
Living with other family	2	2
Living with in-laws	2	1
Rented accommodation	3	3

Table 7.5 Higglers Performing Additional Economic Activities

Economic Activity	Number of Respondents Stating they Undertook Additional Activities	
	Arima	Central Market
Farming	3	3
Sewing	1	2
Food Preparation	1	1
Food Processing	1	-
Domestic	1	-
Odd Jobs	2	-
Carnival	1	-
Hotel Work	-	1
Hairdressing	-	2
Jewellery making	-	1
Craft Production	-	1
Total	10	11

largely unquestioned association of the home as a women's place and undervalued reproductive activities as 'duty' rather than economic productivity.

Higglering Practices: Business, Entrepreneurship and Social Capital

Arima higglers' sell a variety of fresh fruit and vegetables in different amounts. A number of women, particularly the elderly, may sell only a small number of mangoes or limes. Others sell a mixture of ground provisions, local fruits and/or a selection of imported goods. The majority of those interviewed sold reasonable amounts of imported foods, as well as locally supplied products. On one day, Mrs E was selling tomatoes from Holland, garlic and onions from Canada, aubergines from Mexico, and fruit from St Vincent. The majority of imported goods are distributed through Central Market in Port of Spain, where the higglers will travel on certain days of the week, often Wednesdays. Government officials chalk up the day's price for each imported vegetable, on a big board. This is the price which higglers must pay if they buy direct from the suppliers.

A more likely system adopted by traders from outside Port of Spain, is to buy from a regular 'middleman', for a small additional price. By obtaining goods from one middleman (and they are often men) on a regular basis, the higgler states that she will get him to save her the best, undamaged produce for a good price. A long term trading relationship will also lead to credit and storage arrangements.

Rural higglers, such as those from Toco, often prefer to use middlemen as they are wary of Central Market operations, and fear they may be given 'bad goods' from the wholesaler. Part-time higglers may also buy off other higglers who use Central Market as their main trading place, the other female group identified in this chapter. In addition, inter-island higglers bring in products from other islands to trade in a specially designated CARICOM wharf. Arima higglers also buy from local farmers who trade in the market, and from neighbours.

Central Market higglers also gain their produce from a number of suppliers. A Guyanese inter-island trader visits Central Market twice a month in order to sell fruit, and to buy food and luxury items to trade on her return. The three Tobagonians brought plantains, pigeon peas and other ground provisions to sell in Trinidad, but would leave with green vegetables and luxury foods. A middle-aged widow, Mrs W, travels from St Vincent to bring mangoes, and other fruits, which she will sell in the market for up three days. On her return, she likes to buy material, clothes and manufactured items. The ten Trinidadian higglers come to sell produce bought from small farmers, or family plots, and to buy imported goods to sell in their place of origin. For this purpose, they often remain in the market for several days until business is completed.

Higglering is an occupation which requires physical stamina as it involves arduous work. Average daily hours typically range from 8 to 12, often for a six or seven day week. Many of the Central Market higglers will remain at the market for two or three nights before returning home. Patterns of movement do tend to differ between the two groups. All the Arima higglers, with the exception of the school girl, maintained a relatively fixed weekly pattern of movement, although it is always susceptible to change according to demand, and family commitments.

Table 7.6 shows the weekly trading patterns of the Arima higglers, suggesting the large amounts of travel undertaken by these women. Arima higglers favour Wednesday as Central Market day, as many local farmers take their produce to be sold on this day. Many of the higglers also took produce from their own localities to be sold in Central Market, thereby combining the role of buying and selling into a days work. All the respondents used their days at Central Market for socialising, and the buying of goods for their families.

A typical weekly schedule incorporates Mondays and Tuesdays at home, either undertaking additional income-earning activities, or gathering local produce for sale. Higglers have arrangements with local farmers who they visit on a weekly, but often a seasonal, basis. Wednesday appears to be the popular market day for the group, many of whom meet up every week. Following this, Thursdays, Fridays, and Saturdays are popular market days. Sunday is often reserved for the family and other duties such as church, but this depends on whether the higgler has managed to sell all her produce. If she has large amounts of stock left, then she will often trade on the nearby streets at discounted prices. As their profit margins are limited, a small amount of perished stock means that there is less money to buy new supplies the following week.

Central Market higglers tend to be more flexible about their weekly schedules. Although they spend two-three days on average in Central Market, they will also trade on the streets and along their route home. For example, Ms T, lives in Diego Martin where she has arrangements with a number of small growers in the area. She usually spends Wednesdays, Thursdays and Fridays at Central Market, where she also buys imported produce to sell on Saturdays and Sundays in Tunapuna, Diego Martin, or wherever she thinks business will be good.

Despite the vast number of miles covered, only two younger Arima higglers had their own vehicle, although one could not drive and relied on her husband to carry and fetch her. Vehicles owned by extended family were commonly used by Indo-Trinidadian higglers, but the majority of Afro-Trinidadian higglers relied on an arrangement with a friend, or a regular Maxi driver. The main bus terminal, located near to the Central Market, is a gathering place for higglers carrying large sacks of fruit and vegetables to distribute around the country.

The maintenance of social capital, particularly through informal networks, is an important facilitator for the survival of small businesses in Trinidad. The occupation of higglering relies upon the use of a number of informal arrangements with family or friends. This is a process which

Table 7.6 Weekly Trading Patterns of the Arima Higglers

Trader	Mon	Tue	Wed	Thur	Fri	Sat	Sun
Mrs B	Ns	Ns	CM	Ar	Ar	Ar	H
Mrs C	Fm	Fm	CM	Ar	Ar	Ar	H
Mrs D	Ns	HW	H	Ns	Ar	Tc	H
Mrs E	H	Tp	CM	Ar	Ar	Tp	Tp
Mrs F	H	C	CM	Ar	Ar	Ar	Ar
Mrs G	Ns	Ns	Ns	Ar	CM	Ns	Ns
Mrs H	Ns	Ns	Ns	Ar	Ar	Ar	Ns
Mrs I	Fm	Ar	Fm	Fm	Ar	Ar	H
Mrs J	H	C	CM	Tp	Ar	Ar	H
Mrs K	H	C	CM	CM	Ar	Ar	Ar
Mrs L	Fm	Fm	Fm	Ar	Ar	Ar	Ns
Mrs M	H	Ar	CM	Ar	Ar	H	H
Mrs N	Ns	Ns	Ns	Ns	Ar	Ar	Ns
Mrs O	Ns	Ns	Ns	Ns	Ns	Ar	Ns
Mrs P	H	H	CM	Ar	Ar	Ar	H

Key:
H - Home
CM - Central Market
Fm - Farming
C - Collecting produce
Ar - Arima market
Tp - Tunapuna market
Tc - Toco
HW - Highway
Ns - No specified activity

begins inside the household, where extended family living arrangements are utilised to provide sources of child-care and other household duties. The caring of a child by its grandmother, aunt or elder sister, is common throughout Trinidad (Senior, 1991). This pattern is accentuated further within many Indo-Trinidadian households.

Therefore, the traditional female occupation of higglering is essentially maintained by well-established networks of kinship and patronage between the higgler and her suppliers and customers. Most of the higglers interviewed had long-standing relationships with small rural farmers, for whom they sold produce in the marketplace. Money is rarely exchanged until a sale has been made, and higglers tend to follow a rigid pattern seasonal and weekly pattern of trade. Many rural higglers also rely on local truck owners to help them carry their stock to market. Elderly rural higglers may also sell on their produce to another higgler to sell in Port of Spain's central market rather than attend herself. Despite the vast number of miles covered, higglers rarely had their own vehicles and the majority of Afro-Caribbean higglers relied on an arrangement with a friend, or a regular Maxi driver. Likewise, the Central Market where higglers go to purchase imported fruit and vegetables operates a similar system of patronage with the wholesalers and customers. Many higglers indicated that they relied heavily on one or two wholesalers who would give them a good deal. In relation to customers, higglers also tend to depend on patronage from particular families. In some instances, higglers have built a relationship with a household over several decades. Given the increased competition from highway traders, higglers need this system to maintain their businesses. Interestingly, however, higglers have poor networks between themselves. Higglers, who value their independence, are not as willing to assist co-workers in times of trouble as one might expect. Mutual assistance amongst many higglers only seems to be provided in a number of circumstances, mainly at a household level, but rarely in business.

Economic autonomy and independence is of such a high value to Trinidadian women, that few informal business partnerships are found, unless they are instigated by a government scheme. Higglering is not a shared occupation, although it needs other shared arrangements for its survival. Higglers have good stocks of certain types of social capital, such as child-care and household-based networks, and will often have long-term relationships with buyers and sellers which they value. In addition, many utilise friends or regular maxi drivers to transport them and their produce around the country. All Afro-Trinidadian higglers, and one Indo-Trinidadian, had some savings, and many participated in a credit union or informal partnership (sou-sou), thereby trusting their money in others hands. They have few links, however, with outside agencies or wholesalers, and are suspicious of small business schemes. When asked whether they would like to expand their business, or operate with a partner, many of the women would cite their fear of 'not being in charge'. In searching for an explanation for this, Afro-Trinidadian higglers tend to draw upon three factors. Firstly, since slavery, there has been a need for autonomy, a factor which outweighs economic considerations. The need for autonomy and independence is often gender specific, however, as mens' autonomy is largely unquestioned and recognised by society. Secondly, there is a conservatism about business and expansion, as higglers are not great risk takers. Their sole responsibility for their children's welfare, as is often the case, means that spending their earnings on business development is not an option. Thirdly, higglers do not enjoy working together, or relying on other people. This lack of co-operation, it has been argued, is one reason why higglers have been unable to expand their productivity. In times of economic crisis, however, this reluctance to combine labour power has lead to extreme hardship.

Individual autonomy is a privilege not worthy of risk. As Mrs C states, "I have lots of friends, she I know (pointing to a nearby higgler) for near on ten year, but trade wid her, no. Each women 'ere is boss, she may not be boss when she go home and she get licks for not doing de housework, but in here she in control. If she work wid another trader, der be all kinds of fuss 'bout how much dis cost 'n when she go to market. It not worth the bother, so we jus help each other, yes that's what we do and it work good."

By contrast, Indo-Trinidadian family businesses tend to operate on a totally different ideology. Families work collectively together for the good of the whole unit, often combining the economic activity of several households in a patriarchal system of control. This system of social networks allows the development of larger, more profitable businesses, as risks and labour can be shared. It also depends, to a great extent, on the use of unpaid family labour, particularly female.

Of the five Indo-Trinidadian women interviewed, only one operated her business in a similar way to the Afro-Trinidadian higglers. The remaining four women worked for either a father's, or husband's, family agricultural business. These women worked on a irregular basis in Arima market, trading produce grown on their farm, or bought in Central Market accompanied by another family member. In addition, they also worked on the farm, and undertook a range of additional household duties. None of them were actually paid for their labour, but their work was seen as contributing to the household. As a result, none of the women had savings of their own, and they showed little interest in the occupation of higglering, except for the fact that it offered them a break from the home environment.

Rather than being the true entrepreneurs for which they are known, many older higglers are restricted in their earning capacity by their reproductive role, and their fear of losing their autonomy (see also Le Franc, 1988). Higglers' main problems stem from their lack of access to capital, and reliable transport. Solutions to improving the position of higglers in society include the provision of training and market facilities. Despite their success in developing social networks to assist with their household responsibilities, their business networks are spatially and economically limited. Although co-operatives are a good idea, many higglers are unwilling to work as a group. Independence as a work ethic, and the associated lack of social capital, may be the greatest obstacles to business improvement.

Suitcase Trading: The People's Mall, Frederick Street

The People's Mall, or the 'Drag Mall', as it is known locally, is situated on Frederick Street in the heart of the business district of Port of Spain, shown in Figure 7.1. Designed by Prime Minister Eric Williams in the early 1980s as a solution to the insecurity, and the haphazard nature of street trading, it represents a pioneering step towards policies which consider the future of informal sector development. The mall offers the use of small booths to traders of crafts, clothing and jewellery with a rent and tax free agreement. The site was given to a group of male street traders in Port of Spain to develop as they wished without any government interference. Its appearance is misleading as it is not a 'mall' in the modern western sense, but rather a series of small hidden alleyways along which small booths are situated. There are approximately 200 sites, each of a size 8 feet by 6 feet, many of which have a two-storey construction. Due to its dubious reputation for drugs and smuggling, many locals prefer to keep away from the site and tourists are often warned off.

The concept of the Mall was originally designed to give insecure street vendors a chance to build a more secure business (Lloyd-Evans and Potter, 1993). The original Mall owners were taken from their occupations, as simple street vendor's struggling to survive, and offered a space on which to build and consolidate a permanent trading place. Most of the traders started with a simple table and gradually upgraded their patch as their incomes grew. Ten years later, the Mall is a well established trading centre and business place where many well-educated traders operate booths for large profits.

Contrary to popular opinion, these are not insecure and unknowledgeable street sellers, but successful entrepreneurs who have great awareness of the business environment. The booths were initially offered for a small down payment which vendors obtained from their family and friends, but today it is rumoured that booths can be sold informally for as much as TT$60,000 (£8500). The high price comes from the sought after position of the Mall, which occupies one of the most advantageous retail positions on prime economic land in the heart of the CBD (see Figure 7.1). The vendors' reputation for making a good living has pushed the exchange price upwards to the extent that it is unaffordable to many new vendors. Success has had further repercussions, as established vendors are unwilling to move out and let new vendors have a chance to develop a business. A minimal weekly rent of $25.00 in 1991 (£3.00) is paid to the Vendor's Association which provides electricity and

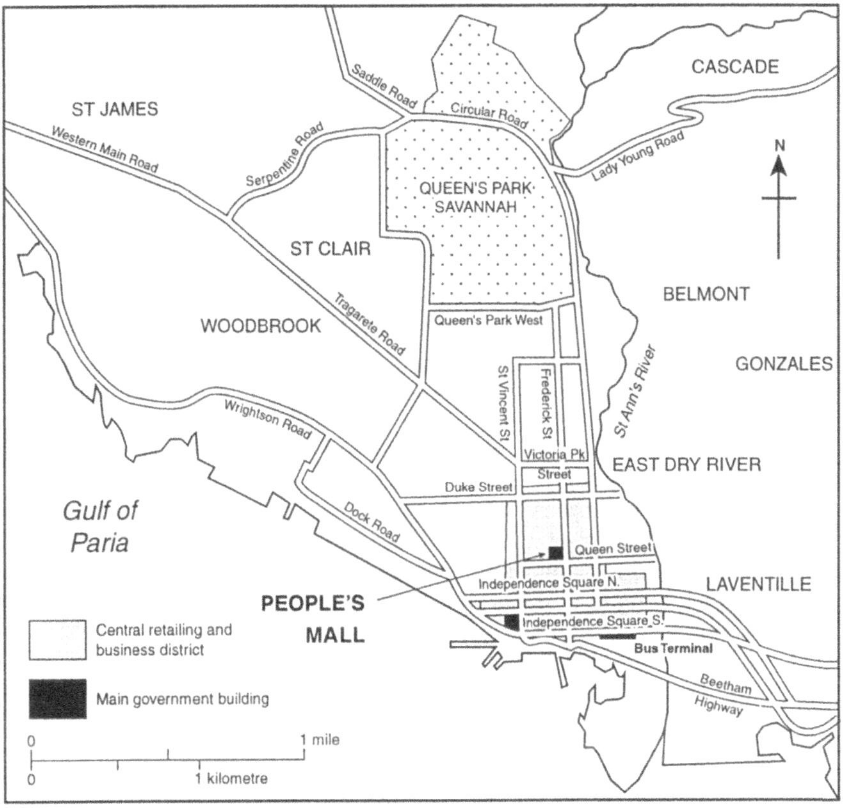

Figure 7.1 Location of the People's Mall, Port of Spain

service facilities, along with a hardship fund to assist vendors in trouble.

As an extension of the traditional nature of street vending, the booths sell mainly clothes, jewellery, records shoes and trinkets. A modern transformation has occurred from the original concept of trading in local products, as the majority of vendors are·selling imported goods. These traders have found their niche in the rapidly globalising economy, a phenomenon which has been documented elsewhere (Teltscher, 1994). The vendors are now commonly known as 'suitcase traders' who sell sought-after imported goods. The vendors will visit the USA, Canada and Venezuela once or twice a month to bring back items.

When the Mall was established, the government granted the vendors a 'licence' to import up to US$8,000 worth of goods each year for sale in the Mall, free of any duty/tax. These licences are still administered by the Vendor's Association but little attention is given to the $8,000 limit, either by the vendors or by customs. Many vendors have contacts in customs who take a small cut of the profits. The unwritten rule appears to be that the vendors can bring in as much as they can carry, hence the term 'suitcase traders'. Suitcase trading of clothes is a risky business, as there is a need to outlay large amounts of capital for flights and expenses. In order to make a profit the trader needs to sell a foreign shirt for TT$300 (£40), a task which is difficult in a recession. Despite this problem, however, the vendors appear to make a decent living.

Until 1992, Trinidad had a strict policy towards imported goods, which restricted the importation of all unnecessary goods. Foreign electrical items, cosmetics, clothes and music were all items which were highly sought after in Trinidad, and the vendors were able to take advantage of this demand. Since 1992, the government has abandoned the negative import list so the advantage of the suitcase traders over other more formal businesses may be lost in the near future. A return visit to Trinidad in September 1992 witnessed the enormous range of foreign goods which were on sale in the formal stores, a pattern which has forced suitcase traders to re-adapt their market strategy to a 'back to their roots' trade in crafts and unusual items.

The booths were originally occupied by male followers of the Rastsfarian culture, hence its other name the 'Rasta Mall'. One respondent stated that the scheme was gender biased, in that the Rastafarian ideology excluded women. As Harrison (1991) comments on her work in Kingston, local followers of Rastafari organise their economic activity along the lines of male dominance. Rastafarian ideology appears to have infiltrated into low-income settlements, and the informal sector in Trinidad. In Rastafarian views, women are clearly seen as dependants, and men must guide their spirituality (Kitzinger, 1969; Rowe, 1980).

This distinct cultural ideology provides a problem for female traders, and those of Indo-Trinidadian backgrounds who are also markedly absent, and it is in this respect that the major flaws of the project are found. The project is firmly embedded in a particular gendered and racialised identity, through social processes which have been reinforced over the years through the social networking of the original traders. As the first traders were relocated from downtown Port of Spain, it is likely that they would have been of African descent due to the social geography of the city. Furthermore, male traders would have found it easier to raise the initial capital than the women, who faced more financial barriers. This discrimination is not surprising when consideration is given to the fact that Eric Williams' political support came for the urban black lower class, many of whom were engaged in informal activities. Today, a reasonable proportion of women, estimated at 20 per cent, work in the Mall, but they are employees of the booth owners, rather than owners in their own right. The interviews presented in this chapter were carried out with 15 Afro-Trinidadian male booth owners.

Profile of a Modern Smuggler: Suitcase Trading in the 'Drag Mall'

The People's Mall exudes an unaesthetic atmosphere in that it is dark, confined and enclosed. For many Trinidadians, it is a forbidden space, a 'no-go' area for fears of rape, theft and drug abuse. The overpowering smell of insense and 'ganga' is off-putting to many would-be customers. There is no doubt that the dealing of drugs and organisation of other illicit activities do take place in the confines of the Mall, but they are carefully hidden activities, and do not interfere with the customer. The booth owners know that any 'bad' behaviour could result in the closing down of their businesses.

A fortunate encounter with an ex-social worker, who used to work in a Port of Spain drug rehabilitation programme, reassured any doubts about undertaking ethnographic research with the booth owners. An introduction to the Vendors Association's leader, enabled the establishment of a network of reliable contacts. Once a mutual trust had been established with one of the 'leaders' who supported my research, I could move at ease throughout the Mall. Despite this association, a number of booth owners were unwilling to talk, but there were plenty who would let me sit in their booth for a morning/afternoon and observe their trading.

Unlike the female traders, many of the booth owners did not like to talk of their personal lives. As a result, only approximate ages were given, which roughly placed the booth owners in their early thirties to forties. Five of the owners were single, one was married, and the remainder were in very loosely arranged unions. By contrast, all the vendors had children, often by more than two women. They see their children often, but do not offer constant financial support, due to their frequent absence from Trinidad. Instead they will often bring gifts back from abroad, such as a radio or clothes. Seven of the vendors also 'visited women' during their travelling, mainly in Miami and Caracas.

All the vendors were of Afro-Caribbean descent, but with a mixed Caribbean background. Two of the vendors were Jamaican, and had arrived in Trinidad as young men hoping to find work in the oil trade. Others had parents from St Vincent, Grenada, Jamaica and Barbados, displaying the effects of migratory patterns of movement in this region. This also had the effect of socialising them into travelling at a young age. Seven traders had lived in a number of islands, with Jamaica and Barbados being the most popular, and two had lived for a time in Canada. Four of the booth owners had 'business interests' in other islands. One young Trinidadian, frequently went to see his 'partner' or 'brother' in Barbados, to take him jewellery, tie-dye and crafts which he sold to tourists. In this respect, the vendors' social networks were geographcailly extensive and based on notions of friendship and shared experiences of African Caribbean 'brotherhood'. Despite the overall Rasta image maintained by the Mall, only five of the booth owners interviewed were true followers of the religion, others had just adopted the familiar dreads, image and dress.

In direct contrast to the female higglers, all the booth operators owned, or jointly-owned, their home in either Laventille, Eastern Main Road, Belmont, Woodbrook, Arima or Tunapuna. None of these areas is associated with the lowest-income settlements, apart from part of Laventille, suggesting that the incomes earned by suitcase traders are higher than other informal workers. Male trader's households seem to have less members than the higglers, as they do not have responsibility for children. Three vendors lived with a brother, or in a house share arrangement with other males. Four vendors did at times have a sister and her children, or mother, to stay but essentially were only responsible for themselves. The remainder lived mainly on their own, although they would sometimes have their children/partner with them. Two booth owners were wealthy enough to support their children and partner in a separate house. Living without commitment is preferred amongst traders, particularly as they are often away for weeks at a time.

One revealing, and unexpected factor was the educational background of traders. Three of the sample had degrees from the University of the West Indies, in Public Administration, Accountancy and Agriculture. Disillusioned with their lower ranking jobs in the civil service and sugar industry, they adopted street trading as a means of survival which allowed them to live a more West Indian lifestyle. This transformation in lifestyle was made in the late 1970s, when the influence of the Black Power Movement was strong. A further three vendors had 'A' levels, whilst the others had all attended secondary school. Such a high level of education poses a problem for theories which state that the informal sector is a haven for formally unqualified workers.

Suitcase traders often employ people to operate their booth. This is a necessity when the owner is buying stock abroad, but also appears to be a trend based on their work ethic. Only four of the traders operated their stall full-time on their own, when they were in the country. When they travel, they enlist the help of 'brothers', or a number of friends, who already trade on the streets. The problem, according to the owners, is one of trust, as the booths contain expensive stock.

Other traders are more willing to employ sales assistants both when they are around, and when they are abroad. They will often employ young women, who are willing to work for lower wages, and 'don't give them problems'. In many cases, trading in the Mall is a part-time occupation, as booth owners prefer the role of travelling. Five of the owners only worked as traders for two days a week, and employed between one or two young women on a rota basis. An additional two vendors operated the business with another friend/brother and shared the workload. A further two only worked in their workshops located above their booths, and the remaining two only visited the Mall to collect money and instruct their workers. All vendors, however, conduct the buying of imported goods themselves, as they do not trust others to do it.

Risk, Entrepreneurship and Global Networks

Unlike the female higglers, the Mall vendors were not overtly concerned with running their business on their own. Instead, they were often happy to share the responsibility and risk with another 'brother'. They were embedded in both local and global networks which they used for finance, travel arrangements, trade and accomodation abroad. Their freedom from household and child-care responsibilities, also allowed them to be more adventurous with investments, and to adopt a very flexible pattern of work. Twelve of the owners had joined the Mall at its outset, and had consolidated their business over a number of years. Starting with nothing more that a wooden stall, they had slowly added wooden walls, roofs and in many cases another storey. Seven of the owners had a second storey extension, which they used as a workshop to assemble goods, and make crafts. Typical products include copper jewellery, tie-dyed T-shirts, pottery, leather shoes, beaded bracelets, and pendants displaying the familiar red, green and yellow motifs. In addition, they also sell a range of other local crafts made in informal workshops, and tourist items bought from formal outlets.

Thirteen of the booths sold a mixture of imported clothes, jewellery, cosmetics and crafts produced by the owner, whilst one booth sold only imported labelled clothes such as jeans. The other was a music booth offering a range of pirate copies of local reggae, Jamaican dub, and expensive imported LPs and tapes. The recording of pirate copies of music does not appear to be an offence worthy of concern in Trinidad. The Mall vendors operate a less fixed pattern of trading than the higglers or female traders. Table 7.7 shows the travelling undertaken by the trader's in the previous month. Most traders travel abroad at least twice a month, but this depends on a number of factors. If a booth does particularly good trade in a particular item, then the owner may refurbish his stocks immediately. Travelling abroad requires large amounts of capital for foreign exchange and expenses. During poor periods of trade, booth owners cannot afford to buy new stock. Rather than follow a strict routine, the trader usually travels when he has shifted a large proportion of his stock, and 'feels that the time is good'. As an international occupation, travelling is also influenced by currency fluctuations, availability of flights and visa availability.

Traders will usually stay out of the country for five days, but on many occasions will extend their stay up to three weeks depending on finances and visas. They tend to adopt a 'see what happens' policy whereby they may stay in a country for a few weeks if the mood takes them. This is particularly the case with Miami, a popular destination, where many have family. They also travel to Jamaica, Puerto Rico, Margarita, and Caracas. Mr A, a successful trader of 12 years standing, now spends his summers in Miami with relatives, whilst his brother runs the booth. A further seven traders had travelled to Europe, with The Netherlands being the most popular destination, and England the second. Suitcase traders appear to adopt a nomadic lifestyle, which conforms to their ideology of work. Work should essentially be enjoyable, and conform to a West Indian identity. Many of the traders scorn white collar workers for trying to emulate colonial lifestyles.

A popular topic of conversation amongst the vendors was the ideology of 'street life' (Lieber, 1981). Many vendors started their working lives selling on the streets, an occupation which affords a meagre existence but provides a valuable experience. Street trading teaches a number of 'tricks' and survival strategies, which are invaluable to the informal sector worker. Young traders learn how to sell, how to be tough, and how to beat the competition. A vendor must always be aware of changing fashions and tastes before his neighbour. Many traders still leave their booths to go to Independence Square, in order to catch those customers who are afraid to visit the Mall, and keep up with the 'street lime'. Although, many of the traders aspire to running successful formal businesses, their ideology of work and the street mentality, may cause them to remain informal workers.

Highway Trading: An Indo-Trinidadian Work Ethic?

East Indians in Trinidad appear to have higher aspirations than any other social group, a factor which is seen to be typical of immigrant families (Brereton, 1979). It is by understanding the historical quest for advancement that the role of the highway trader can be understood. Rather than 'just making do', the Indo-Trinidadian highway trader has extended the size and scope of informal sector retailing, and has transformed the role of subsistence fruit and vegetable selling to successful entrepreneurship.

Highway traders occupy reasonable sized, often consolidated stalls along the West-East and North-South highways in Trinidad (as explained in chapter 5). Their businesses are usually family concerns, and a number of traders may work from one stall. It was not as easy to gain access to the sole owners of the businesses, as they were often family concerns. In all

Table 7.7 Typical Monthly Travelling Patterns of Traders

Respondent	Destination	Number of visits made
A	Miami	1
	Caracas	1
	Barbados	1
B	Miami	2
C	Margarita	2
	Caracas	1
D	Jamaica	2
E	Puerto Rico	2
	Miami	1
F	Caracas	1
G	New York	1
H	Miami	2
	Jamaica	1
I	Barbados	1
	St Lucia	1
J	No Trips	0
K	Caracas	2
L	Miami	1
	Puerto Rico	1
M	Merida, Mexico	1
N	Caracas	1
	Margarita	1
O	Jamaica	1
	Puerto Rico	1
	Barbados	1

cases, the respondent was male. When women were assisting in trading, they were usually not expected to comment. Instead, interviews were undertaken with a family member involved in the operation, such as a brother or son. Five of the interviews conducted were with the owners, six with brothers or another close relative involved in a family venture, and four with full-time employees. In this respect, this sample provides an insight into the lives of both the stall owners, and their employees.

Table 7.8 shows the personal characteristics of the sample and highlights the age distribution of the sample. Once again, ages are only approximate, but show that the employees were all under 30 years. Business owners, and family members were aged between 30 and 50. As expected, amongst an Indo-Trinidadian community, the majority of the men were married. Only the younger men were still single. Union status is frowned upon in their communities, and considered to be disrespectful. Seven of the respondents traded on the Southern Highway, and the other eight on the West-East Highway near Port of Spain. None of the West-East traders lived within the north of the country, instead two lived in San Fernando, one in Caroni, one near Toco, and four in the South near Oropouche and Douglas. This involved much travelling but was undertaken due to income which could be made on this particular highway. The traders located on the Southern Highway also lived far from their trading place with only two employees living near to their place of trading, in Chaguanas, and the remainder in the Central or Southern regions. All the businesses concerned had at one vehicle, with the employees also gaining use of a truck.

An extended family household appears to be the norm amongst highway traders, as this facilitates their business commitments. Only three of the traders lived in a nuclear household, with only their wife and children. The others lived in an extended arrangement, which incorporated from 9 to 25 household members. Two of the traders were working for their wives' brothers, although it is usually the wife who goes to work for the husbands' family. Within the households, however, there are usually six or more adults who work for the business, or bring income into the households. In this respect, highways traders' households are usually more wealthy than their other informal counterparts. The exception to this, are the employees, who gain a meagre wage for their labour (under £100 per month). All the employees had been working for their boss for over three years, often as farm hands. When they are not trading on the highways, they are undertaking other jobs for their employers, such as driving, picking fruit, farming and household duties. Highway traders only employ workers who they have known for many years.

Other family members did not receive a set wage for their work, but shared the profits amongst the male members of the families. One young trader was working for his uncle's business, but complained that his father made him work, as he had lost his job in the sugar industry. His uncle paid him very little, as his father owed him a few favours. The exchanging

Table 7.8 The Characteristics of Highway Traders

Respondent Number	Position of Trader	Age Band of Trader	Marital Status
1	Owner	40-45	Married
2	Brother	35-40	Married
3	Brother (in law)	30-40	Married
4	Employee	18-25	Single
5	Owner	35-40	Married
6	Employee	15-17	Single
7	Son	30-35	Married
8	Owner	45-50	Widowed
9	Owner	40-45	Married
10	Nephew	25-30	Married
11	Employee	18-25	Married
12	Employee	25-30	Single
13	Owner	40-45	Married
14	Son	30-35	Married
15	Brother (in law)	30-35	Married

of labour between families in return for loans or other favours, appears to be common. Unfortunately, females and younger men do not appear to have a say in their career choice, and often work as unremunerated labourers. Their use of unpaid labour, is one of the reasons why East Indian businesses are successful. In contrast to the higglers' work ethic, independence and autonomy are not considered important in highway occupations.

Informal Business Practices

Large amounts of local and imported products are sold by the highway traders from fixed stalls. Apparently, each of the businesses in this sample had its own permanent stall. The majority of the other traders in the area knew which stall belonged to whom, and there was an unwritten code of conduct between them. Stalls were often family concerns, and may be shared on different days of the week. Only three of the stalls, located on the West-East highway were open every day of the week for 16 hours. Highway trading is an activity usually undertaken on three or four days a week, due to the time involved in buying and transporting goods. Interviews with three families operating large stalls near to Port of Spain highlighted their use of the extended family to keep the stalls open for 16 hours a day. A strict division of labour is usually applied to the family network, with some members trading, and other buying from Central Market or transporting. This is an important issue which will be explored in chapter 8.

Once again, imported produce was supplied by daily, or weekly, visits to Central Market. In addition, nine of the traders also farmed produce on their own land, and all the sample used one or two domestic suppliers on a regular basis. The owner of one business had entered into a partnership with a colleague who had a reasonable sized farm. Highway traders tend to use only one supplier at Central Market, who will afford them credit arrangements.

Whilst higglering is a relatively safe and unthreatened occupation, highway trading is subject to theft and police harassment. Many traders identify police attacks as a form of racism, as the police 'don't like Indians making good money'. In addition, although highway vendors occupy some of the most profitable informal locations in Trinidad, their profit margins are subject to greater risk than the higglers. Many traders will go and buy TT$8000 (£120) of wholesale produce from Central Market, and take it back to their stall. The perishibility of vegetables in the heat is high, and they lose large amounts of produce this way. Goods need to be sold in a number of days or large amounts of money are lost. The majority of traders also have to pack up their stalls at night and take their produce back home.

When asked whether they would like to improve their businesses, thirteen of the traders said they needed refrigeration for storage and transportation. The capital needed for these improvements was too high for even the most successful businesses. In addition, twelve traders also wanted to see a reduction in harassment from the authorities, which was extensive in 1991. In their defence, they argued that higglers rarely encounter government opposition.

The main governmental concern with street vending is for the congestion on public highways. The death toll of vendor's on the highways is increasing, as is the number of accidents caused by cars stopping suddenly to purchase goods. The greatest occurrence of highway vending occurs at peak traffic times, as it is a demand-led occupation. The increasing commuter traffic from the East and South, to Port of Spain, has encouraged greater levels of highway trading. A seasonal concern is the number of children who accompany their fathers during school holidays. Drivers often use small children to bring goods to the car, and there have been several fatal accidents.

During the evening rush hour (4-5pm), the highways are blocked by traders walking around stopped cars, and of cars queuing from the inside lane to stop at a stall. The threshold for this type of vending is vast, and as discussed in chapter 5, the money which may be earnt substantial. The West-East corridor contains the greatest levels of trading, as 60 per cent of the working population are employed in the north-west of Trinidad (Town and Country Planning, 1991). Highway traders locate according to whether they want to catch the in-coming or out-going traffic.

Highway traders only invade the streets after careful calculation. Primarily, traders assess the value of the available locations in respect of the following factors: estimation of customers, economic viability, potential customer threshold and likely resistance from other vendors in the area and from the authorities. These questions are resolved by asking friends, contacts and observing the current activity in the area. It is not uncommon for a number of friends to invade an area at once, establishing themselves at different locations. Planners are greatly concerned with the increased level of informal trading which has grown as a result of the recession. The government periodically clears traders away from the main roads and highways, and in 1990 attempted to relocate them elsewhere in a more formalised environment. The violent clearing of traders in the Valsayn area, to a formalised market, is discussed in chapter 9.

Highway traders are providing a much needed service for the new urban classes, who do not have the time to wander around the more traditional market. The highway trader is a more modern version of a traditional higgler. Unlike the higglers, highway traders are not restricted by household responsibilities, or prevented from taking risks due to restrictions on their incomes. The use of a division of labour within an extended family network, is one of the main factors in their success. However, highway traders have not been fortunate in gaining much government support, unlike the suitcase traders, which many argue is a political problem.

Conclusions: Divisions of Labour

The occupational profiles presented in this chapter have highlighted the ways in which different groups of male and female traders adopt varied business practices to earn a living. Petty commodity traders are also embedded in different social networks, networks which are also spatially defined. The higglers of Arima and Central Market, although different in many respects, operated successful but rather limited trading businesses. As research elsewhere has suggested, their trade was generally less well paid although it involved more strenuous work. Women are not as successful in the informal sector as their male counterparts. Reasons for this marginalisation stem from their reproductive responsibilities, and their fear of losing their independence by changing their business. Male traders, on the other hand, are more likely to develop successful informal businesses, and obtain higher incomes. This could be attributed to their ability to disregard family duties and household ties, or to their ideology of work, which due to a broader childhood socialisation, is not as restricted as women's. It may also be linked to their ability to take advantage of extensive social networks, either based on kinship networks as in the case of the Highway traders, or the geographically extensive friendship networks of the Mall vendors.

Having fully explored the nature of the informal activities operated by higglers, suitcase traders and highway traders, and having examined their everyday experiences of work, the next chapter examines the factors which influence their views on work and conditions their experiences of different places in the informal sector. As chapter 8 will show, traders' ideas about work are formed and re-formed through processes which are not only gendered and racialised, but strongly associated with spatial divisions in the labour market.

8 "Like we beggin on de streets": The Gendering of Street Lives and Working Identities

Introduction

As chapter 7 highlighted, poverty is only one factor in explaining the spatial distribution of informal sector employment. The factors which make the informal sector a haven for some workers and an environment of exploitation for others are multifaceted. The main factors, which include access to capital, household responsibilities, social capital and membership of social networks, are all governed by social processes which are conditioned by ideas about gendered and ethnic difference. Social networks, which are built around commonalities, shared values and ways of knowing, are often maintained around gender and kinship ties and are firmly embedded in place. As the division of labour is as much about where you work as it is about what you do, thinking spatially can help us better understand the working experiences of informal entrepreneurs.

Mobility is crucial to informal sector workers, particularly in times of hardship such as those experienced in Trinidad under structural adjustment in the early 1990s. The ability to diversify, or seek new opportunities, is often the key to the survival of petty commodity traders in an increasingly competitive market. The presence of both visible and invisible spatial boundaries often provides obstacles to different groups of traders, particularly women who may not have either the resources or the social networks necessary to overcome problems. Although visible boundaries, such as those developed by the state through legislation and police intervention, are more likely to affect traders equally, invisible spatial boundaries are subject to greater inequalities. During the early 1990s in Trinidad, under conditions of economic austerity, increasing numbers of men have entered informal occupations which were traditionally seen as 'female'. Essentially, male traders are reconstructing these spaces for their own uses.

In Trinidad, the occupations of petty commodity trading and informal commercial importers (ICIs) have provided new opportunities for male entrepreneurs who have been more successful in adapting to changing market conditions. Their ability to out compete many traditional female traders, such as higglers, due to their enhanced access to capital, transport, membership of informal trading networks and business associations, has resulted in their occupation of women's 'spaces'. As a result, many female traders have been marginalised into less competitive territories and business markets. As participation in public spaces is crucial to the survival of poor households, restrictions on women's trading locations can severely reduce their income generation opportunities.

As chapter 7 provided an insight into the daily experiences faced by different groups of informal traders in Trinidad, this chapter investigates the ways in which people's ideas about work help to construct and maintain gendered and racialised divisions of labour in the informal sector. As engagement in work is central to an individual's notion of identity (Lloyd-Evans and Bowlby, 2000), it is important to understand how this construction is influenced by ideas about gender, ethnicity and place. The rhetoric behind this evaluation is based on the belief that an understanding of the factors which influence workers views of different occupations, can assist in promoting more equitable employment opportunities.

As this chapter will show, one of the major obstacles to adopting a more equitable work ethos concerns the established perceptions of work held by individuals and society as a whole. As long as the better paid and higher status jobs in Trinidad are perceived as only attainable by the members of the elite, or those of a specific gender or ethnicity, then inequaility in opportunity between different social groups will remain. The perpetuation of 'accepted' codes of behaviour and working roles in Trinidad still act to constrain many workers to adopt low-paid and low-status occupations. Societal acceptance of a more liberal and non-traditional image of work may assist in raising many informal sector workers' perceptions of their own worth, and their contribution to society. The informal sector is a particularly good place to start, as it already encourages self-employment and non-traditional forms of work. Unfortunately, there still exist many invisible spatial boundaries which translate into very real tensions between traders over issues such as access to markets, capital and business opportunities. In particular, negative ideas about women's roles in the informal sector often present obstacles for those women attempting to cross these divisions.

Men and women conceive and use space differently in the informal sector, but how are these spaces constructed around gendered and ethnic identities? As we have argued in earlier chapters, traditional dualisms which conceptualise space in terms of private/public or inside/outside offer little insight into the lives of informal sector traders. As Massey (1994) argues, such divisions are not absolute and female traders frequently cross boundaries, although this process may result in conflict. As Stitcher (1990) argues, movement into public spheres cannot result in increased power for women if men won't allow it. In Trinidad, women are not confined simply to private or public spaces, but to what Davidson (1996: 116) refers to as "points of intersection". As with individuals, these different places also have their own identities which can serve to maintain social divisions. Therefore, this chapter also examines the images of different places which are constructed by male and female traders.

In order to investigate the most productive method of encouraging a new work ethos, it is important to highlight the views that different individuals hold about work. If a higher profile is given to informal sector occupations, small business development and entrepreneurship, workers' evaluations of their own skills may be raised. As a result, this may encourage certain social groups to be more adventurous in following different career paths. As chapters 5 and 6 have shown, the existence of a clear division of labour is in itself a hindrance to development for many workers.

The informal sector offers a range of different opportunities, and career paths, to those working within its boundaries. As in many social environments, people enter their work place with a perceived, as well as a real set of advantages, and disadvantages. In many cases, there is added pressure related to differences in gender, ethnicity, religion, and background. Images of work are built upon a complex structure of past experiences, education, awareness, childhood socialisation, and environment. Perception of space, is in many cases, of equal importance in constraining people's choice of work. For example, a female worker may not choose to work in certain areas at night, due to her perception that they are unsafe. In this respect, there are many cultural, social and psychological factors that influence the occupations undertaken by informal sector workers.

The previously documented interviews undertaken with the Central Market higglers, the Arima higglers, the suitcase traders, and the highway traders incorporated a detailed section on work. Respondents were asked to talk of their work experiences and views on different occupations, often with regard to place, gender and ethnicity. During the interviews, respondents were encouraged to talk about their work histories, and answer questions which were aimed at identifying their individual ideas about work. Firstly, respondents were asked to state whether, within the context of Trinidad, there was an occupation which they would prefer to undertake. When this question was asked, no stipulations were made as to whether the occupation had to be informal or formal, within practical attainment of the worker, or not. It was left to the individual to make their own assessment of the word 'preferred'. Secondly, participants were asked to identify what they considered to be three 'good jobs', and subsequently, three 'bad jobs', on offer in Trinidad. Once again, individuals were left to interpret whether the question implied three good/bad jobs in the entire country, or only occupations which they considered to be personally on offer to them.

Thirdly, in specific relation to gender, respondents were asked which, if any, were the three jobs most likely to be undertaken by women, and why. As an extension, the conversations progressed to examine whether men and women are suited to particular occupations, and if so, the reasons behind this. Attention was also paid to evaluate whether the participants held strong views on the existence of gender-specific skills. In conclusion, the groups were asked to explore the importance of locational factors in occupational choice/constraint, by discussing whether there were any environments in which the participant would not work.

The results provided a series of detailed perceptions of sixty informal sector workers, outlining their views on their job, the jobs of others, and work as a whole. In order to present the results of the analysis of the wealth of information gained, this chapter is divided into four sections. The first section examines the factors behind occupational desirability, and evaluates the participants' interpretation of the word 'preferred'. This is followed by an analysis of informal sector workers' perceptions of 'good' and 'bad' jobs in Trinidad. Thirdly, attention is paid to the gender division of labour, and whether informants felt that there are specific women's jobs in Trinidad. Finally, as part of the conclusion, attention is focused on the important role of space and the environment.

Occupational Aspirations: The Preferred Occupations of Informal Traders

Despite the fact that informal trading is a popular occupation in Trinidad, there are a number of other jobs which traders would prefer to undertake. Although 84 per cent of the sixty workers interviewed stated that they considered informal trading to be a long-term career choice, 65 per cent of the sample stated that there was an alternative job which they would like to do. Interestingly, the majority of the Central Market and Arima higglers stated their preference for another occupation, whilst the male highway traders and suitcase traders appeared to be more satisfied with their present occupation. In this respect, there is a marked difference in the data based on gender.

Female Traders' Aspirations: Lifecycle and Independence

Despite their decision to undertake higglering as a serious career, 13 of the 15 Central Market higglers cited a job which they would prefer to undertake. The two remaining higglers stated that given the choice, they would rather not work at all. With the exception of one respondent, the Central Market higglers' cited occupations which they could conceivably undertake given their eduction, background and skills. Their interpretation of the word 'preferred' appeared to be associated with their own abilities. A similar pattern was also found in the occupational preferences of the fifteen Arima higglers. In Arima, only one higgler stated that she had no preferred occupation.

Tables 8.1 and 8.2 show the jobs which the Central Market and Arima higglers regarded as a better alternative to their current position. As the list of occupations shows, many higglers confine their perceptions of work

Table 8.1 Job Preferences of Central Market Higglers

Preferred Job	Number of Higglers citing the job as preferred (n=15)	Reasons Given
Shop Owner	2	Status Good business
Hairdresser	2	Enjoyment Fashionable
Suitcase Trader	2	Enjoyment Higher status Success
Teacher	2	Status Satisfaction Public respect Good job
Lawyer	1	Success American
Own Clothes Shop	1	Own business Modern
Hotel Receptionist	1	Easy work Smart job Respect
Own Craft Store	1	Good business Enjoyable
Operate Flower Shop	1	Enjoyment
Prefer not to work	1	Stay at home
No preferred job	1	n/a

Table 8.2 Job Preferences of Arima Higglers

Preferred Job	Number of Higglers citing the job as preferred (n=15)	Reasons Given
Shop Owner	3	Respect Higher income Job security
Office/Clerical	2	Easy Respect Job security
Don't know	2	n/a
Child Care	1	Home-based Easy Life-change related
Seamstress	1	Fashionable
Craft Production	1	Enjoyment Home-based
Carnival Designer	1	Enjoyment Social life Creative
Nurse	1	Caring job Respect
Remain at home	1	Child care Age related
'Business'	1	Higher income Respect
No preferred job	1	n/a

to their own environment and everyday experiences, of which informality is a familiar process. Only one Central Market higgler said she would rather be a lawyer, although she knew she did not have the qualifications, or opportunity, to attain this goal. The remainder of the occupations cited by both groups, such as hairdressing or owning a shop, could conceivably be achieved. Interestingly, many of the cited occupations are part of the informal sector. It also establishes the fact that informal workers do not necessarily aspire to formal sector employment. When given the opportunity to discuss any job they liked, the higglers limited their choice to fit in with their own values, needs and skills.

From the occupations selected, it was clear that Central Market higglers' view the maintenance of their independence as important. In addition, there is also evidence of their aspirations towards modernity and higher status. For example, owning a shop was a popular choice which reflects the desire for business independence. Hairdressing and hotel reception work are perceived as modern and glamorous. Two respondents expressed their desire to be suitcase traders, a job not unlike their own, but one which accords higher status, and allows greater freedom through travel. They felt they were currently unable to do this because they did not have the funds available and contacts abroad.

When a comparison is made with the discussions held with the Arima higglers' interpretation of the construct 'preferred', a number of differences are noted. The older age of the group, outlined in chapter 7, combined with their greater responsibilities in terms of child-care, may explain some of the differences behind their preferred job choices, and more importantly their reasons. Although, their choices still reflect a preference for self-employment, two Arima higglers expressed the desire to take a clerical occupation, as it affords greater ease and security. Staying at home, and/or engaging in child-care, was another alternative suggested by higglers over 60, who would prefer an easier lifestyle. Associated responsibility appears to be an important variable in occupational choice.

The most marked difference between the two samples concerns the reasons behind the higglers' job preferences. As shown in Table 8.3, the reasons given by the Central Market higglers stressed 'higher social status', 'good business' and 'more enjoyment' as the three most important factors. Generally, the Arima higglers did not value modernity, or higher status, as important job requirements.

Table 8.3 shows that increased social respect, and the ability to be fashionable or modern are important considerations for Central Market higglers in Trinidad. As workers in Port of Spain, the higglers are more exposed to the wealth and modernity which have been adopted by the elites. A modern appearance and the following of fashion is important, particularly to younger workers. Left over from the colonial past, public acceptability and peer pressure are important concepts in Trinidad. Status *per se* is often a more important consideration, for the young, than income.

Table 8.3 Social Status versus Job Security: Job Qualities considered Important to Central Market and Arima Higglers

Important Qualities	Number of Higglers Citing Quality	
	Central Market	Arima
Higher social status	3	0
Greater job security	0	4
Good business	3	0
Greater personal enjoyment	3	2
Fashionable/modern image	2	1
Accords greater respect	2	4
Higher income	0	2
Perceived as good job	1	0
Own business	1	0
Successful image	1	0
Easy work	1	2
Higher job satisfaction	1	0
Home-based work	0	1
Smart image	0	1
Age related	0	2
Creative	0	1
Enhances social life	0	1

Economic improvement, or increased earning capacity, did not feature as a motive behind preferred occupational choice, stressing the fact that many of the Central Market higglers' 'preferred occupations' may afford them less income than they gain through higglering, but were still desirable for their status value. It is often assumed that economic improvement, and income, are the greatest influences on peoples' choice of occupations. To the higglers, however, independence is still a popular factor and as such, the ability to be self-employed is one of the most important considerations. This is clearly shown by the fact that the higglers' 'preferred' jobs still involved a high degree of independence. Hairdressing, managing their own store, and suitcase trading, are all occupations which involve self-employment. Few higglers wanted to change their independence for a more secure white collar job in a formal firm, which is often regarded as 'selling out'. In Trinidad small-business development appears to be a more popular occupation, probably as it accords an expression of independence against the colonial past.

The relative importance of status and image, however, appears to change once women takeover responsibility for the household, a factor clearly demonstrated in the interviews held with the Arima higglers. To the older higglers in Arima, public respect was more important, along with increased financial gain and job security, as shown in Table 8.3. Responsibility for children, and the household, overides all other considerations. Preferences for home-based employment indicate that the provision of support for children is a higgler's prime consideration, and one which greatly affects their views on work. Job security and the ability to earn a decent income becomes paramount in their choice of occupation. In this way, women's reproductive reponsibility limits their perception of work, and highlights the important role of gender in constraining occupation choice.

The importance of ethnicity, combined with life-cycle stage, is shown by comparing preferred occupations within the Arima sample. Table 8.4 highlights the differences in Arima higglers' aspirations in relation to their age and ethnicity. The younger members of the group aspire to more formal, white-collar occupations, whilst the older members prefer the more traditional informal qualifications. Furthermore, when ethnicity is considered, it is clear that the Indo-Trinidadian members of the group would prefer to work in clerical, medical and business-related jobs. A similar pattern was also found in the Central Market sample. A number of explanations for this were offered by the Indo-Trinidadian higglers in both groups.

Firstly, they view white-collar jobs as offering greater social acceptability than agriculture. To them, the formal sector accords greater social respect. Secondly, as they do not own the trading businesses, they would prefer an occupation which pays them a fixed salary. Thirdly, movement away from a family business would allow them greater freedom, and the possibility of independence. This line of thought is in

Table 8.4 Age, Ethnicity and Preferred Occupations of Arima Higglers

Preferred Job	Age of Higgler	Ethnicity of Higgler
Stay at home	60-64	Afro-Trinidadian
No preferred job	60-64	Afro-Trinidadian
Don't know	55-59	Afro-Trinidadian
Child-care	50-54	Afro-Trinidadian
Don't know	50-54	Afro-Trinidadian
Craft producer	45-49	Afro-Trinidadian
Carnival designer	45-49	Afro-Trindadian
Shop owner	40-44	Indo-Trinidadian
Shop owner	40-44	Afro-Trinidadian
Shop owner	40-44	Afro-Trinidadian
Nurse	35-49	Indo-Trinidadian
Office work	35-39	Indo-Trinidadian
Seamstress	35-39	Afro-Trinidadian
Office work	25-29	Indo-Trinidadian
Business	15-19	Indo-Trinidadian

contrast to the views of the Afro-Trinidadian higglers, who argued that they would lose their independence by moving out of the informal sector. This demonstrates how workers in the same job can have differing perceptions on the benefits and disadvantages of the occupation. Job perception is often related to both the higglers' household responsibility, and the environment in which they work. Both these factors are heavily influenced by ethnicity. As the majority of Indo-Trinidadian higglers work as unpaid labour for a family business, they see higglering as inhibiting their freedom, social status and personal wealth accumulation. To the Afro-Trinidadian higgler, the job awards them economic autonomy and independence.

Male Traders' Occupational Aspirations: Formality and 'Getting On'

The job preferences expressed by the fifteen suitcase, and fifteen highway, traders differed greatly to those of the higglers. As many of the suitcase traders had previously left white collar jobs to take-up booths in the People's Mall, they did not hold false images on the nature of work available outside the informal sector. Of the fifteen suitcase traders interviewed, only eight stated that they would prefer to undertake another occupation. Their preferred occupations centred around setting up a more established clothing/commodity business in the formal sector, where the fundamental principles of their work would stay the same. Table 8.5 highlights the nature of transition to the formal sector that many of the traders would like to make. Only two of the booth owners stated that they might like to undertake a different occupation altogether. Mr C said that he had thought about establishing a small travel agency which would arrange tours, as he had many contacts abroad. On a similar theme, Mr M had considered moving to Tobago to run a guest house and organise trips to Bucco Reef.

In this instance, the suitcase traders wanted to continue in small business development. Successful suitcase traders are willing to enter the formal sector, unlike the higglers who expressed a definite fear of change. Formal white collar jobs, status and respect are not as important for the male suitcase traders, as they feel that they do not have to work for acceptability and respect. This is also related to the fact that in Trinidad men gain higher respect based on their gender, whilst women feel that they have to earn it.

> As Mr C expresses: "People think they great 'cos dey wear white shirt 'n tie, and they go to air conditioned office every day, dey think dey better than us. But, we laughing cos we done it before, we know that money 'ere is better and ya can enjoy life, for real. That kinda attitude is from your country ya know, everyone 'ere aspire to be white and do office work, working wid your hands is like slavery. We brothers in the Mall, na we don't care for dat kinda attitude, as long as we happy den it don't matter what dey tink of us. Other people mind, it bother dem a whole lot".

Table 8.5 Job Preferences of the Suitcase Traders

Preferred Job	Number of Suitcase Traders citing the job as preferred	Reasons Given
Run Tobago guesthouse	1	Profitable business By the sea
Operate travel agency	1	Enjoys travelling Good business
Buy formal shop	2	Expand business Greater profits Increased profit
Operate export business	2	Has good contacts Import more stock Greater success
Operate small chain of shops	1	Good business Greater income
Formal craft production unit	1	Enjoyment
No preferred job	7	
Total respondents	15	

The views expressed by the highway traders reflect a different ideology. Ten of the fifteen highway traders interviewed said that highway trading allowed them to fulfil their goals of business development, and the accumulation of wealth. The other five respondents worked for a family business on a junior level, and were dissatisfied at the level of respect accorded them, and their low pay. All under the age of thirty, this group of five wanted to break out of family control and lead a more modern lifestyle. Their preferred occupations were ambitious, and may unfortunately be out of their present grasp due to perceptions of their class and social standing.

One young trader wanted to travel by means of working for British West Indian Airways (BWIA), as a steward. The BWIA flight-crew are held in high regard in Trinidad, and are generally made up from young, attractive, fair-skinned and well-educated individuals, who have come from high-income groups. As such, the demand for this job is extremely high due to its links with the 'foreign' and 'exotic', and promotion of jet-setting life-style, which many young Trinidadians aspire to.

Other highway traders were attracted to occupations which they saw to be of higher social status, urban and modern, as shown in Table 8.6. This could be interpreted as a reaction against their own rural and traditional lifestyle. In general, it is the younger members of society who are most dissatisfied with the prospect of remaining in an informal sector occupation. To many, informality restricts their social standing and opportunity to 'get on in life'. As another trader expressed, "trading on de highway is hard work, and when ya go home ya too tired to go out. If I lived in Port of Spain, and worked in the government or someting, I could lime at work, be wid lots of young people and at night I could go to 'Attic' and other clubs. I'd be accepted, but now me just a street trader from Penal, that's not how I want to live me life".

In a post-colonial society like Trinidad, ethnicity has been instrumental in shaping the lives of male petty commodity traders. As the most advantaged gender and ethnic group in Trinidad, Afro-Trinidadian men do not have to struggle for social respect in the same way as other groups. The highway traders' experience of work has been very different. The male highway traders have undertaken their occupational roles as a means to increasing their social status, in a society which has tended to regard them as belonging to its lower echcelons (Clarke, 1984). Few occupational avenues are open to poorly educated Indo-Trinidadians from a lower-income background. An attitude which is similar to that held by the higglers, concerns the highway traders' desire to be treated with greater respect by society as a whole. One middle-aged trader expressed his disatisfaction with the way he was treated by many customers.

> Mr P: "Dey immediately wary of us, almost afraid like we thief their money, or someting. Den they look at us cos our clothes is dirty from carrying vegetables all day, n' you can see dat dey think dey better than us. Sometimes dey talk to us like we stupid or what, and some people always try to pay nothin for the

> fruit n' act like we grateful dey give us someting, like we begging on de streets! Many make us carry der goods to de car, like we servants or what, wid not so much as a thank you. That's de way tings are y' know."

Despite their obvious mistreatment, the traders put up with the job, as it affords them a standard of living, one which they may not be able to make elsewhere. Despite claims of social harmony, prejudice against the lower-income Indo-Trinidadian population in Trinidad is strong, particularly by the middle and higher income groups. Many East Indian families endured racial prejudice for many decades, and they work to overcome it by accumulating wealth. Ironically, many of the traders are regarded as successful businessmen in their neighbourhoods. It is widely known, that a number of the most successful private businesses in Trinidad are owned by East Indian families, and that many of them started their careers as street traders.

Vertovec (1992) has also spoken of the desire to leave traditional lifestyles held by many young Indo-Trinidadians. However, as Sampath (1993) argues, this romantic illusion is far from the reality of the life, as many young rural men would be unemployed if they gave up their jobs in a traditional agricultural occupation. Once again, there emerges a conflict between image and reality amongst Trinidad's informal workers. It is also clear that many young Indo-Trinidadian males perceive working for a large firm, or the government, as a way of attaining independence. To many young traders, independence is interpreted as a breaking away from family control, which also includes the family business. Whilst the Afro-Trinidadian higglers, and suitcase traders, identified working for a large firm as a loss of independence, the Indo-Trinidadian workers saw it as a way of breaking out of a rural, isolated existence. Like work itself, independence is another relative concept, and its meaning is subject to various interpretations.

In the Central Market, higglering is a means of making a living, but one which women may prefer to exchange for another higher status occupation. On the other hand, the Arima higgler values those occupations which accord her independence, job security, and the ability to support her household. More fortunate are the suitcase traders, who have been able to merge ideology with reality, through government assistance. They hold an ideology that work must be in accordance with an agreeable lifestyle, culture and religion. Work, to the older highway traders is undertaken to accumulate wealth, which will eventually enable them to attain greater social acceptance. The younger generation of all groups, however, are more conscious of portraying an image of poverty, rurality and backwardness. To them, work is a process to acquire social acceptability and independence from family tradition. The extent to which traditional informal trading occupations like higglering will remain is debatable, given the different aspirations of the younger generation.

Table 8.6 Job Preferences of the Highway Traders

Preferred Job	Number of Traders citing the job as preferred	Reasons Given
Own business	1	Own boss Higher income More respect
Office work in Port of Spain	2	Modern Social respect Independence
BWIA Steward	1	International Allows travel Independence Social respect
Public sector	1	Better income Live in PoS Good job
No preferred occupation	10	

Perceptions of Good and Bad Jobs in Trinidad: The Influence of Gender, Ethnicity and Space

By identifying occupational characteristics which are important to informal traders, a number of other factors came to light. One noticeable pattern centres upon the confinement of higglers' perceptions of work to traditional female occupations, such as clothing and child-care. Another, is related to perceptions of independence, which differed according to ethnicity and gender. In order to explore these concepts further, respondents were asked to identify what they regarded as three of the best, or 'good', jobs on offer in Trinidad, and also three of the worst or 'bad' jobs. From these responses, identification could be made of the perceived advantages, and disadvantages, relating to different occupations, and of the status which workers' ascribe to their own position in the work force.

"That's a 'Good' Job": The Perceptions of Four Groups of Informal Traders

In general, the occupations which traders' viewed as 'good' could be divided into two categories; jobs which they, or other associates, had direct experience of; and those jobs which they knew little about, but which they perceived to be good due to societal images. For example, one higgler stated that being a seamstress was 'good' from her own experiences. In her mind, a 'good job' afforded independence and the ability to work from home, so she could care for her children. Another trader thought that being a lawyer was a 'good job', as it was portrayed in a popular soap 'the Young and the Restless' as being a glamorous and high status occupation, but she recognised that she had little direct knowledge of the occupation. Trinidadian society tends to interpret a 'good job' as a well-respected formal occupation, which is also modern and internationally recognised. Good examples of these occupations are marketing, insurance or banking, and popular American soaps do little to deconstruct this image. During the discussions, many traders differentiated between what they regarded as a good job in their own social environment, and what society had taught them to recognise as good. These two interpretations produced a variety of responses, and varied both between the four interview groups, and within them.

The occupations which both the Central Market and Arima higglers considered to be 'good', were rather limited in their scope. Table 8.7 highlights the occupations suggested, and provides an indication of the percentage of higglers who selected the same occupation as one of their three responses. A total of 24 different occupations were suggested by the Central Market higglers, and only 19 by the higglers interviewed in Arima. Of the total responses given by the Central Market higglers, owning a shop, working for the government, and the airlines, each accounted for 14 per cent. Although owning a shop and working for the government were also popular with Arima higglers, their most frequently cited 'good job' was office work, with working in the media or in a medical profession, following closely behind. On close examination, however, a number of these jobs have close similarities and as such, may be placed within a limited number of occupational categories based on similar qualities, shown in Table 8.8. It is important to note that some jobs may fall into more than one category. For example hairdressing, which is a traditional female occupation, is often run as a self-employed business.

Many of the occupations chosen by the higglers conform to a traditional ideology of female work, association with self-employment and independence, or the achievement of higher social status through white-collar occupations. Even the white collar jobs suggested, do not occupy high positions on the occupational ladder, as they tend to be administrative, and female dominated. As few high status jobs were mentioned, higglers' perceptions of work appear to be constrained by their own ability, in a similar manner to their preferred occupations. In this respect, women's limited perception of their ability tends to restrict their view of work. This encourages them to look for traditionally female, or low-status occupations. Despite these overall trends, perceptions of work do vary between the Central Market and Arima higglers.

Firstly, Arima higglers' identification of good jobs were more limited than the younger, urban counterparts. Secondly, as displayed in Table 8.8, Arima higglers were less concerned with white-collar office jobs, but were more aware of the 'good reputation' of professional jobs. Only government, and 'office work' were regarded as 'good' by the Arima higglers, not so much for their higher status, but for their job security and 'easy' reputation. Their younger counterparts, who work in Central Market are likely to be more influenced by image and the 'office lime', confirming the important influence of environment and perceived space. A total of 66 per cent of the Central Market higglers also identified their preferred occupation as a 'good job'.

When the suitcase traders were faced with the same discussion, their interpretations of work were more ambitious, and extended beyond their own experiences. As previously discussed in chapter 7, their high level of education and previous formal sector occupations, had provided many of the suitcase traders with an insight into many diverse occupations. More outspoken than the higglers, the suitcase traders stated that they place the greatest value on their own perceptions of good work, and are not influenced by societal pressures and international images.

The second difference between suitcase traders and the higglers, was that where higglers had tended to suggest specific occupations, many of the traders' talked about general occupations and the qualities of 'good jobs'. Their interpretation of the construct 'good job' was inherently different, as a 'good job' was translated as a good way of making a living, thereby identifying activities which to others, particularly the highway traders, may not be construed as 'jobs' *per se*. Table 8.9 illustrates the

Table 8.7 Higglers' Perceptions of 'Good Jobs'

Occupations cited as 'Good Jobs' (three different examples given from each trader)	Number of Times an Occupation was Defined as 'Good' (displayed as a percentage of total responses) (n=45)	
	Central Market Higglers	Arima Higglers
Own shop	14	10
Government	14	10
British West Indian Airlines	10	0
Bank	6	2
Boutique	4	5
Hairdressing	4	2
Teacher	4	7
TV/Media	4	10
Office work	4	14
Clothes industry	4	4
Medical/Doctor	4	10
Dress designing	4	0
Suitcase trading	2	0
Public service	2	0
Lawyer	2	4
Tourist guide	2	0
Craft production	2	0
Church work	2	2
Carnival	2	0
Own farm	2	2
Travel agent	2	0
'Burger boys' (fast food chain)	2	0
Run guesthouse	2	0
Jewellery design	2	0
Own business	0	2
Home production	0	2
Beautician	0	2
Working at airport	0	2
No response	0	10
Total	100	100

Table 8.8 Occupational Categories of Higglers' 'Good Jobs'

Categories of 'Good Jobs'	Number of Times an Occupation was Defined as 'Good' (displayed as a percentage of total responses)	
	Central Market Higglers	Arima Higglers
Clothing/Fashion/Glamour	24	22
Office/White Collar	38	24
Operating Own Business	42	36
Professional Jobs	13	22

Table 8.9 Suitcase Traders' Perceptions of 'Good Jobs'

Occupations cited as 'Good Jobs' (three different examples given from each trader)	Number of Times an Occupation was Defined as 'Good' (displayed as a percentage of total responses)
<u>Specific Occupations</u>:	
Jobs associated with the environment	
Suitcase trading	11
Working in the People's Mall	7
Owning formal clothes stall	11
Small business ownership	7
Fashion/clothing industry	4
Craft production	2
Travel agency	2
Concert promotion	2
Crew for music band	2
Tour guide	2
Distributor	2
Import/export business	2
Smuggling	2
Carnival design	2
Other jobs	
Doctor	2
Government Minister	2
Teacher	2
Oil industry	2
Local Government	2
Work in theatre/arts	2
Sports industry	2
<u>Images of a 'Good Job'</u>	
Flexible working	2
Non-tax paying	2
Own boss	2
Working with 'brothers'	2
Local	2
Working for Trinidad	2
Work which allows you to 'be yourself'	2
Enough money for what you need	2
Enjoyment	2
Street job	2
Travelling job	2
Does some good	2
Total	100

'jobs', and qualities which the traders valued in work.

In a manner similar to other groups, many of the specific occupations suggested by the suitcase traders were associated with their own occupation and working environment. Their satisfaction with suitcase trading as an occupation led many trader's to talk of their favoured jobs in the import/export business, and clothing industry. Small business ownership was also high on the list, as it appeared to be with the the other groups of workers. The booth owners link with Rastafarianism and Afro-Caribbean culture, has also given rise to an interest in local artforms and music. Occupations, which were seen as promoting indigenous culture, were also deemed to be 'good'. Noticeably, many of the jobs suggested by the traders, such as assisting on a music tour, have a high enjoyment factor, but do not provide a stable income. There are probably many occupations which the higglers would also enjoy, but these are not considered to be 'good' jobs as they do not provide stable income for their families, or enable them to run the household. This highlights a fundamental difference between individual perceptions on the purpose of work, and perceptions which are based on age, family responsibility, gender and ethnicity. Many suitcase traders also offered their own images of what a good job entails. They are fortunate to be able to idealise about work, and how it should promote personal beliefs and satisfaction, as demonstrated by a number of responses:

> A good job is one where you make enough money for ya needs, ya rent, ya food, the lime!

> Whatever work ya do is good if it lets ya live how ya want to live, not how any other person say ya have to live. Me, I like a job which I can relate to, as a Rastafarian.

One respondent with a university degree stated:

> If you like what ya do, it's a good job ya know, no matter what others say. People always say 'dat's bad, dat's no good for a boy like you, what do you tink we educate ya for boy'. My family get so vexed when I says I givin' up working for the no good government, and I going on the streets. My mother she not talk to me for months, she real vexed about what her neighbours in Diego would say. Dat's the trouble with Trinidad ya know, everybody moan 'bout about de British, but now they gone everyone wanna act like dem! It's madness! Here in the Mall, people real happy ya know, and dey make a livin, now that's a good job if ya ask me.

The ideology, held by the traders, is commendable and is somewhat radical for Trinidad. However favourable their work ethic appears to be, the day to day reality of a higgler's life, on the other hand, does not allow for indulgence, or the perusal of personal goals. As discussed in chapter 9, political support for a particular ethnic group, in this case the Afro-Trinidadian Vendors' Association, is an important enabler in the informal sector. Unfortunately, history has largely been responsible for the inclusion of the lower-income Indo-Trinidadian workforce into a limited number of occupations, of which agriculture plays a major role.

Amongst the highway traders, there was a definite distinction between perceptions of work according to the trader's age. Older, more established traders observed a work ethic which involved many years of hard work to attain increased wealth, and social status. Highway traders hold no idealised notion of work being enjoyable, or permitting a lifestyle, like that of the suitcase traders. Rather, work is a means to an end, and is best undertaken as a family-based operation. Many highway traders are willing to work long hours in poor conditions, to further their goal of successful business development. The younger traders, who mostly worked as part of a family unit, stated their desire to rebel against this traditional work ethic. Work to them was a means of gaining social acceptance, and a modern Trinidadian, rather than East Indian, lifestyle, a factor shown in Table 8.10.

Many of the jobs discussed by the highway traders conformed to the traditional image of the Indo-Trinidadian domination of agriculture. A number of highway traders perceived farm ownership and associated occupations, such as fruit processing, as good jobs. Indo-Trinidadian acceptability in, and dominance of, agricultural trades may also explain their preference for this type of work. A common theme throughout this chapter has been the popularity of self-employment and small business development, to which the highway traders provide no exception.

Another noticeable pattern, is that many of the jobs are located in male dominated industries, such as construction, and transport. Many of the highway traders still hold an image of work which conforms to a patriarchal model, perceiving work as a male dominated activity, although women's work within the family business, or household, is a necessary addition. This may also be due to the fact that the majority of occupations undertaken by women, are rarely seen as 'good jobs' by others. What is clear, however, is that highway traders' perceptions of work are clearly influenced by the ability to earn a decent living, and achieve social status through occupations which other Trinidadians have abandoned. The younger respondents hold images of work which correspond more with those of the Central Market higglers, than with their older colleagues. In general, 'working for the government' appears to held in high esteem in Trinidad, a factor which may be attributable to Eric Williams' promotion of nationalisation in the 1970s. Government employment is often synonomous with respectability and good work throughout the Third World.

The Gendering of 'Bad Jobs' in Trinidad: Image and Reality

During the interviews, respondents were asked to identify three jobs which they considered to be the most undesirable occupations in Trinidad. This was undertaken to determine whether workers in the informal sector perceive many informal occupations, including their own, to be undesirable, and amongst the worst occupations on offer. Identification of the least desirable occupations in Trinidad, shown in Table 8.11, resulted in a greater consensus between groups as to the nature of a 'bad job'. The responses were subsequently divided into five categories: agricultural, domestic service/industry, trading, miscellaneous and image. The distribution of reponses within these categories highlights a number of interesting patterns.

Firstly, three groups identified general agriculture and farming occupations as bad jobs, despite the fact that the higglers are currently employed in agricultural related occupations. One third of Central Market and Arima higglers, and 40 per cent of suitcase traders, cited farming/agriculture as one of their three most undesirable occupations. Within the same category, 33 per cent of highway traders stated specifically that sugar cane work was a poor job, although it was not mentioned by any female traders. The general dislike of agriculture not only conforms to the societal stigma attached to occupations within it, but highlights its reputation for low wages and back-breaking work. Working in the sugar industry was not held in high regard by the highway traders due to their direct knowledge of the industry, which is now associated with Indo-Trinidadian labour. Other occupations mentioned by the higglers included working with animals, which the Central Market higglers particularly disliked, pluck n' gut, forestry and fruit packing. Many higglers had direct experience of these occupations, and argued that they were arduous, low-paid and traditional in nature.

Secondly, the domestic/service industry category contained the occupations most frequently cited as 'bad'. Not surprisingly, domestic occupations were unanimously regarded as extremely undesirable. In total, 40 per cent of the Central Market higglers, 60 per cent of Arima higglers, 53 per cent of suitcase traders and 46 per cent of highway traders the female-dominated occupation as a 'bad job'. Within this category other frequently cited occupations, by all groups, included working in a fast-food restaurant/bar, cleaning the road and garbage collection. Responses, however, also varied between the four groups.

Images of domestic service consist of hard work, poor conditions, and no respect, which are reminiscent of slavery. To a higgler, domestic service is also characterised by a loss of independence. Many of the other jobs listed are commonly seen to be undesirable, due to their association with poverty and degradation, such as garbage collection, or a service such as waitressing. An important factor which emerged during the interviews, was that 40 per cent of Central Market higglers, and 66 per cent of Arima higglers, had previously undertaken an occupation which they cited as 'bad'. Three important factors may be drawn from this association.

Firstly, as previously noted, people's perceptions of work are preconditioned by their own experiences. Secondly, many women are forced to undertake occupations which they themselves view as

Table 8.10 Highway Traders' Perceptions of 'Good Jobs'

Good Job	Number of Times an Occupation was Defined as 'Good' (displayed as a percentage of total responses)
Jobs suggested by traders aged over thirty	
Small business development	16
Farm ownership	14
Agricultural processing	10
Agro-industry (chemicals, etc.)	10
Market gardening	4
Insurance	2
Finance/money lender	2
Storage and distribution	2
Construction business	2
Government Minister	2
Own business	2
Fishing business	2
Hotel industry - Tobago	4
Hardware	2
Jobs suggested by traders under thirty years of age	
Government	10
Office work	4
Oil industry	4
TELCO (Telephone company)	2
BWIA	2
Own business	2
Lawyer	2
Total	100

Table 8.11 Perceptions of 'Bad Jobs' by Informal Traders

Bad Jobs	Number of Traders who cited an Occupation as a 'Bad Job'			
	Central Market Higglers	Arima Higglers	Suitcase Traders	Highway Traders
Agricultural				
Farming/Agriculture	5	5	6	1
Working with animals	3	1	0	0
Sugar cane worker	2	1	1	5
Pluck n' gut	1	0	0	0
Forestry	0	1	0	0
Fruit packing	1	0	0	0
Domestic/Service Industry				
Domestic	6	9	8	7
Hotel maid	3	0	0	0
Fast food restaurant/Bar	3	2	3	3
Road cleaner	2	3	1	2
Laundry work	1	4	0	0
Housework	0	1	0	0
Working in rum shack	0	2	0	4
Taxi driving	0	1	3	1
Bottle collector	2	0	0	0
Garbage collector	2	4	2	2
Trading				
Lottery ticket seller	4	2	1	3
Highway trading	1	0	1	0
Street trading	1	4	0	0
Suitcase trading	0	0	0	1
Drug trading	0	0	0	5
Miscellaneous				
Begging	1	1	0	0
Working in supermarket	2	3	0	0
Working in Port of Spain	1	0	0	0
Mining	0	1	0	1
Factory work	4	0	6	0
Oil industry	0	0	2	1
Prostitution	0	0	2	3
Police	0	0	2	0
Government jobs	0	0	2	0

Table 8.11 continued

Bad Jobs	Number of Traders who cited an Occupation as a 'Bad Job'			
	Central Market Higglers	Arima Higglers	Suitcase Traders	Highway Traders
As percentage of total traders				
Images of Bad Jobs				
Working in Frederick Street	0	0	0	1
Theft	0	0	0	2
Loss of self-respect	0	0	2	0
'White Jobs'	0	0	3	0
Immoral jobs - drugs, sex, alcohol	0	0	0	1
Women working on street	0	0	0	2

undesirable, for economic reasons. Thirdly, a number of higglers stated that they regarded their own occupation as bad, in comparison to other jobs, as they did not think very highly of their skills or attributes. Lack of confidence in their own worth, and ability, appeared to be widespread for both groups, suggesting their susceptibility to a view of women as being inferior to men, which is portrayed throughout society, and in the media.

Arima higglers had a dislike for domestic-related duties and for occupations associated with 'roughness' and urban living. For example, laundry work, working in a rum shack and taxi-driving featured in the responses. In addition, they were the only group to cite 'housework' as a 'bad job'. Relating back to chapter 7, it may be that the age, responsibility and location of the Arima higglers lead them to identify jobs which are directly known to them, such as laundry, or occupations which contradict their more rural lifestyle and beliefs. Many middle-aged Trinidadian women dislike the rum-shop 'lime', and would associate working in this environment as inappropriate. Other perceptions were a result of individual preferences. For example, one higgler stated that "any work in Port of Spain is bad work".

The Central Market higglers also chose occupations which they associated with distinct urban spaces. In addition to domestic work, Central Market higglers disliked the occupations of hotel maid, working in a restaurant/bar, road cleaning, and bottle and garbage collecting. All these occupations are most frequently found in Port of Spain, where the majority of the country's hotels and restaurants are located. In addition, the dirt and garbage found on the busy streets of Port of Spain increases the need for street cleaners and garbage collectors.

The suitcase traders' and highway traders' responses not only reflected familiarity with their own working spaces, but also dislike for what they see as women's work. Garbage collecting and street cleaning are familiar occupations to both traders as they make a living from the streets. Both groups of traders regarded these occupations as subservient, dirty and low-paid. Interestingly, 26 per cent of the highway traders also stated that working in a rum shack was a bad occupation, due to its association with feting and general promiscuity. Domestic labour and working in a fast-food outlet are both predominantly seen as women's jobs, which are also characterised by low-wages and low-status. Road cleaning and garbage collecting are also seen to be poor occupations. The indentification of many 'bad jobs' as being women's work is a perception that will be discussed in the next section of this chapter.

A number of trading occupations also featured in the survey. Lottery-ticket selling, identified in chapter 6 as another occupation undertaken by women, was seen to be 'bad' by all groups due to its low return. Highway trading, suitcase trading and street trading were also mentioned. A quarter of the Arima higglers expressed 'street trading' as a bad job due to concerns of safety and welfare. Only the highway traders included suit-case trading in this category as they see the occupation as being associated with crime and 'slackness'. Furthermore, 33 per cent mentioned trading in drugs, which suggests that many highway traders' perceptions of work relate more to their moral belief systems, than to other characteristics.

The miscellaneous, and image-related, categories mainly included the responses given by the suitcase and highway traders, highlighting their wider perceptions of work. The suitcase traders perceived a bad job to be one which restricts independence, and does not conform with their informal work ethic. Work associated with the public sector, such as the the government, the police force and the oil industry, is high on their list of undesirable jobs. Factory work was cited by 40 per cent of the suitcase traders as constituting a bad job. Factory work was also frequently mentioned by the Central Market higglers, many of whom had undertaken this type of work previously. Interestingly, both male groups also identified prostitution as a bad job.

A number of suitcase and highway traders responded by offering generalisations, some racialised, on the nature of jobs which they deemed to be bad. For example, the suitcase traders identified jobs which undermined their self-respect, along with what they saw as 'white jobs'. Although the suitcase traders' images of bad jobs reflected their preoccupation with lifestyle and independence, they were also linked to the general pattern of consensus. Whilst stating that many white-collar government jobs were bad, for reasons previously discussed, they also identified domestic service, agricultural occupations, and other service occupations as bad work. Other negative interpretations, included work which placed the employee in a subservient role, work which reduced self respect, and a general anti-institutional attitude.

In a similar manner, Indo-Trinidadian imagery of 'bad jobs' extends to cover those occupations which many of the older traders either considered to be contributing to the moral decline of the country, or which were against their own beliefs. For example, one trader talked about the 'immoral' work which some people do to make money in Trinidad. This included drug smuggling, theft, extortion, working in a rum shack, and prostitution. Furthermore, many highway traders held the general view that women's work is bad, as women should be confined to the home. Two highway traders also commented that women's work on the streets, such as trading, was bad, as women should not work on their own, or in public areas.

Despite individual interpretations on the negative qualities of different jobs, there was a general consensus amongst informal traders that domestic work, service occupations, agriculture, and many other female occupations are considered to be the worst jobs on offer in Trinidad. In order to explore this particular issue further, respondents were asked whether they thought there were jobs in Trinidad which were gender-specific, and if so, they were asked to cite three common women's jobs.

Gendered Jobs: Women's Work in Trinidad

In order to discover whether informal traders perceive certain occupations to be female, the respondents were asked to share their views on this subject. As the views given by both groups of higglers were very similar, the results have been amalgamated. Likewise, comparison will be made only with the responses of the male suitcase traders, as many highway trader's thought that these gender-related questions were unnecessary. This was probably a result of their personal views on gender.

Both the Central Market and Arima higglers stated that there were certain jobs which were almost exclusively undertaken by women, although their individual reasons for this gender division differed greatly. Table 8.12 highlights the jobs which the higglers regarded as being predominently female, and their explanations for this. The higglers identified domestic work, food preparation, making clothes, and their own trading, as typical female occupations in Trinidad. The majority of these occupations are associated with the adoption of perceived female skills, such as a caring mentality, the ability to undertake household duties, food preparation, and cleaning. Other jobs are associated with low pay, poor work and hard labour, and jobs which many men 'won't do'. The explanations given by the higglers for their beliefs can be categorised into three main groups.

Firstly, due to their need for economic autonomy, women are forced into undertaking menial jobs which men 'won't do'. Many higglers talked about the importance of male pride in Trinidad, and their unwillingness to do low status work. Others, supported men's avoidance of these jobs, as they 'deserve better work'. Secondly, women are restricted to occupations which allow them to work from home, or take into account their family duties, a process which had long been recognised. Thirdly, there is a general opinion among women that it is their role or duty to undertake certain occupations as 'that's the way it is'. Many of the older women were scornful of younger women 'trying to be men'. As children, many Caribbean women are socialised into stereotypical female roles by mothers, aunts and grandmothers. This socialisation leads to women believing that they have different skills from men, and that it is societally correct to fulfill these roles. Societal pressure, which enforces traditional codes of behaviour, is a powerful force throughout the Caribbean (Senior, 1991). It is generally accepted by the majority of the higglers that a women's role is predestined, and evolves around motherhood. Many are aware of the societal images which portray women as the caring providers of the nation. They are also fully aware that it is society which expects women to fulfill the roles of secretaries, waitresses and maids, but they are in acceptance of this.

As expected, the suitcase traders offered a more in-depth interpretation of women's work in Trinidad. The general consensus was that due to circumstances, women were limited in their occupational choice, a fact

Table 8.12 Women's Work: Perceptions of Female Traders

Occupational Type	Number of Higglers citing an Occupation as Female-Dominated	Reasons Given
Food Preparation	14	Men won't do it Female skills Perceived skill Taught at home Child socialisation Women know how
Domestic	10	Poor job Hard job Men too proud No respect People want women Men won't clean
Trading	10	Well-paid job Can't do other work Lack of education Family support Independence
Seamstress	10	Taught skills Women like fashion Home-based Women like clothes
Farming	6	Menial Hard work Poor pay
Secretarial	6	Men want women Typing skills Socialisation
Child-care	6	Lots of practice Female skills Men know nothing Home-based
Supermarket work	6	More understanding Men won't do it

Table 8.12 continued

Occupational Type	Number of Higglers citing an Occupation as Female-Dominated	Reasons Given
Hotel maid	4	Women clean better Poor job
Waitressing	4	Customer expectation Too menial for men
Family Care	2	Skills, practice
Craft Production	2	Home-based
Nursing	2	Caring job
Hairdresser	2	Women enjoy it
Beautician	2	Women train for it
Shop Assistant	2	Low wages
Laundry	1	Practice Poor work
Receptionist	1	Firms employ women Societal
Total Responses by 30 Higglers	90	

which is displayed in Table 8.13. Child-care responsibilities force women into taking any type of work they come across, which is usually work which others will not undertake. Furthermore, the suitcase traders recognised that older women may not have had the opportuinity for education or skill acquisition, and therefore they have to fall back on the skills which they accrued as a child, such as sewing, cooking, cleaning.

Despite their recognition that women are often disadvantaged in the labour force, many booth owners failed to comment on why younger women with decent educations still enter traditionally female occupations. Having commented that the concept of the People's Mall was not conducive to the advancement of female traders, many booth owners justified their position by returning to women's roles as mothers.

A number of booth owners were critical of younger women's inability to break away from family pressure and tradition. "Young women know that they not gettin' on, and that they shouldn't be treated with disrespect and poor jobs, but they accept it as their lot. I blame the grandmother's influence, they always pokin in you business saying 'girl help your mother' whilst her brother play in the yard. I tell ma sister all the time 'break away girl', I even offer her job wid me, but she don't know what's best".

Although the trader's fully recognise the problems faced by many female workers, and to a certain extent other ethnic groups, they benefit from the current status-quo. They are able to employ young women on low wages to work on their booths whilst they are travelling. They are fortunate to belong to a successful male-dominated organisation which accords them a well-paid occupation. Ironically, the male traders are more willing to discuss the many reasons why women are restricted to certain occupations, whilst the women interviewed accepted the situation as 'their lot'. Although a change in male attitudes is necessary for progress, the ultimate challenge lies with the ability of female workers to break away from their traditional images of work. However, until the government, and other institutions, work to alleviate some of the pressure exerted by household responsibilty on these women, there is little that they can do.

To further understand how the higglers felt about the status and worth of traditional female occupations, the category of 'women's jobs' was compared with the category of 'bad jobs', to see if there were any associations. A total of 66 per cent of the higglers interviewed had identified an occupation, which they had previously categorised as 'a bad job', as being a 'women's job' in this section of the survey. Occupations such as food preparation, working in a restaurant, farming, and domestic work, amongst others, were regarded by women as being undesirable on the one hand, but typical women's work on the other.

The association of poor jobs with typical women's work, by female workers themselves, suggests that there is a fundamental problem with women's perceptions of their own work, and its value. What is more disturbing, however, is that despite widespread recognition that women are

Table 8.13 Typical Women's Work: Male Perceptions

Specific Occupations	Images of Women's Work
Domestic work	Restricted by children
Higglering	Limited in scope
Shop Assistant	Traditional
Junior office jobs	Household skills
Secretarial	Poorer paid
Seamstress	Subservient
Home-based work	Under-valued
Data Processing	
Factory work	
Reasons	
Societal pressure	
Tradition	
Coping roles of elites/whites	
Unwillingness to change	
Don't stand up for themselves	
Have too many children	
Childhood socialisation	
Men's attitudes	
Government	
TV/Media	

undertaking many of the lowest status, and more undesirable jobs in Trinidad, society has worked towards female acceptance of this process. Chapter 9 presents an analysis of governmental policy, part of which is aimed to assist in altering people's traditional perceptions of work, so that greater equality can develop.

Conclusions: Image and Reality

There is undoubtedly a contradiction in Trinidad between worker's images of work, and reality. Female perceptions of work, which largely reflect the recognition that a women's place is in subservient, or traditional occupations, only serve to produce the motive for continued male repression. Women are often critical of male responsibility, their predeliction for feting, and yet they often defend the image of men as members of the stronger, more powerful, gender for which they should earn more money and get better jobs. If men are recognised as being irresponsible, women often defend them by referring to government policy, unemployment, and male pride, all of which excuse their behaviour. This is a prime example of how lower-income women have been socialised into accepting a traditional set of beliefs, which are thereby perpetuated.

The female higglers tended to hold very critical perceptions of the value of their work, and that of other women. 'Anti-women' attacks in Trinidad, have also been documented by Yelvington's (1993) work in a factory. Strangely, women have survived through the centuries by supporting one another in extended family networks, but often damage their collective power by their critical attitudes towards other women.

This research had shown that womens' occupational choice is constrained by their household responsibilities, their own perceptions of their role, and societal ideology. In addition, it is often only women, who will undertake undesirable jobs such as domestic work, which men refuse to do. As one higgler commented, 'men couldn't be maids, they wouldn't know what to do, and anyway they deserve better work, it's expected of them'. It is this image of expectation, which exerts a most powerful influence on the structure of the division of labour in the informal sector. Although many women did agree, in theory, that they could do other jobs, they stated that it would not 'be right'. To many women the informal sector allows them to support their families in an independent manner.

If, as it is suggested, racialised and gendered perceptions of work do confine workers to a limited set of occupations, this will have adverse affects on the standard of living of certain groups. Where disparities between urban and rural populations, or between agricultural and industrial workers exist, the broadening of people's perceptions on work can go a long way to assist. If workers do not feel constrained by tradition, or family ideology, they are better placed to venture into new occupations.

It is recognised that many workers are forced to undertake certain occupations due to family responsibility, lack of education, and income. Even here, it is still possible for workers to increase their job potential through a transformation of governmental and societal attitudes, and policy prescription. Financial and social disparities in Trinidad are geographically expressed in a number of different ways, such as the inequality between rural and urban areas, street and market environments, peripheral and central commercial areas. In many cases, workers are prevented from working in more profitable areas, due not only to real restrictions in their lives, but also to the ways in which different spaces are seen to be 'East Indian' or 'Afro-Caribbean', friendly or violent, female or male. There is much that the government can do in eradicating false images of space, which will also serve to enhance equality at work.

By advocating the adoption of a more positive view of informal sector work, which ascribes higher values to 'women's work' and alternative methods of work, it is not to suggest that Trinidadian workers should abandon their own belief system. The East Indian work ethic, for example, has many merits based on family co-operation and shared aspirations. What does need to be challenged, is the prevalent image of Indo-Trinidadian traders as backward and of low social status. As documented in this chapter, many highway traders, despite their success, experience hostility from other social groups based on a collective negative image. Likewise, motherhood is a powerful image in the Caribbean, and one which is unlikely to alter. Instead, the government needs to awaken to the important role undertaken by Trinidadian women, and employ ways to assist in their support of the young. Many higglers argued that if they were not solely responsible for their children's welfare, they might be able to develop more dynamic businesses.

Through this series of ethnographic insights into the informal sector, it has been established that people's ideas about work are influenced by three different processes. Firstly, workers build their own perceptions of work, which relate to personal experience and socialisation. These ideas about work are circulated and maintained via social networks which are often based on shared gender and kinship ties. Secondly, workers are influenced by a wider societal ideology on the division of labour, which positions individuals in different jobs according to dominant ideas about appropriate work and behaviour which are influenced by processes of racialised gendering. For example, agricultural occupations are seen as suitable for young Indo-Trinidadian men but defined as undesirable by many Afro-Trinidadian workers. Thirdly, individuals, and groups, face obstacles from their own histories, family responsibilities and economic circumstance. Chapter 9 examines the ways in which some informal sector policies in Trinidad have worked to maintain traditional images of work, and how others attempt to break down the established division of labour. Chapter 9 discusses whether the observations made in this chapter, can be effectively translated into practical policy suggestions. In particular, the ability for women to access productive spaces and command resources is central to understanding their ability to overcome economic hardship.

9 Governmental Response to Informal Employment: Micro Level Support as a Strategy for Development

Introduction

This chapter aims to provide an evaluation of a number of programmes, implemented by the NAR, the government in power until December 1991, which were targeted at assisting informal sector participants and small business development. The first author spent a period of time working in each of the schemes, and in a number of governmental departments, where the data for this chapter were gathered. Following an introduction which considers the history of informal sector legislation in Trinidad, the chapter presents a brief evaluation of the main informal sector programmes which were operative in 1990/1991, and outlines the perspectives of informality held by government departments involved with the sector. Secondly, the chapter focuses specifically on a particularly important programme, the Youth Training and Employment Partnership Programme (YTEPP), where the first author spent a number of weeks working with the participants. Within this section, data collected using social surveying techniques to determine the views of YTEPP participants, are also presented.

Thirdly, consideration is given as to whether current government policies recognise the salience of the gender, ethnic and spatial divisions which characterise the informal sector, and if so, whether there is any attempt to promote greater equality between groups. In conclusion, the chapter highlights the People's Mall as a case study of a successful project discussed in chapters 7 and 8, but one which is gender and ethnic specific. In this light, consideration is given to the benefit of such gender/ethnic specific projects, and whether a uniform series of policies would be more successful in encouraging growth in all areas of informal activity. Finally, the chapter evaluates the role of government policy in overcoming traditional stereotypes and inequality, and asks if the government is also responsible for the lack of opportunity for certain ethnic and gender groups.

According to the government, informal economic activity is not strictly legal in Trinidad, as it escapes detection, legislation and tax. In particular, the police are given the power, under the Highways Act 50, to impound informal traders, those people engaged in 'willful obstruction of the passage-way' or 'vending on the footpath', and vendors displaying goods on railings, buildings, or littering the streets. In the last two decades, the Mayors of Port of Spain and San Fernando have instigated campaigns to clear the streets and highways of informal trading. The justification for periodic street clearing is centred around concern over the congestion of streets, hygiene, nuisance from traders, and unfair competition with the owners of formal stores.

Informal trading was not favoured during the mid 1980s, but tolerance has increased in the 1990s, due to severe unemployment. As in many other developing countries, the current consensus in Trinidad is that informal economic activity is still illegal, although certain activities may be actively encouraged in times of recession (De Soto, 1989; Simon and Birch 1992; Portes *et al*, 1989). Hence, informal sector participants find themselves on insecure ground, being tolerated one month and subject to fines the next.

As a colonial state, Trinidad witnessed a substantial rise in informal street trading and 'hawking', after the emancipation of slaves in the mid 1800s. Many ex-slaves, particularly women, turned to hawking fruit and vegetables grown on their own plots to supplement their income, a topic which was fully explored in chapter 7. In addition, the importation of indentured labour to work on the plantations led to a surge in Syrian, Lebanese and East Indian street hawkers, who traded in cloth, trinkets and household goods in Port of Spain. The colonial authorities tolerated this wave of informal activity as it provided a useful internal distribution mechanism, at no cost to the British government. Despite the government's overall tolerance of the street traders, there were still periodic street clearances, often involving short stays in jail, to show that the government was in control of the situation (Gilmore, 1940). Periodic street clearing exercises, carried out by the police, are a familiar and widely used tool of many government authorities. De Soto (1989), provides a detailed account of the historical evolution of street trading which identifies the early emergence of state repression in many developing countries.

As the number of informal activities in Trinidad began to grow in the 1950s, the government began to show greater concern over the sector's development. The post Second World War colonial government, which encouraged policies of modernisation and industrial growth, regarded the informal sector as a sign of under-development and backwardness. The stigma attached to unemployment and visible informal activity, such as street trading, caused the government to clamp down on the sector, and to encourage traders to utilise government markets. Street vendors are a popular target for government repression, as they are visible and more easily identified than other participants of the sector. Although there are similar legal restrictions on informal production and home-based work, the government has less chance of successfully locating these activities.

As documented in chapter 3, the failure to achieve full employment was at its most evident in the oil boom of the 1960s and 1970s, as Trinidad poured wealth into its industrial base, at the expense of job creation. At this time, a large informal sector was evidence of the government's failure to command the economy. In retaliation, informal workers were regularly fined and jailed, in an attempt to push informal trading underground, and away from the prestige areas of Port of Spain.

By contrast, the 1980s saw new governmental attitudes to informal sector work throughout the developing world, following the collapse of many oil-led economies. Uncontrollable unemployment, poverty and debt lead many governments to reappraise their employment policies (Thomas, 1992). Gradually, with assistance from the International Labour Office, governments turned their attention to the informal sector, which was virtually self-sufficient, required little government support, and appeared to provide an expanding haven for the survival of the urban poor. Towards the late 1980s, the informal sector began to be regarded by governments as a more acceptable alternative to unemployment, as it allowed the reproduction of the labour force at little public expense. Although it was not seen as the most efficient strategy, it was a tolerable alternative to massive poverty, and popular revolution.

An additional momentum behind this change in attitude lay with the increase in the self-help type development strategy, which focused upon helping people help themselves (Mangin 1967; Eyre, 1972; Turner, 1982). Along with the governments of other developing nations, Trinidad recognised that it was unable to sustain an economy which could provide jobs for the labour force in the immediate future. Its inability to provide work, or a suitable alternative in the form of social security, gave the government little choice but to accept the informal sector as a permanent provider of employment.

Towards the late 1980s, the Trinidadian government turned its attention from formal sector job creation to encouraging small business development, and entrepreneurship. The NAR, the party in power until December 1991, attempted to assist the informal sector as a tool for development by employing a variety of different strategies, some of which were more advanced in their conceptualisation than their Latin American neighbours. As part of their overall strategy of promoting a 'people's sector', the NAR recognised the importance of the informal sector in providing jobs in the 1990s.

Continued unemployment had identified the informal sector as a permanent feature of society, and not as a temporary response to economic pressure. Attitudes towards the sector began to change, as its capacity to absorb the increasing numbers of unemployed workers increased. Although a decision had been made to assist informal operations, problems were encountered in devising policies to assist informal sector participants. Problems centred upon the unprecedented growth of the sector, the increasing number of diverse informal occupations in Trinidad, and the wide-ranging location of activities. In addition, the informal sector was adopting a social cause, in that it had begun to be associated with 'people power', indigenous culture and radical political ideology, all of which represented unfamiliar entities to the government.

Support for the sector has lead to a general easing of regulations, and a tolerance of informal growth, by the government in most areas of the country. Not surprisingly, traders and irregular businesses are still being cleared, by force if necessary, from prestigious neighbourhoods, and parts of Port of Spain. One such area is the Queen's Park Savannah, a public park in central Port of Spain, where vendors selling food and coconut water are periodically cleared. One campaign, launched by the Mayor of Port of Spain in June 1990, was met by public outrage in support of coconut vendors in this area.

In line with the actions of other developing countries, the 1990s have seen a more positive response to the dilemma of informal sector growth in Trinidad (Tokman, 1989). Policies of active encouragement and direct assistance to informal sector participants, have emerged in the form of a number of programmes aimed at assisting the informal sector, and bringing it into line with the mainstream economy. In addition, plans have been developed to undertake a wide-ranging study of national informal activity, and the national census has been amended to include questions which relate directly to informality (Central Statistical Office, 1991). At the time of this research, the Trinidad Government were actively promoting a number of informal occupations.

Formalising the Informal Sector: An Evaluation of Public Sector Programmes in Trinidad

In the late 1980s, the Government of Trinidad and Tobago estimated that between 80,000 to 100,000 new jobs would need to be created in order to put a large sector of the youthful population back to work. Solutions to the escalating problem of unemployment centred around job creation schemes that would help workers find sustainable employment. Past job generation schemes, particularly those of the 1970s, had high failure rates due to the schemes being centred solely on financing operations with little additional support. A more successful concept, it appeared, would involve a package of structured support which included practical training and the development of business skills. In addition, the government would provide a financial support system which would distribute loans and grants to prospective entrepreneurs. The target population of the new programmes was to be the 18 to 25 year old age group who were the group facing the greatest difficulties in obtaining work.

The government looked to the informal sector for the solution to youth unemployment. It centred its campaign on creating vehicles for stimulating self-employment, which were largely manifested in the informal sector. Attention was paid to training the young to become self-sufficient entrepreneurs, and future developers of small businesses. The informal sector appeared to be a good area for entrepreneurial expansion, and one which was open to the young and unskilled. More importantly, pressure from society to conform to a western life-style, identified in chapter 8, encourages many young workers to chase high status, white-collar, formal jobs. Policies aimed at assisting the young must therefore confront, and understand, the societal structure which enforces traditional codes of behaviour.

A series of government reports which aimed to identify possible targets for assistance, recognised five major obstacles to employment for the young: a poor attitude towards job creation conditioned by society; a lack of education; the absence of marketable skills; an inability to gain work experience; and barriers to financial and technical support (Ministry of Mobilisation and Planning, 1989). In addition to these obstacles, the present research has identified traditional perceptions of work as another barrier to improvement.

As part of an overall strategy to support the informal sector, the government developed a two-part programme. Firstly, they were interested in receiving policy suggestions from two governmental departments concerned with the operations of the informal sector, the Ministry of Town and Country Planning, and the Ministry of Mobilisation and Planning. Secondly, a number of separate programmes were developed to assist with specific issues such as funding, training or education. In 1991, the main institutions consisted of the Small Business Development Corporation (SBDC), the Labour Intensive Development Programme (LID), the Apprenticeship for Industrial Mobilisation (AIM), YTEPP, and the further development of a number of existing projects, such as the People's Mall in Frederick Street and the traders of Independence Square.

The Ministry of Town and Country Planning

The Ministry of Town and Country Planning is the physical planning tool of the government, and is responsible for development control, land-use planning, highway construction, and urban redevelopment. In relation to the informal sector, the Ministry governs the locations of markets, plans for the development of new roads, highways and pedestrian areas, and is often instrumental in upholding the Highways Laws. As the Ministry's Director stated when interviewed, "the very nature of the informal sector presents problems for planners. Our team work hard for months developing a new traffic scheme, or pedestrian centre, and within weeks informal traders spill onto the pathways, or the roads/obstruct the traffic, and all our plans fall apart. We redevelop an urban area for residential land-use, but informal businesses still operate when they should not. Sometimes they cause danger to themselves, and the public".

The department has had dealings with the informal sector for many years, as informal sector participants are often in breach of formal planning laws. The planners have previously supported street clearing exercises, and although they are more tolerant in the current political climate, they still advocate the formalisation of informal activities. The ideology of the Town and Country Planning Department is built upon formality and order, which is at odds with the nature of informal employment.

There are a number of specific planning concerns which are associated with street vending. These include inadequate retailing space in markets, leading to the overcrowding of vendors in the sidewalks; inadequate facilities for goods display; inadequate garbage disposal for market vendors; traffic congestion resulting from sidewalk crowding; unsafe structures; noise and visual pollution; unaesthetic planning; and non-conformity to design standards.

Of paramount concern is the increase in highway trading, discussed in chapters 5 and 7. According to the planners the death toll of highway traders is increasing as is the number of accidents caused by cars stopping to purchase goods, although statistical evidence could not be found. At peak traffic times, highway traders can be seen weaving around vehicles travelling at 80km speeds or more. The increasing level of commuting from the East and South, to Port of Spain, has led to a rise in the number of highway vendors. During the evening rush hour (4-5pm), the highways are strewn with vendors walking in and around stopped cars, and with cars queuing from the highway to stop at a stall.

In 1991, there was a marked effort to restrict highway trading along the Valsayn, St Augustine, section of the Churchill Roosevelt Highway. The Town and Country Planning Department instructed the clearance of all vendors along this stretch of road, due to concerns over safety. The highway traders saw the movement as an act of discrimination, forced by the residents of the elite housing developments which surround this area. Protests from nearby residents against highway trading had identified the activity as a contributor to the unaesthetic nature of the area and to increases in crime. As a result of the campaign, groups of highway traders were forcibly removed from their stalls, often following violent confrontations with the police. The disturbances reached local news, as many traders faced jail sentences and heavy fines for confronting the police. The traders argued that similar action had not been taken against other trading groups such as the vendors in Port of Spain, and as such the action represented discrimination.

As a solution to the problem, the authorities built a large open market, farther east along the highway. Macoya Market was established to provide market space for the evicted highway traders, so they could continue with their fruit and vegetable trade. A number of basic stalls, and some enclosed units, were also provided. Many traders were forced to relocate to another area, or take advantage of the new market facilities.

The planning department had not consulted the needs of the traders, and there were a number of flaws in the project. Firstly, the market was off the highway, and not as visible as the previous stalls. Many customers did not visit Macoya Market, but took their business to other traders located nearer to Port of Spain, where they were still able to operate. Informal trading is spontaneous, and as highway traders explain, a visit to Macoya is more akin to visiting a supermarket, than a quick stop along the highway. Secondly, the unaesthetic nature of the market, with its confined small stalls, made many customers wary of stopping, particularly at night when traders' business is good.

Thirdly, and most importantly, the market is located on the wrong side of the highway to attract the best custom. Macoya market is situated on the left-hand side of the East-West lane of the highway, and catches the traffic going into Port of Spain in the morning rush-hour. Customers are more likely to purchase goods on their way home from work due to convenience. Few people will buy goods on the way to work, as such goods will perish in the heat. The combination of these factors resulted in a dramatic decline in traders' incomes and after two months, traders gradually began to reappear along the highway in their old locations.

The Macoya example is just one attempt by planners to force informal traders into a formal market environment. When it is poorly planned, and gives no consideration to the needs of traders, then such a scheme is unlikely to be successful. As established in chapters 5 and 6, different participants have different needs, and preferences for location. Although the highway trader favours a random highway location, the Macoya Market scheme may have been of greater use to a more specific group, such as female vendors who are afraid of working along the highway. Given the right environment, a more open planned development and some clever advertising, Macoya market could have provided a traditional market place for female vendors, which would also be popular with customers. Eventually, a type of formalisation, based on the People's Mall ideology, could offer the next stage of the development. Instead by late 1992, Macoya Market was virtually empty.

The Ministry of Mobilisation and Planning

The Social Sector's Unit of the Ministry of Mobilisation and Planning, is responsible for strategic social, economic and planning matters of national importance. The Social Sector's Unit identifies the informal sector as a vibrant component of the economy, which can contribute to the social and economic development of Trinidad, if an active policy of promotion is adopted. The Unit's latest task is to launch an in-depth study into the informal sector which incorporates a sociological profile of the categories of operations and operators. The estimated cost of the project is TT$250,000 (£40,000) and was due to commence in 1993. The Central Statistical Office is also setting up an informal register. International Agencies such as the United Nations Economic Commission for Latin

America and the Caribbean (ECLAC) have also provided some funding for informal sector activities.

Financing the Informal Entrepreneur - the Small Business Development Company Limited (SBDC)

The main objective of the Small Business Development Company Ltd, which was registered in 1989, is to promote the rapid and widespread expansion of small businesses and informal-enterprises in all areas of business activity. The company is interested in providing support for small business development, and has been designed to work closely with graduates from the Youth Training and Employment Policy Partnership (YTEPP). It aims to help informal entrepreneurs by providing four major services. Firstly, and most importantly, there is the 'Loan Guarantee Plan' which was set up to help small and informal sector businesses with no collateral. Furthermore, few entrepreneurs have an established track record to obtain loans from private lending institutions. Loans are provided for the expansion of business, new equipment, or a change of location. The SBDC is supposed to encourage businesses to move away from central Port of Spain to less populated regions of Trinidad in order to promote regional growth. The company states that it aims to lend small amounts of money, not obtainable elsewhere, to those businesses which are uncreditworthy due to the operator's informality or gender. In this way, it helps with the purchase of a small piece of equipment, such as a sewing machine or lawnmower.

The SBDC does not provide the loan itself, rather it guarantees a loan through one of its participating private agencies, or banks. It will guarantee up to 85 per cent of a loan which must not exceed TT$150,000 (£18,000), to new businesses which have been in operation less than one year, and to informal sector operators. The borrower has to be able to put down 15 per cent of the loan as guarantee. The interest rates are variable, but are usually 1 per cent above base rate, and loan periods are of up to 5-7 years, with repayment intervals to be agreed.

The conditions attached to the loan, although not unreasonable, may represent a frightening liability to a street trader. Apart from the financial conditions, the application process provides more obstacles for the informal entrepreneur. In order to be considered for a loan, the applicant must complete a Business Plan. This plan, together with an application form, is sent to the lender who assesses the risk, and then advises the SBDC as to whether they should recommend a guarantee. The most important decisions are still made by the commercial banks, and not the SBDC who are more sympathetic to informal operators. As a result, a large proportion of loan applications are refused and the SBDC had only guaranteed loans prior to 1992.

Despite its good intentions, the programme fails to assist those informal workers, for whom it was designed to help. In addition, although the

SBDC considers a wide-range of businesses, priority is given to energy-related products, agro-industry, light manufacturing and tourism. As shown in chapters 5 and 6, these activities are rarely undertaken by informal operators due to the large amounts of capital required, and the difficulty in establishing manufacturing businesses. Chapter 8 highlighted the fact that these occupations are mostly undertaken by men and as a result, the SBDC indirectly excludes many female entrepreneurs. During an interview, an SBDC advisor stated that they did not like to recommend loans for clothing businesses, catering or trading, as there were already too many of these operating in Trinidad. Before funding polices of this nature are successful in promoting equality in the informal sector, attention needs to be paid to encouraging women to enter manufacturing occupations, and to assisting in the wider societal acceptance of this transformation. In reality, a majority of informal workers in Trinidad who are employed in service industries, will be unable to secure assistance from this scheme.

The Apprenticeship for Industrial Mobilisation (AIM), and the Labour Intensive Development Programme (LID)

AIM, which in also run in conjunction with YTEPP, provides work experience for 4,000 trainees every year. The scheme was based on the Youth Training Scheme (YTS) which was introduced in the UK in the 1980s. AIM, however, was abandoned in 1991 due to allegations of the exploitation of young workers. Other projects, which are co-ordinated under LID, attempt to devise public sector works to make use of unemployed labour, such as road building and housing developments. The impetus behind public works has declined under the restrictions placed by the International Monetary Fund.

The only successful scheme operating in 1991 was the 'Cottage Industry Programme'. This scheme, which was developed under the Labour Intensive Development Plan, focuses upon the garment industry and is one of the only schemes which is of direct benefit to women. The idea is based on the fact that large firms can afford to import cloth in large quantities, thereby reducing production costs and ultimately, the cost of the garment. The informal sector producer, and retailer, cannot compete against the large stores as they do not have the resources, or storage facilities, to purchase large amounts of material. LID buys the material in bulk, and sells it at a cheap rate to the informal entrepreneur in small amounts. It has also assisted with establishing clothes producing co-operatives, often for female workers.

Youth Training and Employment Partnership Programme (YTEPP)

The Youth Training and Employment Partnership Programme was started in 1988, and became a state corporation in October 1991. Recent attention has been focused on the programme by the World Bank, which has agreed to fund 60 per cent of the company's annual expenditure. Mr Leslie Bowrin, Programme Manager, kindly allowed the first author to take an active role within the scheme, provided access to data, gave permission for discussions with participants and ultimately, allowed attendance at board meetings. These included discussion of the informal sector with a team from the World Bank. In return, work was undertaken on the programme, and assistance was given in establishing a review of academic research and literature on informal activity.

The focus behind the programme stems from an ideology which identifies education as one of the most important factors in obtaining successful employment. The Trinidadian government promotes vocational training for a broad range of informal sector occupations, as a major aim of employment policy. The focus of YTEPP is on the trainee adopting an adaptable skill, or trade, along with a keen entrepreneurial spirit. The key words of the scheme are 'train, produce, and market'. It prepares the young unemployed to master skills that will assist them in employment, through the undertaking of a number of different modules. YTEPP is also unique in that its training is geared towards many non-traditional jobs, not usually found in other programmes, but which are commonly offered in the informal sector market. A good example of this is the 'house planning' module, which aims to instruct basic architectural techniques, to assist in informal sector housing projects.

To enter the programme, a prospective trainee must be between the ages of 15-25 years, out of school, and unemployed. Although the scheme aims to facilitate entry into all areas of employment, one of its major aims is to encourage and train young people for self-employment, much of which will be in the informal sector of the economy due to current economic conditions. In this respect, the programme offers specific job skills and hands-on experience, as well as training in small business management and communication skills.

In addition to assisting the young, YTEPP are also trying to reduce stereotyping of jobs in relation to ethnicity, gender and location. Stereotypical beliefs that the best entrepreneurs are from an East Indian background, and that agriculture is an undesirable occupation, are some of the views which YTEPP is trying to change.

Changing Traditional Perceptions of Employment: An Evaluation of YTEPP

This section of the chapter presents a two-fold analysis of the success of the YTEPP project in promoting a new ethos of work, which is based on informal self-employment. Firstly, it presents the results of information collected from YTEPP on the success rates of their trainees. The data available refer to graduates of the scheme who have undertaken a variety of occupations since graduation from the scheme, including small business development, self employment and home-based production. YTEPP produces an annual list of results, which displays the success rates of graduates in obtaining work. A more advanced evaluation is also conducted on graduates who have attained self-employment in the informal sector, or other small business ventures. Details of previous course participation were provided, along with information on the nature of the business, its location, and the trainee's gender and ethnicity.

Secondly, YTEPP gave their permission to interview ten current students, in order to assess their perceptions of different occupations. The group consisted of ten randomly selected students aged between 18 and 21. Following initial discussion, it was decided that personal construct theory, and the associated repertory-grid test, was a suitable method of social analysis (Barker and Richards, 1978; Hudson, 1980; Potter and Coshall, 1984). The use of this technique will be explained later on in this chapter. Although the full results are not included in this chapter due to restrictions of space, the most valuable information, the constructs and contrasts, are presented.

The YTEPP network includes 43 strategically located centres in Trinidad and Tobago, and a wide range of staff. There are 216 contact hours in a vocational skills programme which usually takes between nine and ten months to complete. Each student must take one skills module at a time and he/she can choose from a wide range of occupations. The scheme does not prepare students to become specialists in their chosen field, but will hopefully give them a useful skill which can be adaptable in the fluctuating market place. Post-training support is also given once the students have completed the programme, this either takes the form of assistance to develop their own business's or work experience.

The programme offers courses in fourteen occupational areas: agriculture; applied arts; construction; crafts; electronics; food preparation; mechanics; performing arts; services; family services; garment construction; metal design/fabrications; beauty culture; and tourism. Many of these occupations are frequently found in the informal sector, as shown in this research. The project runs in cycles of nine months, which are divided into five training phases, and are separated by short periods of 'hands-on' experience.

The General Survey on YTEPP Graduates

The latest evaluation of YTEPP students came from graduates who had attended the course in the period of 1988-1989. Data on the occupations and fortunes of these students were compiled in 1990, the year before this research was undertaken. Information on the graduates was divided into several indicators; previous course undertaken, nature of current business, geographical location, gender and hours worked. A total of 67 graduates from the 1988-1989 course had set up small businesses that were still in operation in 1991. Although specific details were not provided, YTEPP estimate that approximately 1000 students go through the scheme each year, and that despite the promotion of self-employment, many opt for waged employment due to perceptions of high status, as discussed in chapter 8.

The distribution of the 67 successful entrepreneurs by gender, showed an almost even distribution of males (50.75 per cent) and females (49.25 per cent). When details of the skill courses undertaken by successful students are documented, a clear gender division is apparent in their choices. Of the 67 entrepreneurs in the survey, only 7 graduates had undertaken a course which was neither specifically male, or female, dominated. By this, reference is made to a 90 per cent or more domination of either male or female students in a course. The distribution of courses according to their gender bias is displayed in Table 9.1.

The table shows that those courses preferred by female participants relate strongly to a number of stereotypical ideas of women's work, previously established in chapter 8. Popular courses included fashion, beauty culture, and catering. Young female trainees were highly concentrated in fashion design and dress making subjects, flower arranging, beauty and hairdressing, catering related subjects, and management. The male dominated courses are associated with typical male occupational roles such as radio/TV repairs, mechanics, electrics and agriculture. The only courses which appealed equally to both male and female trainees are business studies, house design (informal sector architecture), food preparation and plant propagation. These findings support the previously documented ethnographic evidence, which suggests that young workers will opt for a traditional line of work, even when presented with an equal chance to undertaken a range occupational choices.

Furthermore, the popularity of fashion and design courses is evident. Due to the demand by women to enter this line of work, due to its home location and part-time nature, YTEPP have developed four similar courses. Not surprisingly therefore, women who have dress-making skills are likely to find some kind of employment after graduating. This is a reflection of Trinidadian society, as much as it is a reflection of the aspirations of female trainees.

Comparison between course choice, and the type of business set-up after graduation, also reveals gender differences. As illustrated in Table 9.2, women who have taken business-related courses have developed businesses which conform to typical images of female work. For example, four successful female graduates in management were found to have set-up two cafes, a mini-mart, and a crocheting business. Two of their male colleagues, however, had managed to establish an electronics firm which was growing rapidly.

Despite education and skill-enhancement, women are still being channelled into a narrow range of occupational specialisms. Unfortunately, due to the domestic nature of the courses favoured by

Table 9.1 The Distribution of YTEPP Courses According to the Predominant Gender of Participants 1988-1989

Courses where at least 90 per cent of Trainees are Female	Courses where at least 90 per cent of Trainees are Male	Courses where the Predominance of Either Gender is under 90 per cent
Management	Agriculture	Business
Fabric Design	Gardening	House Design
Fashion/Fabric	Radio/TV Repair	Food Preparation
Dressmaking	Tailoring	Plant Propagation
Dress Design	Plumbing	
Flower Arranging	Auto Mechanics	
Applied Art	Auto Electrics	
Beauty Culture	Metal Fabrication	
Hair Culture	House Wiring	
Small Business Development	Photography	
Catering	Carpentry	
Cake Decoration	Craft Production	
	Sound Systems	

Table 9.2 Distribution of Self-Employed YTEPP Graduates According to the Nature of their Business

Course Taken	Nature of Business	Male	Female
Agriculture/Gardening/ Plant Propagation	Vegetation production/ Market gardening/ Budding	5	1
Business Studies	Electronics	1	-
	Crocheting	-	1
Small Business Management	Parlour/cafe	-	2
	Mini-Mart	-	1
Radio/TV Repair	Repair Shops	9	-
Fabric, Fashion, Dress Making and Design	Sewing, Seamstress/ Dressmaking/ Retail	-	13
Tailoring	Tailor Shop	1	-
Plumbing	Plumbing	1	-
Auto Mechanic	Mechanics/Electrician	6	-
Metal Fabrication	Welders	2	-
Flower Arranging/ Child-care	Florist	-	4
Art	Artist	-	-
House Planning	Teachers	1	1
Beauty and Hair	Beauty Parlour/ Hairdressing	-	4
Photography	Freelance	1	-
Carpentry/Craft	Carpenters/Crafts	2	-
Sound Systems	Party Sounds	3	-
Food Preparation	Cafe, Retail, Processing	1	2
Small Catering	Market Vendor	-	2
Cake Decoration	Teacher, Cake Maker	-	2

females, they are often found in the same lower paid occupations after graduation, as they may have entered without training. According to YTEPP, the demand for courses on fashion and design is so high that young women have to be encouraged to undertake another option.

Programme advisors have tried encouraging women to take up electrical repairs, or plumbing, but very few have taken the challenge for fear of being reproached by society, family and peers. Choice also plays a role in gender patterns of occupational stratification in Trinidad, as young women are eager to 'cut style' and keep up with new fashion looks. If it is recognised that preference is also a factor in young women occupying certain occupational roles, then attention needs to be focused upon the reasons behind these choices.

YTEPP Trainees' Perceptions of Typical Informal Occupations

Although the analysis of the YTEPP tracer study provides an insight into the occupational decisions undertaken by young entrepreneurs, the present research wanted to identify the images of work which were held by young workers in the scheme. As YTEPP aims to help trainees overcome stereotypical approaches to work, it was important to identify whether the training programme was successful in this area. A group of 10 participants, 5 male and 5 female agreed to participate in a technique based on Kelly's Personal Construct Theory (1955), the repertory-grid analysis. Each participant was presented, in turn, with a series of common informal sector occupations in Trinidad; vegetable/fruit trader; coconut vendor; doubles seller; clothes producer; repair/trades person; lottery-ticket seller; taxi/maxi-driver; domestic worker; clothes vendor; snow-cone (ice-cream) vendor; suitcase trader. These occupations were selected by the informal traders, which participated in the ethnographic interviews, as the most popular informal jobs in Trinidad.

Repertory grids are constructed by presenting each individual with the study objects or elements, the occupations, in sets of three or 'triads'. The participant is asked to state the way in which two of the elements are alike and thereby, different from the third. The similarity is defined as the construct, and the difference as the contrast, both of which are recorded in the form of a grid. When a construct has been suggested, all other elements can then be assessed in relation to it. Triads continue to be shown to the participant until no further constructs are given (Fransella and Bannister, 1977).

A completed grid displays a series of perceptions, held by the participant, which relate to the selection of occupations. For example, it may be established that a participant views taxi-driving and coconut selling as male-dominated occupations as opposed to domestic work, which they perceive to be women's work. In this respect, the grids display a series of personal perceptions on the nature of occupations in Trinidad. The results may be subjected to factor analysis (Potter and Coshall, 1984), but due to restrictions in length, a detailed analysis of the results is not required in this research. Rather, it is sufficient for the purpose of this chapter to present a selection of the constructs and contrasts which were given for the different occupations. Table 9.3 displays the constructs and contrasts which were forthcoming from the participants.

The constructs can be grouped into ten categories: gender-related; income-related; status-related; location-related; job characteristics; image-related; ethnicity; skill requirements; product-service-related; and age-related. The most frequently cited responses referred to gender, income, status, location, image, ethnicity, and job characteristics such as self employment and part-time work. These results further support the argument that gender, ethnicity, space, status and ideology, as well as income, exert an important influence on the job choices of informal workers. Other individually cited constructs relate directly to the nature of Trinidadian society, such as the desire to hold a job which is sociable, and allows the mixing of work with pleasure. Tables 9.4 to 9.7 highlight the respondents' perceptions of different occupations according to a number of construct/contrast pairs which relate to gender, status, image, ethnicity.

Table 9.4 shows the response to the construct/contrast pair male-dominated/female-dominated, where over 90 per cent of the respondents cited that an occupation was strictly gender-specific. Respondents stated that lottery-ticket sellers, domestic workers, clothes vendors and clothes producers were predominantly female occupations. The only occupation which was not unanimously agreed upon, was the vegetable/fruit trader, which was cited by one respondent as also being a female occupation. Table 9.5 shows those occupations which were regarded as being of high and low-status. Here, the only suitcase trader, the repair/trades person, the Taxi/Maxi-driver and the clothes producer were deemed to hold relatively high-status occupations. The other informal occupations were all seen to be of low-status.

Table 9.6 provides information on which occupations the YTEPP trainees regarded as offering a modern or traditional image. The occupations of suitcase trader, repair/trades person, Taxi/Maxi-driver, and clothes producer are seen to be modern, as well as high-status. In addition, the snow-cone vendor was also seen to be a modern occupation, possibly as it is also predominantly an urban occupation. Respondents also classified occupations according to an image of ethnicity, in particular the association of a number of occupations with workers of East-Indian descent was most noticeable. Table 9.7 highlights those occupations which are seen to be dominated by East-Indian workers: vegetable/fruit trader, coconut vendor, doubles vendor, Taxi/Maxi-driver, and snow-cone vendor. These occupations were also regarded by 90 per cent of respondents as being male-dominated, a factor which also illustrates the lack of visible informal activity by Indo-Trinidadian female workers.

Finally, Table 9.8 shows the interesting association between the respondents' perceptions of the gender, status and ethnicity ascribed to the

Table 9.3 The Constructs/Contrasts Most Frequently Cited by YTEPP Participants

Construct/Contrast Number of Respondents	Using Constructs
Gender-related	
Male dominated/Female dominated	10
Income-related	
High income/Lower income	9
Large/Small Investment required	5
Status-related	
High status/Low status	9
Location-related	
Urban based/Rural based	8
Fixed location/Flexible location	7
Street location/Home location	3
Job Characteristics	
Full-time/Part-time	8
Self employment/Not self employment	7
Main occupation/Secondary occupation	2
Future career potential/No potential	2
Difficult work/Less difficult work	1
Seasonal work/Not seasonal work	1
Social job/Unsociable job	1
Image-related	
Modern job/Traditional job	8
Family-based/Non-family based	4
Ethnicity	
East Indian dominated/Not East Indian	6
Skill Requirements	
Requires education/No education	6
Skilled/Unskilled	3
Product/Service-related	
Associated with food/Not associated	2
Tourist oriented/Non-tourist	1
Imported/Local resources used	1
Age-related	
Older workers/Younger workers	1

Table 9.4 Gender Perceptions of Respondents of Informal Occupations

Occupations Regarded by over 90 per cent of Respondents as being either Male Dominated or Female Dominated	
Male Dominated Occupations	Female Dominated Occupations
Vegetable/Fruit Trader	Lottery Ticket Seller
Coconut Vendor	Domestic Worker
Doubles Vendor	Clothes Vendor
Repair/Trades Person	Clothes Producer
Taxi/Maxi Driver	
Snow-cone Vendor	
Suitcase Trader	

Table 9.5 Perceptions of the Status of Informal Occupations by Respondents

Occupations Regarded by over 90 per cent of Respondents as being High Status or Low Status	
High Status Occupations	Low Status Occupations
Suitcase Trader	Lottery Ticket Seller
Repair/Trades Person	Domestic Worker
Taxi/Maxi Driver	Doubles Vendor
Clothes Producer	Clothes Vendor
	Vegetable/Fruit Trader
	Coconut Vendor
	Snow-cone Vendor

Table 9.6 Perceptions of the Image of Informal Occupations by Respondents

Occupations Regarded by over 80 per cent of Respondents as being Modern or Traditional	
Modern Occupations	Traditional Occupations
Suitcase Trader	Lottery Ticket Seller
Repair/Trades Person	Domestic Worker
Taxi/Maxi Driver	Doubles Vendor
Clothes Producer	Clothes Vendor
Snow-cone Vendor	Vegetable/Fruit Trader
	Coconut Vendor

Table 9.7 Perceptions Relating to the Ethnicity of Informal Occupations by Respondents

Occupations Regarded by over 80 per cent of Respondents as being Dominated by Indo-Trinidadian Workers	
Occupations dominated by Indo-Trinidadian Workers	Occupations not dominated by Indo-Trinidadian Workers
Vegetable/Fruit Trader	Lottery Ticket Seller
Coconut Vendor	Domestic Worker
Taxi/Maxi Vendor	Clothes Vendor
Doubles Vendor	Suitcase Trader
Snow-cone Vendor	Repair/Trades Person
	Clothes Producer

occupations. Firstly, three of the four occupations which respondents perceived to be female were regarded as being of low-status. The low-status given to lottery-ticket sellers, clothes vendors and domestic workers was also identified in the research presented in chapter 8. Table 9.8 identifies clothes production as the only higher-status occupation which is deemed to be women's work, a factor which also came to light in chapter 8. Secondly, all of the occupations which were cited as being dominated by Indo-Trinidadian workers, with the exception of Maxi-Taxi-driving, were identified as low status.

In summary, the exercise showed that low-status occupations in the informal sector are seen by many to be either women's work, or associated with Indo-Trinidadian workers. Other occupations such as repair/trades-person and suitcase trader, were seen to be of higher status, predominately male and not usually undertaken by Indo-Trinidadian workers. It would appear, that despite efforts to promote greater equality through training schemes, YTEPP trainees hold similar stereotypical perceptions of work as the older operators discussed in chapters 7 and 8.

Youthful Perceptions of Informal Sector Occupations: Policy Suggestions

The data on YTEPP graduates indicate that even in this innovative training scheme, there is a marked gender division between courses chosen by participants, and their subsequent careers. The course is still following a similar trend as in the 1990-1991 study, over 87 per cent of the female participants opted for courses which assimilate females' domestic role, such as catering, hairdressing and fabric design. Unfortunately, as young women as still choosing to undertake courses in traditionally 'female' skills such as hairdressing and dress-making, it appears that greater effort is needed to either assist women to develop more successful businesses in these areas, or to help them diversify. Encouragement through a scheme such as YTEPP is not enough on its own, particularly as young adults come to YTEPP with pre-determined ideas of occupations. Instead, a broad policy of re-educating children about work is needed throughout their schooling. Even so, many of the trainees talked of the pressure from their parents, and other relatives, to go into certain careers. One female trainee said that she had chosen to do a course in electronics, but had been forced to change her mind by her father, who said that electronics was not a suitable occupation for a woman. The counter attempt to encourage men to undertake clerical and design classes has been even more unsuccessful.

Another interesting pattern which emerged from the data concerns the relationship between the geographical location of the graduate's home, and their chosen occupation. Location, particularly the difference between rural and urban areas, is an important factor in the minds of the young. Furthermore, despite heightened demand for domestically produced food in Trinidad, agricultural businesses were greatly under-represented in all regions of the country, except Caroni, where there is a tradition of Indo-

Table 9.8 Respondents' Perceptions of Gender, Ethnicity and Status of Informal Occupations

Occupations Regarded by over 80 per cent of Respondents as being Associated with Female Work, Indo-Trinidadian Domination or Low Status		
Occupations dominated by Female Workers	Occupations dominated by Indo-Trinidadian Workers	Occupations which are perceived to be of Low Status
Lottery Ticket Seller	-	Lottery Ticket Seller
Domestic Worker	-	Domestic Worker
Clothes Vendor	-	Clothes Vendor
Clothes Producer	-	-
	Vegetable/Fruit Trader	Vegetable-Fruit Trader
	Coconut Vendor	Coconut Vendor
	Doubles Vendor	Doubles Vendor
	Snow-cone Vendor	Snow-cone Vendor
	Taxi/Maxi Driver	-

Trinidadian agriculture. Here, male graduates, mostly of East Indian descent, have returned to their home villages to establish family businesses in vegetable marketing. Agricultural businesses are more likely to qualify for grants and loans from government agencies, and credit unions, and represents a growth area for young entrepreneurs.

YTEPP instructs its students on the numerous openings in agricultural production, market gardening and food processing for young entrepreneurs, but very few graduates wish to work in this area. The increasing demand for specialist western foods, such as mushrooms, could hold potential for a good business investment and yet, the challenge has rarely been taken up. Unfortunately, very few graduates of YTEPP would consider agriculture as a future career, due to its association with East Indian roots and underdevelopment. Only one graduate was able to obtain a loan from YESS (Youth Enterprise Support Scheme) and the SBDC, to start a rabbit meat production unit, which highlights the governments' desire to encourage small-scale agricultural production.

The failure to pioneer change is one of YTEPP's greatest concerns, as adaptability will be one of the most important skills in the future job market. Despite marked success in training students for entrepreneurship, YTEPP is still facing difficulties in eradicating the traditional perceptions of occupations, which are largely responsible for shaping career paths in Trinidad. Not surprisingly, policies which have been aimed at particular societal groups have tended to have better success rates in encouraging entrepreneurship and co-operation, conforming perhaps to the idea that it is still the desire of many groups to remain isolated. Whether this is an ethically sound policy is a debatable question. The widespread racialisation of occupational identities in the Trinidadian labour market presents obstacles to the ultimate goal of equal opportunity. This work has already demonstrated the difficulties of female workers in competing for governmental assistant with male groups, such as the People's Mall vendors. The important questions rest on whether a series of policies individually tailored to the different needs of ethnic and gender groups would lead to the general improvement of small businesses, and the status of the entrepreneur, or whether, it would only deepen spatial polarity in Trinidadian society.

Conclusions: Equal Opportunities and Policy Prescriptions for the Informal Sector in Trinidad

A good example of an informal project, in terms of entrepreneurial success, is the People's Mall in Port of Spain, which has been a base for informal trading for over 10 years. During the ethnographic interviews with the suitcase traders in the People's Mall, an in-depth discussion was held with a well-established booth owner concerning the ideology of the Mall in terms of informal sector development. The inclusion of the interview held with Mr B, a middle-aged booth-owner, who had been involved with the Mall since it was pioneered in 1980, is used to highlight the benefits and dis-benefits of government schemes as seen from within the informal sector. Mr M plays the role of spokesman, and general overseer of the booth owner's welfare due to his knowledge of government affairs and the law. He also assists other vendors with book-keeping and legal advice, as he strongly advocates the need for traders to organise their businesses in a professional manner if they wish to be taken seriously by the government.

As discussed in chapter 7, the original concept of the Mall was based on assisting insecure street vendors to build a stable business. Mr B, along with most of the traders, started with a simple stall, and upgraded his patch as his income grew. Twelve years after its inception, the Mall is a well established trading centre where many experienced and educated traders now operate successful businesses. The booths were initially offered for a small down payment, which vendors obtained from their family and friends, but today it is rumoured that booths can be sold informally for as much as TT$60,000 (£8,500). The high price comes from the sought after position of the Mall in Frederick Street, one of the most advantageous retail positions in the Central Business District. The traders' reputation for making a good living has increased the exchange price by such an extent that it is unaffordable to new street vendors. Success has also led to reluctance, on the part of the existing tenants, to move out of the Mall to give more inexperienced traders a chance to move away from the streets.

To secure a booth today, a young trader needs both a good business plan and a reasonable amount of capital. Entry into the People's Mall is as difficult as gaining space in a formal sector shopping mall, and contradicts the reported ease of entry into informal employment. Mr B also stated that many Trinidadians who have retired, or been made redundant from the public sector, invest in a booth, as a silent partner. In this respect, there are many absentee owners who each employ between two to three people, many of whom are women with young families. In total, the success of the Mall has contributed to the maintenance of at least 600 households.

One of the most interesting elements of the discussion with Mr B centred upon the political persuasions of the suitcase traders, and their present conflict with the government. Despite the fact that the People's Mall was founded by the Williams government, and that its existence is still based upon government permission, the Mall presents a political dilemma for the NAR administration. Politically, there is an underlying feeling of militancy and aggression in the Mall, which is one reason for the reluctance of the government to assist the traders in their next goal.

After twelve years in a small protected environment, many of the booth owners want to gain places in a formal sector mall in Port of Spain. Despite many individual attempts by traders to rent shop space, they are often refused leases for unsubstantiated reasons. Mr B feels that the government is confident that it can control the traders in a confined space, but fear that they may provide political opposition if they are spread out in the wider business community. There is also much bad feeling between the traders and the formal business community, due to the proximity of the Mall to many department stores. Formal store owners feel that the vendors have unfair advantage in the market, as they are exempt from paying tax, import duties and rent. At the time of the interview, local businessmen were campaigning to move the traders from their prime position in Frederick Street to a peripheral location on Wrightson Road, which resulted in a wave of violence and aggression.

According to Mr B, the aggressive culture surrounding the Mall can be attributed to the fact that the majority of vendors have endured a life on the streets, accompanied by police and societal oppression. These feelings have manifested into a general distrust of government policies. When asked to further explain the booth owners' position on the government's attempt to assist the informal sector, Mr B commented that:

> We haf a 'ard life on d'streets, when we first set up der wer all kind of aggression n' violence and fights wid police n' dem.

When asked whether the booth owners were aware of the government schemes to help traders, he replied:

> Yer, yer, dey always trying to do someting or other but dey always target de wrong groups! Youth training like YTEPP is OK, but what 'bout all d'people who is older and canna get help? The problem is dey don't understand street culture cos dey don't ask us what we need. They think we stupid or what? We're good business people!

The general feeling amongst traders appears to one of hostility towards the government. Although Mr B and his associates were aware of the YTEPP and SBDC schemes, their negative feeling towards any governmental assistance is typical of informal sector participants. Mr B highlighted a number of reasons why current government schemes appear to be unpopular. Firstly, he stated that the young are not the only group which need assistance. There are still many unemployed workers, in their late 20s, who have young families to support. This is particularly the case with young women, who Mr B recognised as one of the most vulnerable groups. Secondly, the Small Business Development Company Ltd, which is located in a prestigious office complex, does not offer an atmosphere which is conducive for traders. It operates on a technocratic basis, which is hostile to many street workers. Thirdly, and most importantly, informal workers are afraid of losing control of their businesses, a fear which was also held by the higglers. At this point, Mr B drew an analogy between the World Bank and the Trinidadian economy. Fourthly, he stated that informal participants should not be treated as uneducated or 'un-business like', arguing that a trader who has managed to make a living on the basis of his own creativity knows 'business'.

The unwillingness of informal workers to become involved in government schemes, based on past experiences, is a major reason why many schemes fail. Mr B is correct in arguing that government researchers should be sent onto the streets to ask informal traders what assistance they need, but he never refers to the fact that his business success is attributable to a government project. When asked about what traders really want, Mr B commented that "people need help without conditionality". Although this is an ideal scenario, the government is accountable, and needs to monitor its investments. It was generally agreed that self-help projects, like the Mall, have been the most successful in assisting small business development, but that this assistance must not end there.

Street trading has dramatically increased in the last few years, and a new generation of traders is now in need of assistance. Primarily, the established vendors of the People's Mall need assistance to formalise themselves in the marketplace. They need help to re-locate to a new mall, one that is still local in character and design, and in a prime location such as the burnt out sites of Charlotte Street. The scheme would undoubtedly be more successful if a time schedule was brought into the equation. For example, vendors might trade freely for a period of say six years, and could then be assisted in gaining retailing space elsewhere in the formal retail market. This in turn would provide an ongoing movement of traders through the system, as more street traders would get a chance to develop their businesses, and the government would be able to reap its own benefits in terms of future revenue from taxes (Lloyd-Evans and Potter, 1993). At present the vendors are setting up meetings with the government to discuss leasing more land for new vendors. In addition, Mr B is attempting to set up his own official company, with a few others, on a co-operative basis to see if it is a successful model.

As a final note, Mr B commented on his view that increased co-operation between different groups of informal traders was also needed. Twelve years from its start the Mall is still a gendered and often racialised environment, and Mr B recognises that this is not conducive to the general development of the informal sector. Mr B states that in general, Afro-Trinidadian male traders have been more fortunate in gaining tolerance, and assistance, from the government. It is his personal view that this is not right, and that other traders, particularly women should also be given help. However, he believes that different groups have different requirements, and that an identical model of the People's Mall might not work for other groups. Instead, the Trinidadian government needs to consider location, the cultural identity of the group, and their business strategy, before suggesting any similar self-help schemes.

Before real success can be acheived, in terms of assisting informal workers, the government needs to pay attention to the rigid divisions present in the informal sector. These divisions, based on gender, ethnicity and space, must be addressed if there is to be a move towards a more equitable and dynamic informal sector in Trinidad. Following the acceptance of this fact, the government has two possible courses of action.

The first is to assist groups on an individual basis, which will require the development of policies specifically tailored to the groups' needs. For example, highway traders might benefit from assistance to develop safer outlets, but still in prime locations. This line of action, however, does little to change the pre-existing divisions of employment based on traditional perceptions, and economic constraints. In this respect, many female workers would still find themselves in low-paid and low-status occupations, despite receiving some form of governmental assistance.

The second option, is based on encouraging, and promoting, horizontal and vertical mobility in the occupational hierarchy, for all groups, regardless of age, gender or ethnicity. A more wide-ranging programme of equal opportunities, aimed at broadening Trinidadian perceptions of occupations and work in society, would be needed. Here, attention could focus upon the re-education of workers, using popular culture such as the media, to assist in the breaking down of ethnic and gender divisions in the workplace. If this was successful, informal sector workers would reap the benefits in terms of being able to consider, and attain, a wider range of work options.

In addition, a more 'grassroots' based adaptation of the types of programmes discussed in this chapter, could be employed to provide support for workers, particularly women, to make these changes. Good policies, such those of YTEPP and the self-help schemes, will only succeed when society becomes more open to change. However, due to Trinidad's past, the country will always be subject to internal divisions. This fact is highlighted by a recent self-help scheme located in Port of Spain. Following discussions with the People's Mall, the People's National Movement (PNM) who returned to power in December 1991, initiated a similar scheme in Independence Square in 1992, called Tent City. Here the government built modern retail units for street vendors, and petty commodity producers, who had previously operated in Independence Square. Despite an attempt to attract a wider cross-section of vendors, which has encouraged a small number of women, the scheme is still dominated by Afro-Trinidadian vendors. This is partially due to the fact that many Indo-Trinidian traders prefer to remain away from central Port of Spain, due to their preferences for a quieter, and more rural, location. A degree of spatial preference will always remain in a racialised society like Trinidad, and it must be recognised as an important component in shaping the informal sector.

10 The Socio-Spatial Geography of the Informal Sector in Trinidad

The informal sector has always played a major role in Caribbean development. Although it has been widely argued that the informal economy is most important in times of recession as it compensates for formal sector retrenchment, Trinidad's informal sector has always provided work for a diverse cross-section of the population. As there are different processes of informalisation at play at any given time, this monograph has sought to place the informal sector in its socio-spatial context during the early 1990s. A central aim of this research, therefore, has been to relate the working experiences of one particular sub-sector to the wider socio-economic processes that have shaped workers' lives.

As explained in chapter 2, the informal sector adopts the social, economic and spatial characteristics of its locality. In Trinidad, recent austere economic conditions have impacted upon a fragmented labour market to produce varying opportunities and obstacles for different informal workers. In recent political history, state tolerance of informal employment has fluctuated between the active encouragement of micro-enterprise and the periodic police clearance of vendors from public highways. In Trinidad, the informal sector affords opportunities for self-employment, and income earning activity, which would otherwise be unavailable in the present economic climate. From the colonial period to the present day, Trinidad's informal sector has provided jobs for its growing urban and rural population. From street trading and taxi driving to home production, the informal sector is becoming an increasingly important provider of work, but one which is spatially complex and highly gendered. Informality attracts large numbers of participants from all social backgrounds, who utilise the sector for different purposes. On the one hand, there are the subsistence operators who engage in the sector as a survival strategy, and on the other, there are petty capitalists who take advantage of the alternative economic structure offered by the informal sector. Rather than exclusively providing opportunities for the lower-income social groups, the informal sector also provides a haven for many educated, middle-income operators who engage in informal activity on a regular basis. Even in the upper echelons of the community, many business practices are more informal than formal due to the nature of Trinidadian society.

Within the obscure boundaries of Trinidad's informal sector, the existence of petty commodity trading represents one of the most important, and visually prominent, activities. A large proportion of Trinidad's informal operators engage in a trading-related business, with production and service jobs occupying a smaller role. The occupation of trading is distinctly divided between two major types of products; agricultural and food trading, and the vending of petty commodities and non-food items. These two sub-sectors have their own distinct identities, and reflect different characteristics in terms of participants and location of businesses.

Food retailing maintains an important function in providing incomes in the informal sector in Trinidad. The informal food distribution system is essential to the operation of Trinidad's economy, with the sector taking a major role in the nationwide distribution of domestic and imported foods. At the heart of the agricultural system, there are networks of trading businesses largely operated by Indo-Trinidadian families. Even today, the prominence of the highway trading of fruit and vegetables is one of the most noticeable representations of the informal economy. Despite the profitability associated with highway vending, the occupation is generally regarded as low-status and 'backward' within society as a whole.

On the other hand, workers of Afro-Trinidadian descent who engage in the agricultural sector tend to do so on a less frequent, or non-permanent basis, as they generally undertake minor roles. Afro-Trinidadian women are often found at the lower end of the agricultural and food vending spectrum. The traditional female occupation of higglering still affords independence and economic autonomy for many women in Trinidad, but it is increasingly becoming confined to rural areas and urban markets. Few Afro-Trinidadian men undertake a food-related occupation, which many view as a 'poor' job, and as such, they are not prominent in the sector except in specific urban environments such as central Port of Spain. As discussed in chapter 6, occupations related to the trading of non-food products are more likely to be undertaken by workers of Afro-Trinidadian descent.

There exists a large literature on the informal sector in the developing world that explores many of the social and economic factors which shape the work experiences of individuals, but this monograph has drawn particular attention to two important processes which have not been given due attention in previous work.

Firstly, this research has argued that an appreciation of how and why informal labour markets are shaped by processes of racialised gendering (Brah, 1994), is essential for an in-depth understanding of the experiences of informal workers in a post-colonial society. The processes through which ideas about appropriate work are constructed are often firmly embedded in particular places and communicated and maintained by social networks. In multi-ethnic societies like Trinidad, ideas about work are often racialised as a direct result of historical factors as well as more contemporary notions held about ethnicity and cultural difference.

Moreover, these processes have important implications in terms of the effectiveness of government policies designed to help vulnerable workers.

Secondly, through an examination of the different ways in which male and female petty commodity traders enter the informal sector and utilize different working environments for their own survival, this research has highlighted the importance of understanding women and men's contrasting notions of space and place. These processes, which are highly influential in constructing images of work and identity, have largely been overlooked in existing studies of the informal sector. In particular, research has shown that perceptions of 'place' and working identity exert strong influences on men and women's employment choices, career opportunities and daily lives. Without the more formalized regulation of its structure and operation, informal labour markets provide ideal environments in which to explore how notions of appropriate work held by individuals, and their communities, structure divisions of labour.

Gendered and Racialised Spaces in Trinidad's Informal Sector

There is marked gendered and ethnic polarisation of workers within Trinidad's informal sector, and the petty commodity sector provides a good example of how processes of racialised gendering become spatially represented. As previous chapters have explained, Trinidad's ethnic and gendered cleavages structure the informal labour market to produce barriers and opportunities for workers in a rapidly globalising economy. Through an exploration of the working experiences of men and women, this research has examined the ideas which individuals and groups construct about the jobs they do and the places they work. Notions of identity, which are inherently linked to gender, ethnicity and class, play a central role in the construction of these goals and aspirations, and they are central to the embeddedness of certain groups in particular jobs.

The ethnographic profiles of traders presented in chapters 7 and 8, outlined the ways in which informal occupations are both gendered and racialised, and how they become spatially defined. An individual's occupational choice is often constrained by traditional and cultural beliefs that become associated with different groups of traders and specific places. A major part of this research aimed to evaluate perceptions of work held by respondents to determine the extent to which ideas about gender, ethnicity and place are responsible for spatial polarity in the informal sector.

Racialised and gendered working identities often stem from stereotypical ideas which identify particular types of work as more 'suitable' for men or women from different ethnic backgrounds. At any one time, there will be competing versions of 'suitability' which are circulating the labour market according to the positionality of actors in the labour market. The extent to which ideas about appropriate working behaviour become translated into occupational segregation in the workplace depends on a variety of external factors such as the supply and demand for different types of labour, the institutional framework and prevailing macro-economic conditions, as well as less tangible processes like social capital creation. These processes combine to shape the informal sector in a particular locality. In Trinidad, as in many other post-colonial societies, the informal sector is a multi-faceted space characterized by visible and invisible boundaries, which shape the opportunities of those seeking work.

Earlier chapters drew attention to important divisions of labour found in Trinidad's informal sector. In spatial terms, this research has highlighted the ways in which gender and ethnicity combine to reproduce marked occupational stratification throughout Trinidad's informal sector. Divisions, in terms of product specialisation, gender and ethnicity, are quite marked in Trinidad, even over short distances. On the whole, female workers tend to operate limited trading businesses, restricted by their fear of taking risks, a factor which is largely dictated by their family responsibilities. As a result, female traders in Trinidad are not generally as successful as their male counterparts. In the Caribbean, notions of respectability, motherhood and aspirations combine with the realities of daily lives, like family responsibilities and lack of capital, to produce a segmented informal labour market.

Many women interviewed in this research expressed an uneasy contradiction between their ideas about ideal gender roles and the way they live. For example, most higglers wanted more equal opportunities for their daughters but still expected them to adopt distinctly gendered roles in the household and be confined to the market or the yard. The yard is an important space for Caribbean women as it is a place where productive and reproductive activities take place and has been identified as a site of power for many women (Senior, 1991). The street, however, is deemed to be a more acceptable space for young boys, and they are familiar with the 'lime' from an early age. Ideologically, many women still remain in informal occupations due to their desire to be independent, which a more formalised job may not allow. Even within the informal sector, women often under-value their worth and economic contribution to the economy. Furthermore, and as a result of their reluctance to engage in business partnerships with other traders due to concerns over trust, women generally have weaker levels of social capital which they can utilize to expand their businesses or call upon in times of vulnerability. There is some evidence to suggest, however, that young suitcase traders (ICIs) are positioning themselves in secure sou-sou type arrangements for the purposes of raising funds and sharing risks. In contrast, male socialization and their membership of social networks give male workers an in-built confidence, which encourages them to be more ambitious in the labour market.

Place identity, particularly in relation to the difference between rural and urban environments, also exerts influence over the nature of workers and occupations in a number of specific places. In general, informal food traders of Indo-Trinidadian descent more densely populate the highways. Although male Indo-Trinidadian traders dominate the agricultural sector in the main, they often find themselves in competition with part-time Afro-Trinidadian women in localities nearest to Port of Spain. For the majority of informal occupations, locations in close proximity to downtown Port of Spain appear to attract workers of Afro-Trinidadian descent. This is partially explained by the fact that a higher proportion of the Afro-Trinidadian population reside in Port of Spain, but it is also indicative of a number of other forces. Firstly, interviews with traders confirmed that Port of Spain is traditionally associated with a more urban, Afro-Trinidadian culture, a factor that often dissuades other informal sector workers from working in this area. The nature of businesses located in Port of Spain are also specific, and tend to be production and craft-oriented, rather than agriculturally-related. In this way, the spatial geography of the island influences the nature and form of the informal sector. In a similar manner, 'the South' of the country is commonly associated with Indo-Trinidadian culture and settlement. For example, the Southern Highway was completely dominated by traders of Indo-Trinidadian descent, exemplifying their continued links with agriculture and original settlement patterns.

Spatial divisions in the informal sector in Trinidad appear to mirror the spatial polarity of the country as a whole. Place identities, which are closely associated with particular gendered and racialised identities, help to shape an informal sector which channels Afro-Trinidadian and Indo-Trinidadian men and women into different informal jobs. In particular, women are generally confined to work in a limited number of occupations, and locations. Two prime examples are the general exclusion of women working along the highways, and in downtown Port of Spain. Explanations centre on both social and economic reasons, but there are also more subtle forces at work, which relate to perceptions of specific environments. Research showed that many women perceive areas such as the highways to be 'unsafe', 'dangerous', and a bad environment in which to work.

In this respect, the Eastern Main Road provides another excellent example of the fragmented nature of similar informal sector occupations. Afro-Trinidadian workers are frequently located in regional/local urban centres (sub centres), such as central Port of Spain, Tunapuna, Arima, Sangre Grande, and Manzanilla. By contrast Indo-Trinidadian workers and to a lesser extent women from different ethnic backgrounds, constitute a greater percentage of the workforce in more rural locations and suburban areas, for example, residential areas in Port of Spain and routeways between urban centres.

Afro-Trinidadian traders generally expressed a preference for working with other people in a 'work-lime', whilst many Indo-Trinidadian family businesses work near to their own communities, or in isolation. Working with friends or like-minded people, a factor which is central to the notion of 'cultural capital' is often viewed as an important component of job satisfaction in Trinidad, and one which is generally seen as a benefit of informal sector work. Interestingly, in areas where Afro-Trinidadian male operators are dominant, there is a noticeable lack of female and Indo-Trinidadian male traders. There is a similarity, however, between the spatial distribution of female workers and Indo-Trinidadian workers, as traders are often found working within similar urban areas. Both groups hold a preference for working away from downtown Port of Spain and in busy, Afro-Caribbean 'male' areas. The market centres of Tunapuna and Arima offer a more friendly and pleasant environment, which is in contrast to the perceived danger and 'hassle' of central Port of Spain. Female traders are understandably attracted to areas where other women work, although by undertaking an informal occupation they are still able to maintain their independence and individual autonomy. These are important reasons, which explain the popularity of higglering amongst women, even though they may have aspirations towards other jobs. In the informal sector, social networks are a necessary job requirement, which higglering in a market environment often provides.

Having understood the gendering of the labour market, it is important to examine how these processes represent themselves spatially. Places maintain their own distinct gendered and racialised identities, which provide an assertive influence over workers and jobs across Trinidad. As earlier chapters elucidated, there are a number of geographically distinct areas in Trinidad which are associated with different types of work.

Working Boundaries: Different Spaces and Social Networks

It is well known that occupations are gendered, and that jobs associated with household and reproductive activities are generally seen as 'appropriate' work for women. As explained in earlier chapters, stereotypical ideas about women's work are often grounded in spatial metaphors that associate women with 'private', 'household' and 'familial' spaces. Although chapter 2 critically discussed the problems associated with using spatial dichotomies of 'public/private' and 'production/reproduction', particularly in the informal sector which by its nature defies conventional boundaries on many levels, they do provide a basic analytical framework on which to build a more complex picture of the ways in which the informal labour market is segmented between places as much as it is between jobs. So, the vending of fruit and vegetables is identified as 'higglering' (women's work) when it is conducted in traditional markets and other quasi 'private' spaces which are seen to be an extension of the household, but the job becomes masculinised when trading is removed to a very public and often 'dangerous' place like a busy highway.

Spatial processes influence and shape the opportunities and barriers that face informal sector workers. Spatial boundaries are highly gendered and many female traders are prohibited from working in many locations because of the invisible forces which are at play. For example, many female clothes traders preferred to work in Arima and in semi-rural locations, due to their perceptions that these are acceptable spaces for women. Although women are confined to work in certain locations due to child-care, income and family responsibility, their ideas about work are also influenced by gendered and racialised ideas about acceptable work for women 'like them'. Such ideas are communicated and exchanged via social networks, and are often expressed through stories about particular jobs and places being 'unsafe' and 'bad'. As a result, female informal traders are often associated with working in 'confined spaces' and 'inbetween' spaces such as markets or the household yard.

Men's use of public space, it had often been argued, is not so restricted and could be regarded as 'every place', but processes of racialised gendering also work to structure the opportunities open to different ethnic groups. In relation to the labour market, discourses between racialised ethnic groups in Trinidad are focused on the skills and attributes of 'others' in determining their suitability for different types of work (see Yelvington, 1995). For example, ideas about suitable work for Indo-Trinidadian men which are often centred on notions of family responsibility and decency, prevent young highway traders from seeking alternative jobs in places which are seen to be associated with bad living and criminality. In the informal sector, as in the wider labour market, the nature of occupational stereotyping is directly influenced by subtle notions of racial suitability, preference for certain occupations and a distinct imagery of 'otherness'. As a result, spatial divisions in society work to maintain the *status quo*, particularly in preventing certain ethnic or gender groups from attaining better jobs. Chapter 9 presents some good examples of how political schemes often assist particular social groups at the expense of marginalizing others, albeit if it is an unintentional process. As long as individuals, and their communities, continue to be associated with particular sets of gendered and racialised working identities, the labour market will continue to be a divisive and inequitable space.

However, ideologies which link women to reproductive activities and men to more public modes of production can always be negotiated, particularly in times of economic necessity. The gradual take over of food trading by Indo-Trinidadian men is just one example of the fluidity of working identities in the informal sector. By shifting the location of fruit and vegetable vending away from traditionally feminised spaces to places that exclude women, male traders have succeeded in changing the division of labour in their favour. By changing the spatial relations under which an activity is conducted, men and women can restructure productive activities to suit their own goals, thus sometimes challenging stereotypical notions of the gendering of labour market change over time.

As chapter 2 suggests, there are many intermediary spaces within the community that are accessible to women from the household and it is essential that these business environments are given continued support in policy initiatives. As chapter 9 highlighted, new developments designed to assist informal vendors have often excluded female workers. In Trinidad's informal sector, competition over territory and prime economic space often displays itself in gendered and ethnic polarization, a situation that will remain unchanged without institutional intervention. Social networks actively work to exclude competition from other social groups and stories about violence and safety serve to enforce Port of Spain's association with hostility and violence. However, as suggested earlier, territorial dominance can change over time as new groups of workers challenge the existing regime. In the mid-1990s, young female suitcase traders were increasing their business power by using their social networks and homes to sell goods to other women and middle-income customers.

Working aspirations and daily practices are firmly embedded in place and in the social networks that help to shape and maintain a job's identity. Within Trinidad's informal sector, 'bad jobs' were more likely to be associated with working in particular places than with a specific occupation. Similar research undertaken by Lloyd-Evans in the British labour market has also confirmed the fact that individuals identify working environments and qualities such as 'fitting in' to be of greater importance than the job itself (Lloyd-Evans and Bowlby, 2000). Increasingly, it appears that a sense of belonging to a group or network, or being with like minded people, is of greater importance than the task at hand, particularly if jobs are low paid and arduous. This factor, combined with the hierarchical structure of market participation and produce specialisation, forces some workers into a narrow margin of occupations. As previously discussed, female workers often gravitate towards more 'feminised' environments where they feel secure in the company of other women, but these networks are rather weak and are rarely used for business purposes. Other researchers have documented the difficulties associated with uniting Caribbean women in business ventures or cooperatives. As Peake and Trotz (1999) comment, sisterly solidarity is difficult to engender across racialised divisions in the Caribbean. In relation to social capital, it appears that the existence of social networks alone is an insufficient base on which to build economic assets. Without trust and reciprocity, social capital cannot be successfully developed and maintained.

Conclusions: Towards a Reappraisal of Work

Poor perceptions of work in the informal sector, partly built on tradition and modernity, are hindering the occupational, and social, mobility of many workers. They also restrict the flow of workers between occupations, and add to the general failure of society to recognize informality as a socially acceptable form of work. It is clear that there needs to be a reappraisal of work which awards increased status to all workers, not just those in formal occupations. If general perceptions of informal work are altered for the better, then this in turn will result in greater social acceptability for all workers, particularly in terms of acquiring business loans and government assistance.

This research has called into question the established rhetoric on the informal sector which largely ignores the gendering of space as an influential factor in explaining marked divisions in business opportunities. Through exploration of the ways in which different groups of workers become embedded in particular places and social networks, and how these processes are structured by notions of gendered and racialised identity, it is hoped that this research will offer an alternative framework for the study of the gendering of labour markets in developing countries. Although gendered and racialised identities are largely resistant to change, this research offers clear examples of how male and female workers can restructure spatial boundaries to suit their own goals, thus sometimes challenging stereotypical notions of working identity.

Bibliography

Abdullah, N. (1991), 'Ethnicity, mating patterns and fertility', in S. Ryan (ed) *Social and Occupational Stratification in Contemporary Trinidad and Tobago*, Institute of Social and Economic Research, University of the West Indies, St Augustine, Trinidad.

Afshar, H. (ed) (1985), *Women, Work and Ideology in the Third World*, Tavistock, London.

Afshar, H. and Barrientos, S. (eds) (1999), *Women, Globalization and Fragmentation in the Developing World*, Macmillan, Basingstoke.

Ahiram, E. (1966), 'Distribution of income in Trinidad and Tobago, and a comparison with distribution of income in Jamaica', *Social and Economic Studies*, vol.15(1), pp.209-14.

Amin, S. (1996), 'On development: for Gunder Frank', in S.C. Chew and R.A. Denemark (eds), *The Underdevelopment of Development*, Sage, London.

Amis, P. (1995), 'Making sense of urban poverty', *Environment and Urbanization*, vol.7, pp.145-157.

Anderson, P. (1987), 'Informal sector or modern labour market? Towards a synthesis', *Social and Economic Studies*, vol.36(3), pp.149-176.

Anderson, P. and Witter, M. (1994), 'Crisis, adjustment and social change: a case study of Jamaica', in E. Le Franc (ed), *Consequences of Structural Adjustment: A Review of the Jamaican Experience*, Canoe Press, University of the West Indies, Kingston, Jamaica.

Anthias, F. and Yuval-Davis, N. (1992), *Racialised Boundaries: Race, Nation, Gender, Class and Anti-Racist Struggle*, Routledge, London.

Anthony, M. (1975), *Profile of Trinidad; An Historical Survey from the Discovery to 1900*, Circle Press, Port of Spain, Trinidad.

Antrobus, P. (1990), 'Gender Implications of the Development Crisis', in G. Beckford and N. Girvan (eds), *Development in Suspense*, Friedrich Elbert Stiftung, Jamaica.

Appadurai, A. (1986), 'Introduction: Commodities and the politics of value' in Appardurai, A. (ed), *The Social Life of Things: Commodities in Cultural Perspective*, Cambridge University Press, Cambridge.

Appadurai, A. (1990), 'Disjuncture and difference in the global cultural economy' in M. Featherstone (ed), *Global Culture: Nationalism, Globalisation and Modernity*, Sage, London.

Auty, R.M. (1989), 'Trinidad and Tobago: a program for policy reform and renewed growth', *World Bank Country Study*, World Bank, Washington.

Barker, D. and Richards, P. (1978), 'Repertory grid methodology and environmental images in rural Africa', paper presented to a joint meeting of the *IBG Quantitative Methods Study Group and Developing Areas Study Group*, London.

Barrow, C. (1986), 'Finding the support: a study of strategies for survival', *Social and Economic Studies*, vol.35(2), pp.131-76.

Barrow, C. (1988), 'Anthropology, the family and women in the Caribbean', in P. Mohammed and C. Shepherd (eds), *Gender in Caribbean Development*, Women and Development Studies Project, University of the West Indies, Trinidad and Tobago.

Beachey, R.W. (1957), *The British West Indies Sugar Industry in the Late 19th Century*, Blackwell, Oxford.

Beckford, G.L. (1972), *Persistent Poverty: Underdevelopment in Plantation Economies of the Third World*, Oxford University Press, New York.

Beckford, G.L (1975), *Caribbean Economy: Dependence and Backwardness*, Institute of Social and Economic Research, St Augustine, Trinidad.

Beechey, V. (1987), *Unequal Work*, Verso, London.

Bell, R.R. (1970), 'Marriage and family difference among lower-class negro and East Indian women in Trinidad', *Race*, vol.12(1), pp.59-73.

Beneria, L. and Sen, G. (1981), 'Accumulation, reproduction and women's role in economic development', *Signs: Journal of Women in Culture and Society*, vol.7(2), pp.279-98.

Bentley, G. and Henry, F. (1969), 'The Chinese in Trinidad', in F. Henry (ed), *McGill Studies in Caribbean Anthropology*, McGill University, Montreal.

Besson, J. (1987), 'A paradox in Caribbean attitudes to land', in J. Besson and J. Momsen (eds), *Land and Development in the Caribbean*, Macmillan, London.

Besson, J. (1993), 'Reputation and respectability reconsidered: a new perspective on Afro-Caribbean peasant women, in J. Momsen (ed), *Women and Change in the Caribbean: A Pan-Caribbean Perspective*, Croom Helm, London.

Best, L. (1980), 'International co-operation in the industrialization process: the case of Trinidad and Tobago', in *UNIDO, Industry 2000-New Perspective*, Collected Background Papers, UNIDO.

Bhabba, H. (1983), 'Difference, discrimination and the discourse of colonialism', in F. Barker *et al* (eds), *The Politics of Theory*, University of Essex, Colchester.

Bhabha, H. (1990), *Nation and Narration*, Routledge, London.

Bhavnani, K. and Phoenix, A. (eds) (1994), *Shifting Identities, Shifting Racisms*, Sage, London.

Bondi, L. (1990), 'Feminism, postmodernism and geography: space for women?', *Antipode*, vol.22, pp.156-67.

Borde, P.G.L. (1982), *The History of the Island of Trinidad under the Spanish Government, Vol. 2*, Paria Publishers, Port of Spain.

Brah, A. (1994), '"Race" and "culture" in the gendering of labour markets', in H. Afshar and M. Maynard (eds), *The Dynamics of Race and Gender: Some*

Feminist Interventions, Taylor and Francis, London, pp.151-171.
Braithwaite, L. (1953), *Social Stratification in Trinidad*, Institute of Social and Economic Research, University of the West Indies, Mona, Jamaica.
Breman, J. (1976), 'A dualistic labour system? A critique of the 'informal sector' concept', *Economic and Political Weekly*, vol.11, pp.1870-6.
Brereton, B. (1979), *Race Relations in Colonial Trinidad 1870-1900*, Cambridge University Press, Cambridge.
Brereton, B. (1981), *A History of Modern Trinidad, 1783-1962*, Heinemann, London.
Brereton, B. (1993), 'Social organisation and class, racial and cultural conflict in nineteenth century Trinidad', in K. Yelvington (ed), *Trinidad Ethnicity*, Macmillan, London.
Bromley, R. and Gerry, C. (1979), *Casual Work and Poverty in Third World Cities*, John Wiley, Chichester.
Brown, L.D. and Ashman, D. (1996), 'Participation, social capital, and intersectoral problem solving: African and Asian Cases', *World Development*, vol.24, pp.1467-1479.
Brydon, L. and Chant, S. (1989), *Women in the Third World: Gender issues in Rural and Urban Areas*, Edward Elgar, Aldershot.
Camejo, A. (1971), 'Racial discrimination in employment in the private sector in Trinidad and Tobago', *Social and Economic Studies*, vol.20(3), pp.294-318.
Carby, H. (1983), 'White woman listen! Black feminism and the boundaries of sisterhood, in Centre for Contemporary Cultural Studies, *The Empire Strikes Back*, Hutchinson, London, pp.212-235.
Cardoso, H. (1976), 'The consumption of dependency theory in the US', paper submitted to the *Third Scandinavian Research Conference in Latin America*, Bergen, June 1976.
Cardoso, H. and Faletto, M. (1969), *Dependencia y Desarollo en America Latina*, Siglo, Mexico, (English translation in 1979), *Dependency and Development in Latin America*, University of California Press, Berkeley.
Carrington, E. (1967), 'The post war political economy of Trinidad and Tobago', in N. Girvan and O. Jefferson (eds), *Readings in the Political Economy of the Caribbean*.
Carrington, E. (1971), 'Trinidad's post war economy, 1945-1950: industrialisation by invitation in Trinidad since 1950', *Readings in the Political Economy of the Caribbean*, New World Group, Kingston.
Castells, M. (1977), *The Urban Question: A Marxist Approach*, Edward Arnold, London.
Castells, M. and Portes, A. (1989), 'World underneath: the origins, dynamics and affects of the informal economy', in A. Portes, M. Castells and L.A. Benton (eds), *The Informal Economy: Studies in Advanced and Less Developed Countries*, Johns Hopkins University Press, Baltimore.
Central Statistical Office (1985), *Population and Housing Census 1980*, Volumes 1-7, Republic of Trinidad and Tobago.

Central Statistical Office (1986), *Annual Statistical Digest 33*, Republic of Trinidad and Tobago.

Central Statistical Office (1987), *Annual Statistical Digest 34*, Republic of Trinidad and Tobago.

Central Statistical Office (1988a), *Annual Statistical Digest 35*, Republic of Trinidad and Tobago.

Central Statistical Office (1988b), *Continuous Sample Survey of Population, Labour Force Figures*, Republic of Trinidad and Tobago.

Central Statistical Office (1989), *Annual Statistical Digest 36*, Republic of Trinidad and Tobago.

Central Statistical Office (1989), *Labour Force Bulletin*, Republic of Trinidad and Tobago.

Central Statistical Office (1989), *Labour Force Report, 1988-1989*, Republic of Trinidad and Tobago.

Central Statistical Office (1990), *Annual Statistical Digest 37*, Republic of Trinidad and Tobago.

Central Statistical Office (1991), *Annual Statistical Digest 38*, Republic of Trinidad and Tobago.

Central Statistical Office (1991), *Bulletin on Wages and Labour Productivity*, Republic of Trinidad and Tobago.

Central Statistical Office (1991), *Population and Vital Statistics Report 1988-1989*, Republic of Trinidad and Tobago.

Central Statistical Office (1992), *Annual Statistical Digest 39*, Republic of Trinidad and Tobago.

Chant, S. (1985), 'Single-parent families: choice or constraint? The formation of female-headed households in Mexican shanty towns, *Development and Change* 16, 635-56.

Chant, S. (1987), 'Family structure and female labour in Queretaro, Mexico', in J. Momsen and J. Townsend (eds), *Geography of Gender in the Third World*, Hutchinson, London.

Chant, S. (1991), *Women and Survival in Mexican Cities: Perspectives on Gender, Labour Markets and Low-Income Households*, Manchester University Press, Manchester.

Chant, S. (1997), *Women-headed Households: Diversity and Dynamics in the Developing World*, Macmillan, Basingstoke.

Chant, S. and McIlwaine, C. (1995), *Women of a Lesser Cost: Female Labour, Foreign Exchange and Philippine Development*, Pluto Press, London.

Cheng, L.L. and Gereffi, G. (1994), 'The informal economy in East Asian development', *International Journal of Urban and Regional Research*, vol.18(2), pp.914-219.

Clarke, C.G. (1974), 'Urbanisation in the Caribbean', *Geography*, vol.59, pp.223-32.

Clarke, C.G. (1984), 'Pluralism and plural societies: Caribbean perspectives', in C. Clarke, D. Ley and C. Peach (eds), *Geography and Ethnic Pluralism*, Allen and Unwin, London.

Clarke, C.G. (1986), *East Indians in a West Indian Town: San Fernando, Trinidad, 1930-70*, George Allen and Unwin, London.

Clarke, C.G. (1989), 'Jamaica', in R.B. Potter (ed). *Urbanisation, Planning and Development in the Caribbean*, Mansell, London.

Clarke, C.G. (1993), 'Spatial pattern and social interaction among Creoles and Indians in Trinidad and Tobago' in K. Yelvington (ed), *Trinidad Ethnicity*, Macmillan, Basingstoke.

Clarke, E. (1957), *My Mother who Fathered Me: A Study of the Family in Three Selected Communities in Jamaica*, George Allen and Unwin, London.

Connolly, P. (1985), 'The Politics of the informal sector: A critique', in N. Redclift and E. Minigione (eds), *Beyond Employment*, Longman, London.

Conway, D. (1981), 'Fact or uncontrolled peripheral settlement in Trinidad: or how different conclusions arise from the same data', *Ekistics*, vol.286, pp.37-43.

Conway, D. (1984), 'Trinidad's mismatched expectations', *Planning and Development Review*, vol.26, pp.12-22

Conway, D. (1986), 'Caribbean migrants: opportunistic and individualistic sojourners', *UFSI Report* 24, Hanover, New Haven, 15.

Conway, D. (1989), 'Trinidad and Tobago', in R.B. Potter (ed), *Urbanisation, Planning and Development in the Caribbean*, Mansell, London.

Corbridge, S. (1986), *Capitalist World Development: A Critique of Radical Development Geography*, Macmillan Press, London.

Cornia, G.A. (1990), 'Investing in human resources: health, nutrition and development in the 1990s, in K. Griffin and J. Knight (eds), *Human Development and the International Development Strategy for the 1990s*, Macmillan, London.

Craig, S. (ed) (1982), *Contemporary Caribbean*, Maracas, Trinidad.

Crocker, D.A. (1991), 'Towards development ethics', *World Development*, vol.19, pp.457-483.

Cross, M. (1972), *The East Indians of Guyana and Trinidad*, Minority Rights Group, London.

Cross, M. and Heuman, G. (eds) (1988), *Labour in the Caribbean*, Macmillan, London.

Cuales, S. (1989), 'Participation in formal and informal sectors of the economy: are women entrepreneurs?, *Research Papers, Institute of Social and Economic Research*, University of the West Indies, Trinidad.

Curtin, P.D. (1969), *The Atlantic Slave Trade: A Census*, The University of Wisconsin Press, Madison.

Dagenais, H. (1993), 'Women in Guadeloupe: the paradoxes of reality', in J. Momsen (ed), *Women and Change in the Caribbean: A Pan-Caribbean Perspective*, James Currey, London.

Daniels, P.W. and Lever, W.F. (eds) (1996), *The Global Economy in Transition*, Longman, London.

Davidson, G.M. (1996), 'The spaces of coping: women and poverty in Singapore', *Singapore Journal of Tropical Geography*, vol.17(2), pp.113-131.

Davies, R. (1979), 'The Informal sector or subordinate mode of production? A model', in Bromley and Gerry (eds), *Casual Work and Poverty in Third World Cities*, John Wiley, Chichester.

De Soto, H. (1989), *The Other Path: The Invisible Revolution in the Third World*, I.B.Taurus, London.

Deere, C. *et al* (eds) (1990), *In the Shadows of the Sun: Caribbean Development Alternatives and US Policy*, Westview Press, Colorado.

Demas, W.G. (1965), *The Economies of Development in Small Countries with Special Reference to the Caribbean*, McGill University Press, Montreal.

Dirks, R. (1987), 'Resource fluctuations and competitive transformations in West Indian slave societies', in C.D. Laughlin and I.A. Brady (eds), *Extinction and Survival in Human Populations*, Columbia University Press, New York.

Dos Santos, M. (1970), 'The structure of dependency', *American Economic Review*, vol.60(21), pp.245-259.

Drakakis-Smith, D. (1990), 'Food for thought or thought about food: urban food distribution systems in the Third World', in R.B. Potter and A.T. Salau (eds), *Cities and Development in the Third World*, Mansell, London and New York.

Durant-Gonzales, V. (1985), 'Higglering: Rural women in the internal market system in Jamaica', in P.I. Gomes (ed), *Rural Development in the Caribbean*, Hurst and Co, London.

Ellis, P. (ed) (1986), *Women of the Caribbean*, Zed, London. Reprinted in 1988.

Elson, D. (1983), 'Jeans and the international division of labour', *Links*, vol.17.

Elson, D. and Pearson, R. (1981), 'Nimble fingers make Cheap Workers: An analysis of women's employment in Third World export manufacturing', *Feminist Review* (Spring 1981), pp.87-107.

England, K. (1991), 'Gender relations and the spatial structure of the city', *Geoforum*, vol.22(2), pp.135-148.

Evans, P. (1996), 'Government action, social capital and development: reviewing the evidence on synergy', *World Development*, vol.24, pp.1119-1132.

Eyre, A. (1972), 'The shanty towns of Montego Bay, Jamaica', *Geographical Review*, vol.62, pp.394-413.

Farrell, T.M.A. (1978), 'The Unemployment Crisis in Trinidad and Tobago: its current dimensions and some projections to 1985', *Social and Economic Studies*, vol.27(2), pp.161-178

Farrell, T.M.A. (1980), 'The Roots of Unemployment', *Social and Economic Studies*, vol.29(3), pp.297-331.

Farrell, W. (1989), 'The IMF and the Trinidad and Tobago letter of intent', *ASSET*, vol.7(2), University of the West Indies Press.

Fernandez Kelly, M.P. (1995), 'Social and cultural capital in the urban ghetto: Implications of the economic sociology of immigration', in A. Portes (ed), *The*

Economic Sociology of Immigration: Essays on Networks, Ethnicity and Entrepreneurship, Russell Sage Foundation, New York, pp.213-247.

Frank, A.G. (1967), *Capitalism and Underdevelopment in Latin America*, Monthly Review Press, New York.

Frankenberg, R. (1993), *White Women, Race Matters: The Social Construction of Whiteness*, Routledge, London.

Fransella, F. and Barrister, D. (1977), *A Manual for Repertory Grid Techniques*, Academic Press, London.

Geertz, C. (1963), *Agricultural Involution: The Process of Ecological Change in Indonesia*, University of California Press, Berkeley.

Gerry, C. (1979), 'Small-scale manufacturing and repairs in Dakar: A survey of market relations within the urban economy', in R. Bromley and C. Gerry (eds), *Casual Work and Poverty in Third World Cities*, John Wiley, Chichester.

Gibson, E. (1986), 'Underemployment and unemployment of Caribbean women', *Bulletin of Eastern Caribbean Affairs*, vol.11(2), pp.39-45.

Gilbert, A. and Gugler, J. (1992), *Cities, Poverty and Development*, Oxford University Press, Oxford.

Gilmore, H.W. (1940), *The Beggar*, University of North Carolina Press, North Carolina.

Gilroy, P. (1987), *There Ain't No Black in the Union Jack*, Hutchinson, London.

Girvan, N. (1973), 'The development of dependent economies in the Caribbean and Latin America: review and comparison', *Social and Economic Studies*, vol.22, pp.121-132.

Girvan, N. (ed) (1990), *The Debt Problem of Small Peripheral Economies: Case Studies from the Caribbean and Central America*, Association of Caribbean economists (ACE).

Goldschmidt-Clermont, L. (1990), 'Economic measurement of non-market household activities. Is it useful or feasible?', *International Labour Review*, vol.129(3), pp.279-302.

Government of Trinidad and Tobago (1963), *National Physical Development Plan, Trinidad and Tobago 1959-63*, Development Planning Series, Republic of Trinidad and Tobago.

Government of Trinidad and Tobago (1968), *National Physical Development Plan, Trinidad and Tobago 1964-68*, Development Planning Series, Republic of Trinidad and Tobago.

Government of Trinidad and Tobago (1972), *White Paper on Public Sector Participation*, Republic of Trinidad and Tobago.

Government of Trinidad and Tobago (1973), *East Port of Spain*, Development Planning Series, Republic of Trinidad and Tobago.

Government of Trinidad and Tobago (1974), *National Physical Development Plan, Trinidad and Tobago 1969-74*, Development Planning Series, Republic of Trinidad and Tobago.

Government of Trinidad and Tobago (1975), *The Capital Region*, Development Planning Series, Republic of Trinidad and Tobago.

Government of Trinidad and Tobago (1978), *National Physical Development Plan, Trinidad and Tobago*, Development Planning Series, Republic of Trinidad and Tobago.

Government of Trinidad and Tobago (1989), *The Capital Region*, Development Planning Series, Republic of Trinidad and Tobago.

Government of Trinidad and Tobago (1991), *Medium Term Macro Planning Framework*, National Planning Commission 1989-1995, Republic of Trinidad and Tobago.

Government of Trinidad and Tobago (1991), *National Census 1990*, Republic of Trinidad and Tobago.

Grannovetter, M. (1973), 'The strength of weak ties', *American Journal of Sociology*, vol.78, pp.1360-1380.

Green, D. (1995), *Silent Revolution: The Rise of Market Economics in Latin America*, Cassell, London.

Hall, S. (1992), 'New ethnicities', in J. Donald and A. Rattansi (eds), *Race, Culture and Difference*, Lawrence and Wishart, London, pp.252-259.

Hanson, S. and Pratt, G. (1995), *Gender, Work and Space*, Routledge, London.

Haraway, D. (1991), *Simians, Cyborgs and Women: The Reinvention of Nature*, Routledge, London.

Harewood, J. (1971), 'Racial Discrimination in Employment in Trinidad and Tobago', *Social and Economic Studies*, vol.20(3), pp.267-93.

Harrison, F. (1988), 'Women in Jamaica's urban informal economy: Insights from a Kingston slum' *Niewe West-Indische Gids*, vols.62(3/4), pp.103-28.

Harrison, F. (1991), 'Women in Jamaica's urban informal economy: Insights from a Kingston slum, in Mohanty', Torres and Russco (eds), *Third World Women and the Politics of Feminism*, Indiana University Press.

Hart, K. (1973), 'Informal income opportunities and urban employment in Ghana', *Journal of Modern African Studies*, vol.11, pp.61-89.

Hart, K. (1989), *Women and the Sexual Division of Labour in the Caribbean*, Consortium Graduate School of Social Sciences, University of the West Indies, Kingston, Jamaica.

Hart, K. (1990), 'The idea of the economy: six modern dissenters', in R. Friedland and A.F. Robertson (eds), *Beyond the Marketplace: Rethinking Economy and Society*, Aldine de Gruyter, New York.

Heller, P. (1996), 'Social capital as a product of class mobilization and state intervention: industrial workers in Kerala, India', *World Development*, vol.24, pp.1055-1071.

Henry, R.M. (1975), 'A note on income distribution and poverty in Trinidad and Tobago', *Central Statistical Office Research Papers*, vol.8, pp.1-29.

Henry, R.M. (1988), 'The state and income distribution in an independent Trinidad and Tobago' in S. Ryan (ed), *The Independence Experience 1962-1987*, Institute of Social and Economic Research, St Augustine, Trinidad.

Hettne, B. (1994), *Development Theory and the Three World*, second edition, Longman, Harlow.

Hintzen, P. (1981), *Capitalism, Socialism and Socio-Political Confrontation in Multi-Racial Developing States: A Comparison of Guyana and Trinidad*, unpublished PhD thesis, Yale University.

Hintzen, P. (1985), 'Ethnicity, class and international capitalist penetration in Guyana and Trinidad', *Social and Economic Studies*, vol.34(3), pp.56-69.

Hirschmann, A.O. (1958), *The Strategy of Economic Development*, Yale University Press, New Haven, CT.

Hope, K.R. (1986), *Urbanization in the Commonwealth Caribbean*, Westview Press, Hirschmann, A.O. (1958), *The Strategy of Economic Development*, Yale University Press, New Haven, CT.

Hudson, R. (1980), 'Personal construct theory, the repertory grid method and human geography', *Progress in Human Geography*, vol.4, pp.346-59.

Hussmann, R. (1990), *Surveys of Economically Active Population, Employment, Unemployment and Underemployment: An ILO Manual on Concepts and Methods*, International Labour Office Publications, Geneva.

International Labour Organisation (1964), *World Employment Programme*, International Labour Conference.

International Labour Organisation (1970), *Towards Full Employment: A Programme for Colombia*, ILO, Geneva.

International Labour Organisation (1972), *Employment, Incomes and Equality: A Strategy for Increasing Productive Employment in Kenya*, ILO, Geneva.

International Labour Organisation (1988), *World Employment Review*, International Labour Office, Geneva.

International Labour Organisation (1995), *World Employment 1995*, International Labour Office, Geneva.

International Labour Organisation (1996), *World Employment 1996/7: National Policies in a Global Context*, International Labour Office, Geneva.

International Labour Organisation (1998), *World Employment Report 1998-99: Employability in the Global Economy: How Training Matters*, International Labour Office, Geneva.

James, C.L.R. (1993), *C.L.R. James' Caribbean: A Reader*, Macmillan, London.

Johnson, H. (1987), The Chinese in Trinidad in the late-nineteenth century', *Ethnic and Racial Studies*, vol.10(1), pp.82-95.

Jordan, L. (1984), 'Women in food marketing: A Caribbean perspective', *Research Papers of the Women and Development Unit (WAND)*, University of the West Indies, Barbados.

Kabeer, N. (1994), *Reversed Realities: Gender Hierarchies and Development Thought*, Verso, London.

Kanji, N. (1995), 'Gender, poverty and economic adjustment in Harare, Zimbabwe', *Environment and Urbanisation*, vol.7(1), pp.37-56.

Katzin, M.F. (1959), 'The Jamaican country higgler', *Social and Economic Studies*, vol.8(4), pp.421-435.

Katzin, M.F. (1960), 'The business of higglering in Jamaica', *Social and Economic Studies*, vol.9(3), pp.297-331.

Kitzinger, S. (1969), 'Protest and mysticism: The Rastafari cult of Jamaica', *Journal for the Scientific Study of Religion*, vol.8, pp.240-62.

Lautier, B. (1990), 'Wages relationship, formal sector and employment policy in South America', *Journal of Development Studies*, vol.26, pp.278-98.

Lawson, V. (1990) 'Work force fragmentation in Latin America and its empirical manifestations in Ecuador', *World Development*, vol.18(3), pp.641-58.

Le Franc, E. (1989), 'Petty trading and labour mobility: Higglers in the Kingston Metropolitan Area', in K. Hart (ed), *Women and the Sexual Division of Labour in the Caribbean*, Consortium Graduate School of Social Sciences, University of the West Indies, Mona, Jamaica.

Le Franc, E. (ed) (1994), *Consequences of Structural Adjustment: A Review of the Jamaican Experience*, Canoe Press, University of the West Indies, Kingston, Jamaica.

Lefebvre, H. (1991), *The Production of Space*, Blackwell, Oxford.

Lewis, O. (1966), 'The culture of poverty', *Scientific American* 215 (October), pp.19-25.

Lewis, W.A. (1950), 'The industrialisation of the British West Indies', *Caribbean Economic Review*, vol.2, pp.1-61.

Lewis, W.A. (1954), 'Economic development with unlimited supplies of labour', *The Manchester School of Economic and Social Studies*, vol.22(2), pp.139-191.

Lewis, W.A. (1955), *The Theory of Economic Growth*, George Allen and Unwin, London.

Leys, C. (1977), 'Underdevelopment and dependency: critical notes', *Journal of Contemporary Asia*, vol.7(1), pp.42-63.

Lieber, M. (1976), '"Liming" and other concerns: the style of street embedments in Port of Spain, Trinidad', *Urban Anthropology*, vol.5, pp.319-334.

Lieber, M. (1981), *Street Life: Afro-American Culture in Urban Trinidad*, Schenkman, New York.

Lloyd, P. (1979), *Slums of Hope: Shanty Towns of the Third World*, Penguin, Harmonsworth.

Lloyd-Evans, S. (1997), 'Gender, ethnicity and social capital in Trinidad's informal sector', paper presented at the Annual Conference of the Society for Latin American Studies, 4-6 April 1997, St. Andrew's University.

Lloyd-Evans, S. and Bowlby, S. (2000), 'Crossing boundaries: Racialised gendering and the labour market experiences of Pakistani migrant women in Britain', *Women's Studies International Forum*, vol.23(4), pp.461-474.

Lloyd-Evans, S., Bowlby, S. and Mohammad, R. in association with the Pakistani Community Centre, Reading (1996), *Pakistani Women's Experiences of the Labour Market in Reading: Barriers, Aspirations and Opportunities*, Report II for Reading Borough Council.

Lloyd-Evans, S. and Potter, R.B. (1992), 'The informal sector of the economy of the Commonwealth Caribbean', *Bulletin of Eastern Caribbean Affairs*, vol.17(3), pp.26-40.

Lloyd-Evans, S. and Potter, R.B. (1993), 'Government response to informal sector retailing trading: the People's Mall, Port of Spain, Trinidad', *Geography*, vol.78(3), pp.315-318.

Lowenthal, D. (1972), *West Indian Societies*, Oxford University Press, Oxford.

Lucas, C.P. (1890), *A Historical Geography of the British Colonies*, Clarendon Press, Oxford.

MacEwan Scott, A.M. (1979), 'Who are the self-employed?', in R. Bromley and C. Gerry (eds), *Casual Work and Poverty in Third World Cities*, John Wiley, Chichester.

MacEwan Scott, A.M. (1986a), 'Industrialisation, gender segregation and stratification theory', in R. Crompton and M. Mann (eds), *Gender and Stratification*, Polity Press, Cambridge.

MacEwan Scott, A.M. (1986b), 'Women and industrialisation: Examining the "female marginalisation" thesis', *Journal of Development Studies*, vol.22(4), pp.649-80.

Madge, C. (1993), 'Boundary disputes: comments on Sidaway 1992', *Area*, vol.25, pp.294-299.

Madge, C. (1997), 'Ethics of research in the Third World', in E. Robson and K. Willis (eds), *Postgraduate Fieldwork in Developing Areas: A Rough Guide*, Developing Research Group Monograph No.9, DARG, Keele University Press.

Maldonado, C. (1995), 'The informal sector: legalization or laissez-faire?', *International Labour Review*, vol.134(6), pp.705-28.

Mangin, W. (1967), 'Latin American squatter settlements: a problem and a solution', *Latin American Research Review*, vol.2, pp.65-98.

Mason, B. (1988), 'Jamaican working-class women: Producers and reproducers', in M. Simms and J. Malveaux (eds), *Slipping through the Cracks: The Status of Black Women*, Transaction Books, Oxford.

Massey, D. (1994), *Space, Place and Gender*, Polity Press, Cambridge.

Massiah, J. (1989), 'Women's lives and livelihoods: A view from the Commonwealth Caribbean', *World Development*, vol.17(7), pp.965-977.

Massiah, J. (1993), *Women in Developing Economies: Making Visible the Invisible*, Berg/UNESCO, Oxford.

McAffe, K. (1991), *Storm Signals: Structural Adjustment and Development Alternatives in the Caribbean*, Zed, London.

McDowell, L. (1993), 'Space, place and gender relations – Part I. Feminist empiricism and the geography of social relations', *Progress in Human Geography*, vol.17(2), pp.157-179.

McDowell, L. and Sharp, J.P. (eds) (1997), *Space, Gender, Knowledge: Feminist Readings*, Arnold, London.

McIlwaine, C. (1995), 'Gender, race and ethnicity: concepts, realities and policy implications', *Third World Planning Review*, vol.17(2), pp.237-243.

McIlwaine, C. (1996), 'The negotiation of space among sex workers in Cebu City, the Philippines', *Singapore Journal of Tropical Geography*, vol.17(2), pp.150-164.

McGee, T.G. (1979), 'The poverty syndrome: making out in the southeast Asian city', in R. Bromley and C. Gerry (eds), *Casual Work and Poverty in Third World Cities*, John Wiley, Chichester.

Milroy, B.M. and Wismer, S. (1994), 'Communities, work and public/private sphere models', *Gender, Place and Culture*, vol.1, pp.71-90.

Ministry of Mobilisation and Planning (1989), *Annual Labour Market Information Study of the Social Sector's Unit*, Republic of Trinidad and Tobago.

Ministry of Mobilisation and Planning (1990), *Annual Labour Market Information Study of the Social Sector's Unit*, Republic of Trinidad and Tobago.

Mintz, S.W. (1964), Foreword to Guerra and Sanchez, R. (eds) *Sugar and society in the Caribbean: An Economic History of Cuban Agriculture*, Yale University Press, New Haven.

Mintz, S.W. (1974), *Caribbean Transformations*, Aldine, Chicago.

Mintz, S.W. (1985), *Sweetness and Power: The Place of Sugar in Modern History*, Viking, New York.

Mintz, S.W. (ed) (1987), *Crisis in the Caribbean Basin*, Sage, Beverley Hills.

Miraftab, F. (1996), 'Space, gender and work: home-based workers in Mexico', in E. Boris and E. Prugl (eds), *Homeworkers in Global Perspective: Invisible No More*, Routledge, London.

Mitchell, J.F. (1989), *Caribbean Crusade*, Concept Publishing, Vermont.

Mohammed, P. (1994), 'Nuancing the feminist discourse in the Caribbean', *Social and Economic Studies*, vol.43(3), pp.135-67.

Mohanty, C. (1991), 'Introduction: cartographies of struggle: Third World women and the politics of feminism', in C. Mohanty, A. Russo and L. Torres (eds), *Third World Women and the Politics of Feminism,* Indiana University Press, Bloomington.

Momsen, J. (1984), 'Gender versus ethnic pluralism in Caribbean agriculture', in C. Clarke, D. Ley and C. Peach (eds), *Geography and Ethnic Pluralism*, Allen and Unwin, London.

Momsen, J. (1987), 'The feminization of agriculture in the Caribbean', in J. Momsen, and J. Townsend (eds), *Geography and Gender in the Third World*, Hutchinson, London.

Momsen, J. (ed) (1993), *Women and Change in the Caribbean: A Pan-Caribbean Perspective*, James Currey, London.

Momsen, J. and Kinnard, V. (eds) (1992), *Different Places, Different Voices: Gender and Development in Africa, Asia and Latin America*, Routledge, London.

Moore, H. (1988), *Feminism and Anthropology*, Polity, Cambridge.

Moose, J. (1993), *Half the World, Half the Chance: An Introduction to Gender and Development*, Oxfam Publications, Oxford.

Moser, C.O.N. (1978), 'Informal sector or petty commodity production: Dualism or dependence in urban development?', *World Development*, vol.6, pp.1041-64.

Moser, C.O.N. (1984), 'The informal sector reworked: viability and vulnerability in urban development', *Regional Development Dialogue*, vol.5, pp.135-78.

Moser, C.O.N. (1996), 'Confronting crisis: a comparative study of household responses to poverty and vulnerability in four poor urban communities', *Environmentally Sustainable Development Studies and Monograph Series* 8, World Bank, Washington DC.

Moser, C.O.N. and Levy, C. (1986), 'A theory and methodology of gender', *DPU Gender and Planning Working Paper 11*, University of London, pp.3.

Moser, C.O.N. and McIlwaine, C. (1997), 'Household Responses to Poverty and Vulnerability: Confronting Crisis in Commonwealth, Metro Manila, the Philippines', *Urban Management Program Policy Paper* 23, World Bank, Washington DC.

Myrdal, G. (1968), *Asian Drama*, Pantheon, New York.

Myriad, G. (1957), *Economic Theory and Underdeveloped Areas*, Duckworth: London.

Newson, L.A. (1976), *Aboriginal and Spanish Colonial Trinidad: A Study in Culture Contact*, Academic Press, London.

Nicholls, D.G. (1971), 'East Indians and black power in Trinidad', *Race*, vol.12(4), pp.283-326.

Ostrom, E. (1996), 'Crossing the great divide: co-production, synergy, and development', *World Development*, vol.24, pp.1073-1087.

Pahl, R.E. (1988), *On Work*, Basil Blackwell, Oxford.

Pantin, D. (1989), *Into the Valley of Debt: An Alternative Road to the IMF/World Bank Path*, Ferguson, Trinidad.

Peach, C. (1984), 'The force of West Indian island identity in Britain', in C. Clarke, D. Ley and C. Peach (eds), *Geography and Ethnic Pluralism*, Allen and Unwin, London.

Peake, L. and Trotz, A. (1999), *Gender, Ethnicity and Place: Women and Identities in Guyana*, Routledge, London.

Pearson, R. (1993), 'Gender and technology in the Caribbean: new work for women?', in J.H. Momsen (ed), *Women and Change in the Caribbean*, James Currey, London.

Pearson, R. (1994), 'Gender relations, capitalism and Third World industrialisation', in L. Sklair (ed), *Capitalism and Development*, Routledge, London.

Phillips, D. (1985), 'Women traders in Trinidad and Tobago', *Economic Commission for Latin America ECLAC*, Port of Spain, Trinidad.

Portes, A. (1995), *The Economic Sociology of Immigration: Essays on Networks, Ethnicity and Entrepreneurship*, Russell Sage Foundation, New York.

Portes, A., Castells, M. and Benton, L.A. (eds) (1989), *The Informal Economy: Studies in Advanced and Less Developed Countries*, Johns Hopkins University Press, Baltimore.

Portes, A. and Sensenbrenner, J. (1993), 'Embeddedness and immigration: notes on the social determinants of economic action', *American Journal of Sociology*, vol.98, pp.1320-1350.

Portes, A. and Walton, J. (1981), *Labor, Class and the International System*, Academic Press, New York.

Potter, R.B. (1981), 'Industrial development and urban planning in Barbados', *Geography*, vol.66, pp.225-28.

Potter, R.B. (1985), *Urbanisation and Planning in the Third World*, Croom Helm, London.

Potter, R.B. (1989), *Urbanization, Planning and Development in the Caribbean*, Mansell, London.

Potter, R.B. (1993a), 'Basic needs and development in the small island states of the Eastern Caribbean', in D. Lockhart and D. Drakakis-Smith (eds), *Small Island Development*, Routledge, London.

Potter, R.B. (1993b), 'Urbanization in the Caribbean and trends of global convergence-divergence', *Geographical Journal*, vol.159(1), pp.1-21.

Potter, R.B. and Coshall, J.T. (1984), 'The hand analysis of repertory grids: an appropriate method for Third World environmental studies', *Area*, vol.16, pp.315-322.

Potter, R.B. and Dann, G.M.S. (1990), 'Dependent urbanisation and retail change in Barbados, West Indies', in R.B. Potter and A.T. Salau (eds), *Cities and Development in the Third World*, Mansell, London.

Potter, R.B. and Lloyd-Evans, S. (1998), *The City in the Developing World*, Longman, Harlow.

Putnam, R.D. (1993), *Making Democracy Work: Civic Traditions in Modern Italy*, Princeton University Press, Princeton NJ.

Quijano, A. (1974), 'The marginal pole of the economy and the marginalised labour force', *Economy and Society*, vol.3, pp.393-428.

Radcliffe, S. (1994), '(Representing), post-colonial women: authority, difference and feminisms', *Area*, vol.26(1), pp.25-32.

Rakowski, C.A. (1994), 'Convergence and divergence in the informal sector debate: a fouc on Latin America, 1984-92', *World Development*, vol.22(4), pp.501-16.

Ramesar, M.D. (1976), 'Patterns of regional settlement and economic activity by immigrant groups in Trinidad:1851-1900', *Social and Economic Studies*, vol.25(3), pp.187-215.

Rampersad, M. (1991), 'The measurement of the informal sector in Trinidad and Tobago', *Central Statistical Office Research Papers*, Central Statistical Office, Republic of Trinidad and Tobago: Port of Spain, Trinidad.

Redclift, N. and Sinclair, M.T. (eds) (1991), *Working Women: International Perspectives on Labour and Gender Ideology*, Routledge, London.

Reddock, R. (1988), 'Race, class and gender: Gender issues and the future of the Caribbean', *Papers of the Institute of Social and Economic Research*, St Augustine, Trinidad.

Reddock, R. (1991), 'Social mobility in Trinidad and Tobago 1960-1980', in S. Ryan (ed), *Social and Occupational Stratification in Trinidad and Tobago*, ISER, St Augustine, Trinidad.

Reddock, R. (1994), *Women, Labour and Politics in Trinidad and Tobago: A History*, Zed Books, London and New Jersey.

Reynolds, L.G. (1969), 'Economic development with surplus labour: some complications', *Oxford Economic Papers*, vol.21, pp.89-103.

Richardson, B.C. (1975), 'Livelihood in rural Trinidad in 1900', *Annals of the Association of American Geographers*, vol.65, pp.240-51.

Richardson, B.C. (1992), *The Caribbean in the Wider World, 1492-1992*, Cambridge University Press, Cambridge.

Rivera, M. (1987), 'Women and economic analysis in the Caribbean: A look at the underground economy debate', *paper presented at the First Conference of Caribbean Economists*, July 3-6, 1987, Jamaica.

Roberts, G.W. and Braithwaite, L. (1967), 'Mating amongst East Indian and non-Indian women in Trinidad', *Research Papers, Central Statistical Office*, Port of Spain, 148-85.

Roberts, G.W. and Byrne, J. (1966), 'Summary statistics on indenture and associated migration affecting the West Indies, 1834-1918', *Population Studies*, vol.20, pp.125-34.

Robinson, A.N.R. (1971), *The Mechanics of Independence; Patterns of Political and Economic Transformation in Trinidad and Tobago*, Cambridge University Press.

Robson, E. and Willis, K. (eds) (1997), *Postgraduate Fieldwork in Developing Areas: A Rough Guide*, Developing Areas Research Group Monograph No.9, DARG: Keele University Press.

Rogerson, C.M. (1988), 'The underdevelopment of the informal sector: Street hawking in Johannesburg', *Urban Geography*, vol.9(6), pp.549-567.

Rogerson, C.M. and Hart, D.M. (1989), 'The survival of the 'informal sector': the shebeens of black Johannesburg' *GeoJournal*, vol.12(2), pp.153-66.

Rojas, E. (1989), 'Human settlements of the Eastern Caribbean: Development problems and policy options', *Cities*, vol.6, pp.243-58.

Roldan, M. (1985), 'Industrial outworking: struggles for the reproduction of working-class families and gender subordination', in N. Redclift and E. Mingione (eds), *Beyond Employment: Household, Gender and Subsistence*, Basil Blackwell, Oxford.

Rostow, W.W. (1960), *The Stages of Economic Growth: A Non-Communist Manifest*, Cambridge University Press, London.

Rouse, I. (1986), *Migrations in Prehistory*, Yale University Press, New Haven.

Rowe, M. (1980), 'The women in Rastafari', *Caribbean Quarterly*, vol.26(4), pp.13-21.

Ryan, S. (1972), *Race and Nationalism in Trinidad and Tobago*, University of Toronto Press, Toronto.

Ryan, S. (ed) (1991), *Social and Occupational Stratification in Trinidad and Tobago*, Institute of Social and Economic Research, University of the West Indies, St Augustine, Trinidad.

Ryan, S. and Stewart, T. (eds) (1994), *Entrepreneurship in the Caribbean*, Institute of Social and Economic Research, University of the West Indies, St Augustine, Trinidad.

Safa, H. (1981), 'Runaway shops and female employment: the search for cheap labour', *Signs*, vol.7(2), pp.418-33.

Safa, H. (1986), 'Economic autonomy and sexual equality in Caribbean society', *Social and Economic Studies*, vol.35(3), pp.1-22.

Safa, H. (1990), 'Women and industrialisation in the Caribbean', in S. Stitcher and J. Parpart (eds), *Women, Employment and the Family in the International Division of Labour*, Macmillan Press, London.

Sampath, N.M. (1993), 'An evaluation of the creolisation of Trinidad East Indian adolescent masculinity', in K. Yelvington (ed), *Trinidad Ethnicity*, Macmillan, London.

Santos, M. (1979), *The Shared Space: the Two Circuits of the Urban Economy in Developing Countries*, Methuen, London.

Sauer, C.O. (1966), *The Early Spanish Main*, University of California Press, Berkeley.

Scotland, L.H (1983), 'The Petroleum Windfall, Government Activity and Economic Performance in Trinidad and Tobago', paper presented to the first annual conference on Trinidad and Tobago Economy, Holiday Inn, Port of Spain, Nov 18-19, 1983.

Scott, A.M. (1994), *Divisions and Solidarities: Gender, Class and Employment in Latin America*, Routledge, London.

Seers, D. (1969), 'A step towards a political economy of development', *Social and Economic Studies*, vol.18(3), pp.156-172.

Senior, O. (1991), *Working Miracles: Women's Lives in the English-speaking Caribbean*, Institute of Social and Economic Research, University of the West Indies, James Currey, London.

Sethuraman, S.V. (1976), 'The urban informal sector: concept, measurement and policy', *International Labour Review*, vol.114, pp.69-82.

Sethuraman, S.V. (1978), 'The informal urban sector in developing countries: Some policy implications', in A. de Souza (ed), *The Indian City*, Manohor, New Delhi, pp.1-15.

Sethuraman, S.V. (1981), 'The urban informal sector in developing countries: Employment, poverty and environment', *International Labour Office*, Geneva.

Sheridan, R. (1973), *Sugar and Slavery: An Economic History of the British West Indies, 1623-1775*, Johns Hopkins University Press, Baltimore.

Sidaway, J. (1992), 'In other worlds: on the politics of research by 'First World' geographers in the 'Third World'', *Area*, vol.15(3), pp.403-410.

Silverman, D. (ed) (1997), *Qualitative Research: Theory, Method and Practice*, Sage, London.

Simon, D. and Birch, S.L. (1992), 'Formalising the informal sector in a changing South Africa: small-scale manufacturing in the Witwatersrand', *World Development*, vol.20(7), pp.1029-1045.

Simpson, G.E (1954), 'Begging in Kingston and Montego Bay', *Social and Economic Studies*, vol.3(2), pp.197-211.

Singer, H.W. (1970), 'Dualism revisited: a new approach to the problems of the dual society in developing countries', *Journal of Development Studies*, vol.7, pp.60-75.

Standing, G. (1999), 'Global feminisation through flexible labour: a theme revisited', *World Development*, vol.27(3), pp.583-602.

Stewart, F. (1995), *Adjustment and Poverty: Options and Choices*, Blackwell, Oxford.

Stitcher, S. (1990), 'Women, employment and the family: Current debates', in S. Stitcher and J.L. Parphart (eds), *Women, Employment and the Family in the International Division of Labour*, Macmillan, London.

Stitcher, S. and Parpart, J.L. (1990), *Women, Employment and the Family in the International Division of Labour*, Macmillan, Basingstoke.

Stubbs, J. (1993), 'Women and Cuban smallholder agriculture in transition', in J.H. Momsen (ed), *Women and Change in the Caribbean*, Indiana University Press, Bloomington, Indiana.

Taylor, P.J. (1986), 'The World-system project', in R.J. Johnston and P.J. Taylor (eds), *A World in Crisis? Geographical Perspectives*, Basil Blackwell, Oxford.

Teltscher, S. (1994), 'Small trade and the world economy: informal vendors in Quito, Ecuador', Economic Geography, vol.70(2), pp.167-187.

Thomas, C.Y. (1988), *The Poor and the Powerless: Economic Policy and Change in the Caribbean*, Latin American Bureau, London.

Thomas, J.J. (1992), *Informal Economic Activity*, Harvester Wheatsheaf, Hemel Hempstead.

Thomas, J.J. (1995), *Surviving the City? The Urban Informal Sector in Latin America*, Pluto, London.

Thomas-Hope, E.M. (1992), *Explanation in Caribbean Migration*, Macmillan Press, London.

Tokman, V. (1978), 'An exploration into the nature of informal-formal sector relationships', *World Development*, vol.6(9-10), pp.1065-75.

Tokman, V. (1989), 'Policies for a heterogeneous informal sector in Latin America', *World Development*, vol.17(7), pp.1067-1076.

Town and Country Planning (1991), *Port of Spain Development Plan*, Republic of Trinidad and Tobago.

Turner, J.F.C. (1982), 'Issues in self-help and self-managed housing', in P. Ward (ed), *Self Help Housing: A Critique*, Mansell, London.

Turnham, D. (1993), *Employment and Development: A New Review of Evidence*, International Labour Office Publications, Geneva.

Udall, A.T. and Sinclair, S. (1982), 'The luxury unemployment hypothesis: a review of recent evidence', *World Development*, vol.10, pp.49-62.

United Nations Centre for Human Settlements (Habitat) (1996), *An Urbanizing World: Global Report on Human Settlements 1996*, Oxford University Press for the UNCHS, Oxford and New York.

United Nations Development Report (1992), *Human Development Report 1992*, Oxford University Press, Oxford.

United Nations Development Report (1994), *Human Development Report 1994*, Oxford University Press, Oxford.

United Nations Development Report (1998), *Human Development Report 1998*, Oxford University Press, Oxford.

United Nations Development Report (1999), *Human Development Report 1999*, Oxford University Press, Oxford.

Vaiou, D. (1992), 'Gender divisions in urban space: beyond the rigidity of dualist classifications', *Antipode*, vol.24(4), pp.7-262.

Vertovec, S. (1990), 'Religion and ethnic ideology: The Hindu youth movement in Trinidad', *Ethnic and Racial Studies*, vol.13(2), pp.225-49.

Vertovec, S. (1992), *Hindu Trinidad: Religion, Ethnicity and Socio-Economic Change*, Macmillan Press, London.

Wallerstein, I. (1974), *The Modern World System, Capitalist Agriculture and the Origins of the European World Economy in the Sixteenth Century*, Academic Press, London.

Warner-Lewis, M. (1991), *Guinea's Other Suns: The African Dynamic in Trinidadian Culture*, Majority Press, Dover.

Watts, D. (1987), *The West Indies: Patterns of Development, Culture and Environmental Change since 1942*, Cambridge University Press, Cambridge.

Weeks, J. (1975), 'Policies for expanding employment in the informal urban sector of developing economies', *International Labour Review*, vol.111, pp.1-13.

Wellings, P. and Sutcliffe, M. (1984), '"Developing" the urban informal sector in South Africa: The reformist paradigm and its fallacies', *Development and Change*, vol.15, pp.517-50.

Westwood, S. and Radcliffe, S. (1993), 'Gender, racism and the politics of identities in Latin America', in S. Radcliffe and S. Westwood (eds), *Viva: Women and Popular Protest in Latin America*, Routledge, London and New York.

Williams, C.C. and Windebank, J. (1998), *Informal Employment in the Advanced Economies*, Routledge, London.

Williams, E. (1962), *History of the People of Trinidad and Tobago*, Andre Deutsch, London.

Williams, E. (1970), *From Columbus to Castro: The History of the Caribbean, 1492-1969*, Andre Deutsch, London.

Willis, K. (1996), 'Negotiating dualisms: women, locality and employment opportunities in Oaxaca City, *Singapore Journal of Tropical Geography*, vol.17(2), pp.195-212.

Witter, M. and Kirton, C. (1990), 'The informal economy in Jamaica: some empirical exercises', Working Paper no.36, Institute of Social and Economic Research, University of the West Indies, St Augustine, Trinidad.

Wolf, E.R. (1982), *Europe and the People Without History*, University of California Press, Berkeley.

Wood, D. (1968), *Trinidad in Transition: The Years After Slavery*, Oxford University Press, London.

World Bank (1993), *World Bank Development Report*, Oxford University Press, Oxford.

Worrell, D. (1987), *Small Island Economies: Structure and Performance in the English-speaking Caribbean Since 1970*, Praeger, New York.

Yelvington, K. (1993), *Trinidad Ethnicity*, Macmillan Press, London.

Yelvington, K. (1995), *Producing Power: Ethnicity, Gender and Class in a Caribbean Workplace*, Temple University Press, Philadelphia.

Young, K. (1989), *Serving Two Masters*, Allied Publishers, Ahmedabad.

Index

For Product Safety Concerns and Information please contact our EU representative GPSR@taylorandfrancis.com Taylor & Francis Verlag GmbH, Kaufingerstraße 24, 80331 München, Germany

Batch number: 10725921

Printed by Printforce, the Netherlands